John Markoff is a senior writer for *The New York Times* who has coauthored *Cyberpunk: Outlaws and Hackers on the Computer Frontier* and the bestselling *Takedown: The Pursuit and Capture of Kevin Mitnick, America's Most Wanted Computer Outlaw*. He lives in San Francisco, California.

Praise for *What the Dormouse Said*

"At the core of *Dormouse* lies a valid and original historical point."
—*The New York Times*

"A convincing case. . . . This makes entertaining reading."
—*The New York Times*

"Evocative" —*Newsweek*

"Fascinating" —*Computerworld*

"Fascinating . . . Markoff is a wonderful writer and storyteller, and he effortlessly weaves together the stories of the main cast of characters. The individuals had the most unusual knack for crossing paths, and Markoff's ability to show these sometimes tangential—but always important—relationships, without losing the thread of the story, is impressive."
—*The Christian Science Monitor*

"Nobody writes about computer technology better than Markoff, who gives us insights into the people, history and societal pressures that drive breakthroughs and new developments. Here he convincingly traces the birth of personal computing to the counterculture ethos of the Bay Area in the '6os."
—*San Jose Mercury News*

"Shows how almost every feature of today's home computers . . . can be traced to two Stanford research facilities that were completely immersed in the counterculture. . . . The combustive combination of radical politics and technological ambition is laid out so convincingly, in fact, that it's mildly disappointing when, in the closing pages, Markoff attaches momentous significance to a confrontation between the freewheeling Californian computer culture and a young Bill Gates only to bring the story to an abrupt halt. Hopefully, he's already started work on the sequel." —*Publishers Weekly* (starred review)

"A lively prehistory of Silicon Valley and its brilliant denizens of yore. . . . Technogeeks will know much of this history already, but Markoff does a fine job of distilling it here while pointing out how much bleaker the world might be if the pioneers had just said no." —*Kirkus Reviews*

"Striking. . . . a fine job of recording the history of that exceptional time. Both informative and entertaining, this book should appeal to a broad audience of technology readers."   —*Library Journal*

"Thanks to the cunning of history and the wondrous strangeness of Northern California, the utopian counterculture, psychedelic drugs, military hardware and antimilitary software were tangled together inextricably in the prehistory of the personal computer. Full of interesting details about weird but not arbitrary connections, John Markoff's book tells one of the oddest—because truest—of California tales and thereby helps illuminate the still unsettled legacy of the Sixties."
> —Todd Gitlin, author of *Media Unlimited* and *The Sixties: Years of Hope, Days of Rage*

"It is easy to see how the personal computer has shaped contemporary culture. But how did contemporary culture shape the emergence of the personal computer? In this innovative, lively narrative, veteran technology reporter and cultural critic John Markoff demonstrates how the values and obsessions of the 1960s, especially as centered in the San Francisco Bay Area, created the environment for the emergence of the personal computer as social tool and cultural catalyst."
> —Kevin Starr, author of *Coast of Dreams: California on the Edge, 1990–2003*

"John Markoff's wonderful recounting of the origins of personal computerdom makes a mind-blowing case that our current silicon marvels were inspired by the psychedelic-tinged, revolution-minded spirit of the Sixties. It's a total turn-on."   —Steven Levy, author of *Hackers, Crypto*, and *Insanely Great*

"Beautifully written, *What the Dormouse Said* does that important job of placing in a historical context the development of modern computer technology. It tells us not only what happened, but why. These people changed our world as much as any group ever and now I understand not only how it came to be but also why it was probably inevitable."
> —Robert X. Cringely, author of *Accidental Empires* and host of the PBS series *Triumph of the Nerds*

"Reviled and demonized, then trivialized by the official culture it so exuberantly opposed, the counterculture of the 1960s nevertheless remains the 2000-pound gorilla in the china closet of recent American history. With elegance and efficiency, *What The Dormouse Said* charts one of the most important and overlooked songlines from that mind-expanding moment. Tune in, turn on, boot up!"
> —Jay Stevens, author of *Storming Heaven: LSD and the America Dream* and *Burning Down the House*

What the Dormouse Said

How the Sixties Counterculture Shaped the Personal Computer Industry

JOHN MARKOFF

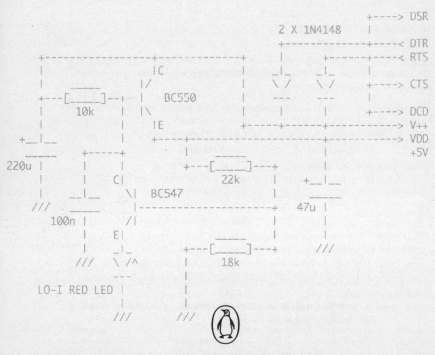

PENGUIN BOOKS

PENGUIN BOOKS

Published by the Penguin Group
Penguin Group (USA) Inc., 375 Hudson Street, New York, New York 10014, U.S.A.
Penguin Group (Canada), 90 Eglinton Avenue East, Suite 700, Toronto,
Ontario, Canada M4P 2Y3 (a division of Pearson Penguin Canada Inc.)
Penguin Books Ltd, 80 Strand, London WC2R 0RL, England
Penguin Ireland, 25 St Stephen's Green, Dublin 2, Ireland (a division of Penguin Books Ltd)
Penguin Group (Australia), 250 Camberwell Road, Camberwell,
Victoria 3124, Australia (a division of Pearson Australia Group Pty Ltd)
Penguin Books India Pvt Ltd, 11 Community Centre,
Panchsheel Park, New Delhi–110 017, India
Penguin Group (NZ), cnr Airborne and Rosedale Roads, Albany,
Auckland 1310, New Zealand (a division of Pearson New Zealand Ltd)
Penguin Books (South Africa) (Pty) Ltd, 24 Sturdee Avenue,
Rosebank, Johannesburg 2196, South Africa

Penguin Books Ltd, Registered Offices:
80 Strand, London WC2R 0RL, England

First published in the United States of America by Viking Penguin,
a member of Penguin Group (USA) Inc. 2005
Published in Penguin Books 2006

10 9 8 7 6 5 4 3 2 1

THE LIBRARY OF CONGRESS HAS CATALOGED THE HARDCOVER EDITION AS FOLLOWS:
Markoff, John.
What the dormouse said—: how the sixties counterculture shaped
the personal computer industry / John Markoff.
p. cm.
Includes bibliographical references and index.
ISBN 0-670-03382-0 (hc.)
ISBN 0 14 30.3676 9 (pbk.)
1. Microcomputers—History.   2. Computers and civilization.   3. Nineteen sixties.   I. Title.
QA76.17.M37   2005
004.16—dc22   2004061181

Printed in the United States of America

When logic and proportion
Have fallen sloppy dead
And the White Knight is talking backwards
And the Red Queen's "Off with her head!"
Remember what the dormouse said:
Feed your head!
Feed your head!
Feed your head!

—Grace Slick, Jefferson Airplane, "White Rabbit" (1966)

PREFACE

There are, generally speaking, two popular accounts of the invention of personal computing.

The first roots the PC in the exploits of a pair of young computer hobbyists–turned–entrepreneurs, Stephen Wozniak and Steven Jobs. Wozniak, the story goes, built a computer to share with his friends at the Homebrew Computer Club, a ragtag group that began meeting on the San Francisco Midpeninsula in the spring of 1975. His high school friend, Steve Jobs, had the foresight to see that there might be a consumer market for such a machine, and so they went on to found Apple Computer in 1976.

The second account locates the birthplace of personal computing at Xerox's fabled Palo Alto Research Center in the early 1970s. There, the giant copier company assembled a group of the nation's best computer scientists and gave them enough freedom to conceive of information tools for the office of the future. Out of that remarkable collection of talent came a computer called the Alto, the forerunner of today's desktops and portables. Although Xerox is reputed to have "fumbled the future" by not commercializing the device successfully, the dozens of spin-offs that resulted from PARC became the basis for one of Silicon Valley's most oft-told fables: that in 1979 Jobs visited PARC and took away with him the idea of the graphical user interface.

Both stories are true, yet they are both incomplete.

This book is about what came before, about the extraordinary convergence of politics, culture, and technology that took place in a period of less than two decades and within the space of just a few square miles. Out of that convergence came a remarkable idea: personal computing, the notion that one person should control all of the functions of a computer and that the machine would in turn respond as an idea amplifier. By the late 1960s, that idea was already in the air on the San Francisco Midpeninsula.

Before the arrival of the Xerox scientists and the Homebrew hobbyists, the technologies underlying personal computing were being pursued at two government-funded research laboratories located on opposite sides of Stanford University. The two labs had been founded during the sixties, based on fundamentally different philosophies: Douglas Engelbart's Augmented Human Intellect Research Center at Stanford Research Institute was dedicated to the concept that powerful computing machines would be able to substantially increase the power of the human mind. In contrast, John McCarthy's Stanford Artificial Intelligence Laboratory began with the goal of creating a simulated human intelligence.

One group worked to augment the human mind; the other to replace it.

Although the two groups had only sporadic contact during the sixties, within each lab was a handful of researchers and engineers who early on understood a fundamental truth about the microelectronics industry then taking root in Santa Clara Valley: Unlike with any previous technologies, the very nature of the silicon chip would inexorably lead to an increase in the power of computing. Moreover, as the transistors etched onto silicon wafers shrank in size, the pace of the process would accelerate. For each reduction of the size of transistors by half, the area for circuits on a chip quadrupled. Computer speed and capacity would continue to increase while costs fell and the size of computers shrank. It was a straightforward insight, but for those who made the leap it was the mind-expanding equivalent of taking a psychedelic drug.

In 1965, Intel cofounder Gordon Moore noted the phenomenon,

which was later known as Moore's Law and which became Silicon Valley's defining principle. By the 1980s and 1990s, Moore's Law had emerged as the underlying assumption that governed almost everything in the Valley, from technology to business, education, and even culture. The "law" said the number of transistors would double every couple of years. It dictated that nothing stays the same for more than a moment; no technology is safe from its successor; costs fall and computing power increases not at a constant rate but exponentially. If you're not running on what became known as "Internet time," you're falling behind.

Although Moore received the intellectual credit for the paradigm, his law had actually been uncovered some years earlier by a handful of computing pioneers who were among the first to contemplate the new semiconductor-manufacturing technology based on photolithographic printing of transistors and logic circuits on the surface of silicon wafers. At the beginning of the 1960s, a small group of computer designers and engineers working with integrated circuits had realized that the technology held stunning economic implications, and not just for moon shots and nuclear-tipped missiles. As semiconductor-manufacturing capabilities were refined, it became apparent that computing, then in the hands of just a few, would eventually be available to everyone.

To these pioneers, the trajectory was obvious. As a result, while the early machines used by researchers at the Stanford laboratories were neither desktop-size nor personal, the central ideas of interactivity and individual control quickly became ingrained in everything they designed. The *idea* of personal computing was born in the sixties; only later, when falling costs and advancements in technology made it feasible, would the box itself arrive.

The engineers' insight did not take place in a vacuum, however. The shrinking silicon chip did not emerge in isolation from the surrounding world but grew out of the twin geopolitical challenges of placing a man on the moon and squeezing navigational circuitry into the nosecone of an ICBM. Today, this is hard to appreciate, particularly because the pace of the semiconductor industry has made progress seem almost mechanistic as each new generation of chips arrives like clockwork. In a similar fashion, the two Stanford laboratories came into existence in a remarkable place during an extraordinary time. The San Francisco Midpeninsula during the sixties and early seventies witnessed an epochal intersection of science, politics, art, and commerce, a convergence comparable to that at such landmark places in history as Vienna after World War I.

Beginning in the fifties, the computer had come under attack as a symbol of large, centralized, bureaucratic institutions. Lewis Mumford, writing in *The Myth of the Machine: The Pentagon of Power,* asserted that the electronic computer had been created in opposition to human freedom and denounced the computer technicians who worked at creating superhuman machines. In the course of a single decade, however, that worldview changed. Computing went from being dismissed as a tool of bureaucratic control to being embraced as a symbol of individual expression and liberation. The evolution of the perception of the computer mirrored other changes in the world at large.

By the end of the 1960s, the United States had been transformed by a broad political and social upheaval that stripped away the comfortable middle-class veneer of the previous decade. The civil rights, psychedelic, women's rights, ecology, and antiwar movements all contributed to the emergence of a counterculture that rejected many of America's cherished postwar ideals. The computer technologies that we take for granted today owe their shape to this unruly period, which was defined by protest, experimentation with drugs, countercultural community, and a general sense of anarchic idealism.

Stewart Brand has argued in his essay "We Owe It All to the Hippies" that "the counterculture's scorn for centralized authority provided the philosophical foundations of not only the leaderless Internet but also the entire personal-computer revolution."[1] Theodore Roszak has advanced a similar argument in *From Satori to*

Silicon Valley (1986), a monograph that traces the rise of the personal-computer industry to countercultural values of the period.

In fact, the New Left and the counterculture were then split between modern-day Luddites and technophiles. Some espoused an antitechnology, back-to-the-land philosophy. Others believed that better tools could lead to social progress. Brand's toolcentric worldview, epitomized by one of the decade's most popular and influential books, the *Whole Earth Catalog* (1968), made the case that technology could be harnessed for more democratic and decentralized uses. The catalog ultimately helped shape the view of an entire generation, which came to believe that computing technologies could be used in the service of such goals as political revolution and safeguarding the environment.

Brand was the first outsider to catch a glimpse of this new cybernetic world and discern the parallels between mind expansion through the use of psychedelic drugs and through the new kinds of computing that were being developed around the Stanford campus. In 1972, he assembled a series of vignettes about the emerging computer scene into a *Rolling Stone* article: "Spacewar: Fanatic Life and Symbolic Death among the Computer Bums." Two years later, he expanded the article into the book *II Cybernetic Frontiers* (1974), in which he became the first to popularize the term "personal computer." Brand caught the spirit of the times perfectly in his *Rolling Stone* piece, which describes how one of the nation's most advanced computer-research laboratories was transformed in the evenings into a video-game arcade. "These are heads, most of them," he wrote. "Half or more of computer science is heads."[2]

Brand was right. Listen to the stories of those who lived through the sixties and seventies on the Midpeninsula, and you soon realize that it is impossible to explain the dazzling new technologies without understanding the lives and the times of the people who created them. The impact of the region's heady mix of culture and technology can be seen clearly in the personal stories of many of these pioneers of the computer industry. Indeed, personal decisions frequently had historic consequences.

■ ■ ■

If you put a stake in the ground at Kepler's, an eclectic bookstore run by pacifist Roy Kepler that was located on El Camino Real in Menlo Park beginning in the 1950s, and drew a five-mile circle around it, you would have captured Engelbart's Augment research group at SRI, McCarthy's Stanford Artificial Intelligence Laboratory, and Xerox's Palo Alto Research Center, as well as the hobbyists who made up the People's Computer Company and the Homebrew Computer Club.

It is not a coincidence that although it was at the periphery of the established computing world, California is where personal computing first emerged. For most of its history, the computing establishment had been centered in the upstate New York mainframe factories of IBM and in the research laboratories and the emerging high-technology world surrounding MIT and Cambridge. Beginning in the sixties, however, the Midpeninsula, a relatively compact region located between San Jose and San Francisco, became a crucible not only for political protest and a thriving counterculture but also a new set of computing paradigms.

An argument can be made that the seeds of personal computing were planted simultaneously on both the East and West coasts. Certainly the idea of a single-user computer was alive around Route 128 in Massachusetts as well as on the Midpeninsula in the 1960s. Work had started on the LINC, the brainchild of MIT physicist Wesley A. Clark, as early as May 1961. That machine was used for the first time at the National Institute of Mental Health in Bethesda, Maryland, the following year to analyze a cat's neural responses. The LINC appeared just a year before Ivan E. Sutherland's Ph.D. thesis describing a remarkably innovative software-design program called Sketchpad. That program, which ran on an early MIT-designed TX-2 minicomputer, was the first program to embody a complete graphical user interface.

With figures like Sutherland, Vannevar Bush, J. C. R. Licklider, Robert Taylor, Theodor Nelson, and the computer hackers[3] at MIT, all of the intellectual ingredients for personal computing existed on the East Coast. Why, then, did the passion for the PC and later the PC industry emerge first around Stanford?

The answer is that there was no discrete technological straight line to the personal computer on the East Coast. What separated the isolated experiments with small computers from the full-blown birth of personal computing was the West Coast realization that computing was a new medium, like books, records, movies, radios, and television. The personal computer had the ability to encompass all of the media that had come before it and had the additional benefit of appearing at a time and place where all the old rules were being questioned. Personal computers that were designed for and belonged to single individuals would emerge initially in concert with a counterculture that rejected authority and believed the human spirit would triumph over corporate technology, not be subject to it.

The East Coast computing culture didn't get it. The old computing world was hierarchical and conservative. Years later, after the PC was an established reality, Ken Olson, the founder of minicomputer maker Digital Equipment Corporation, still refused to acknowledge the idea: He publicly asserted there was no need for a home computer. Digital, though it had pioneered the minicomputer, machines intended for corporate departments and laboratories, underestimated the significance of the personal computer until it was far too late to catch up with the West Coast.

In the sixties, the community surrounding Stanford University was a bundle of contradictions. Outwardly, it was a sleepy college community, complete with leafy, tree-lined streets, a properly stuffy neighborhood dubbed "Professorville," understated shopping districts, and *Leave It to Beaver* high schools. But the Midpeninsula had never been a completely American-as-apple-pie Levittown. There had long been a bohemian fringe in the Bay Area, dating far back to the immigrant culture that created California, and even in the fifties and early sixties there was an undercurrent that ran at cross-purposes to the middle-class mainstream.

On the surface, the area's economy was driven by the rise of the military-industrial complex. Early on, Stanford University spun off electronics companies such as Varian, Ampex, and Hewlett-Packard, and after World War II the Midpeninsula had become a center for high-technology military manufacturing and research and development. To the south, the Midpeninsula was bounded by Lockheed Missiles and Space Corporation, which was building the Polaris nuclear missile; to the north was the Stanford Research Institute, serving as a think tank for both military and industrial concerns.

But there were growing cracks in the facade. Outwardly middle-class, Palo Alto hid a more complex reality below the surface. The town played cameos in influential novels. Both Clancy Sigal's *Going Away*, the largely autobiographical tale of a blacklisted Hollywood screenwriter, as well as Thomas Pynchon's *The Crying of Lot 49* commence in Palo Alto. The bohemian spirit embodied by Dean Moriarty in Jack Kerouac's *On the Road* animated a tiny counterculture. It was not, however, the sort of openly radical counterculture that has long defined Berkeley, on the other side of the bay. In the sixties, the Midpeninsula was a different kind of melting pot, with folk music and a beat scene as well as a tiny radical left. In *Positively Fourth Street*, Robert Hajdu describes how in the early fifties a Pete Seeger concert at Palo Alto High School ultimately had a life-changing influence on David Guard, a Stanford student and founding member of the Kingston Trio. Joan Baez also attended the same concert with her sister Mimi and remembered it as a "major moment" in her life.

And, of course, there was the Grateful Dead. Originally a pizza-parlor folk-rock band known as the Warlocks, during the mid-sixties the Dead literally became the house band for the Midpeninsula, their concerts offering a ready-made identity for members of all of the area's unruly threads of political and cultural unrest. The group had emerged directly from a set of wrenching, mind-expanding LSD parties orchestrated by Ken Kesey and his Merry Pranksters called Acid Tests, which would transform the culture of the Midpeninsula and ultimately the rest of the country.

Now, more than three decades later, the sixties are at best a hazy apparition. The joke, of course, is that if you can remember the sixties, you weren't really there. Today, it's easy to laugh at the long hair, headbands, VW buses, and love beads that were trademarks of the counterculture. Two fingers held aloft in a V no longer stood for victory but for peace, and millions of people united in idealistic causes ranging from civil rights to ending the war in Vietnam. How unlike the cynical, selfish nineties, or even our own increasingly uncertain decade.

It's easy to forget, too, especially from the vantage point of today's "just say no" antidrug morality, and almost impossible to understand how different attitudes were toward drugs during the sixties. LSD, in particular, has become an incendiary subject. Demonized today, its impact is glibly dismissed. Yet four decades ago, LSD was a defining force in a cultural war. Consider the June 28, 1966, issue of *Look,* which reported on California and its "turned-on" people. "Many Californians, among them honor students and leading professionals, have used the drug in a most 'serious' manner, under careful controls," the magazine reported. "These people have tried LSD neither for kicks nor therapy, but to gain glimpses of new and rich worlds of consciousness."[4]

For those who grew up during the 1960s, though, the decade is still a touchstone, having transformed everyone who lived through it—and that is especially true for many of the computer scientists, entrepreneurs, and hackers whom I interviewed for this book. Over and over again in my research, I ran into engineers and programmers who came to computing research in the sixties to avoid military service. While it was a convenient way of avoiding being drafted to fight in Vietnam, that generation was also certain it was going to change the world. Even those who weren't standing at the barricades were deeply caught up in a set of events that was to thoroughly change America over the course of a decade and a half. It seemed inevitable that the old order would collapse and that a different, more spiritual path—to somewhere—lay just ahead.

For some of Silicon Valley's most influential figures, the connection between personal computing and the counterculture has not been forgotten. Early in 2001, I met with Apple's cofounder, Steve Jobs. I have interviewed Jobs dozens of times over two decades and have come to know his moods well. This was not one of our better conversations. A photographer had accompanied me, and if there is one way to insure that Apple's mercurial chief executive will be irritated, it is to attempt to take his picture during an interview.

After only a handful of photographs, Jobs threw the photographer out, and things went downhill from there. Jobs was in a particularly bad mood. However, as our session ended, he sat down in front of one of his Macintosh computers to demonstrate a new program he had introduced earlier that morning before the legions of faithful. iTunes was to turn any Macintosh into a digital music player that stored and played CDs or music downloaded from the Internet. It included a simple visualization feature that conjured up dancing color patterns that pulsed on the computer's screen in concert with the beat of the music.

Obviously pleased with the feature, Jobs turned to me with a slight smile and said, "It reminds me of my youth." I responded by mentioning the names of several of Silicon Valley's best-known pioneers who had taken psychedelic drugs in the 1960s. That ignited an unexpectedly candid and passionate response. It is widely known that Jobs, a dropout from Reed College in Portland, had experimented with drugs and pursued a countercultural lifestyle both before and after helping found the quirky computer maker. Despite the fact that he now flies around the world in his own corporate jet and has a personal net worth of more than one billion dollars, Jobs has maintained deep emotional ties to the era in which he grew up.

He explained that he still believed that taking LSD was one of the two or three most important things he had done in his life, and he said he felt that because people he knew well had not tried psychedelics, there were things about him they couldn't understand. He also said that his countercultural roots often left him feeling like an outsider in the corporate world of which he is now a leader.

Over the span of three decades, much of the original spirit of the sixties has been lost. For many today, the era serves almost as a historical Rorschach test: either an idealistic moment in time, symbolized by a protester placing a flower in the barrel of the gun, or a target for a conservative pundit like *Newsweek* columnist George Will to rail against, whether because of the evils of LSD or the millions of lives said to be ruined by the hedonism of the Grateful Dead.

The sixties likewise serve a similar function for attitudes about information technology. Today, the modern computing industry has become divided into two warring camps: On one side, giant Microsoft champions the private ownership of information. Software, the company believes, is a commodity to be bought, sold, and jealously guarded. Opposed to Microsoft are growing legions of computer programmers who have formed an open-source movement that is committed to the idea that information should be free and that shared software can be used to animate increasingly powerful computers.

The schism between information propertarians and information libertarians divides not only the computer industry but increasingly the entire digital world, affecting the consumer electronics, recording, and motion-picture industries. The defenders of information as private property make the case that unregulated information availability, whether in the form of file sharing or in the doctrines of the open-source movement, is a fundamental threat to industry as well as innovation. Led by Microsoft and the recording and film industries, there is a great cry that the vandals are at the gates and that

information sharing is the digital-age equivalent of the threat communism posed to developing industrialism in the nineteenth and
twentieth centuries.

When societal benefits are weighed against those of private interests, however, the consequences of allowing information to be
shared without restriction become more nuanced. Consider the
roots of Silicon Valley. The transistor was invented at AT&T's Bell
Laboratories in New Jersey, but the giant telecommunications company was later forced to license the invention freely under the terms
of an antitrust settlement with the Justice Department. The Valley's
very existence—the product of the most dramatic technological and
entrepreneurial boom in the nation's history—was made possible by
the enforced availability of the transistor.

Likewise, the hacker's ethos of sharing information lies at the
very heart of the explosive growth of the personal computer. It is not
a coincidence that, during the sixties and early seventies, at the
height of the protest against the war in Vietnam, the civil rights
movement, and widespread experimentation with psychedelic
drugs, personal computing emerged from a handful of government-
and corporate-funded laboratories, as well as from the work of a
small group of hobbyists who were desperate to get their hands on
computers they could personally control and decide to what uses they
should be put.

Science fiction writer William Gibson has said, "The future's already arrived; it's just not evenly distributed yet."[5] That observation
is particularly true of a tiny microcosm that was as localized but has
become as influential in the world as fifteenth-century Florence was
when it gave the world the Renaissance half a millennium ago.

■■■

This book grew out of a spirited dinner held several years ago on a
Sausalito, California, houseboat. The evening was an informal reunion of a computer-industry pioneer—Douglas Engelbart—with a

small group of people who had once worked for him: Bill and Roberta English and Bill and Ann Duvall. Also present was Ted Nelson, an itinerant writer, inventor, and social scientist who can best be described as the Don Quixote of computing. Nelson was a contemporary of Engelbart in the sixties, and the two men had pursued many of the same innovations.

Engelbart, however, had been the first to demonstrate a vision that led directly to today's computing world. He came early on to understand that computing had the potential to range far beyond crunching numbers. He foresaw that computers would become machines that could help human beings communicate and extend the reach of their intelligence.

When he began his crusade in the sixties, computing was almost exclusively the province of a handful of scientists, giant corporations, and the military. Several years earlier, Engelbart had begun to sketch a remarkable plan outlining a new set of information tools based on powerful computers. From that original inspiration, both personal computing and the Internet ultimately emerged. A soft-spoken man with a mane of prematurely silver hair, Engelbart was able to launch in 1963 a leading-edge computer-science experiment funded by the air force, NASA, and the Pentagon because he had been able to capture the attention of several far-seeing scientists who were at the time working in the Pentagon as program managers.

While it was a singular vision, Engelbart's "Augmentation Framework" was brought to life by a small band of researchers who were deeply influenced by the political and cultural climate of the Mid-peninsula. Indeed, within Stanford Research Institute, the research center where Engelbart began his work in Menlo Park, his researchers came to be seen as the lunatic fringe.

In the midst of this engineers' world of crewcuts and white shirts and ties arrived a tiny band distinguished by their long hair and beards, rooms carpeted with oriental rugs, women without bras, jugs of wine, and on occasion the wafting of marijuana smoke. Just walking through the halls of the SRI laboratory gave a visitor a visceral sense of the cultural gulf that existed between the prevailing model of mainframe computing and the gestating vision of personal computing.

Setting aside its countercultural trappings, Engelbart's view of the future of computing in the sixties ran directly counter to the precepts of the mainstream of the computing business. The era was dominated by a belief that artificial intelligence was at hand and would soon create a world populated by thinking machines. Engelbart's notion of creating work groups where human intelligence was instead "augmented" by computers was thought of as quaint and beside the point. It might be suited for the office, or it could improve the skills of a secretary, but it certainly could not be considered real computer "science."

Indeed, Engelbart's augmentation philosophy was in many ways the polar opposite of the ideal of artificial intelligence, which sought to replace humans with machines. AI was in fashion both elsewhere in SRI and on the other side of the Stanford campus, where John McCarthy, a brilliant mathematician and computer-science researcher who had come from MIT, was busy creating his own research center, the Stanford Artificial Intelligence Laboratory. SAIL, as it came to be known, served as a second source for the ideas, people, and technology that were to come together beginning in 1970 at Xerox PARC. Yet though SAIL and Augment were philosophically opposed, the labs shared a computer hacker culture and deeply antiauthoritarian outlook. Funded by the Pentagon's Advanced Research Projects Agency, at the height of its most creative and unconstrained period, SAIL served as a home to many of the most inventive minds in the computing world. SAIL was as unconventional as it was innovative. Researchers lived in the attic above their offices, encounter groups met in the steam tunnels in the basement, and from that tumult emerged the technological insights that would help reshape both Silicon Valley and the entire world during the next decade.

At dinner with Engelbart, I realized that, in spite of reading widely about the history of Silicon Valley and computing, I wasn't familiar with the stories being told that evening. What struck me was that the tales weren't about the technologies but rather about the lives of the researchers themselves, their personal relationships, the drugs they took, the sex they enjoyed, the rock and roll they listened to, and the political protest in which they took part.

I've attempted to set down some of that history before it is lost. The stories collected in this book set out to explore the brief period in a turbulent place that gave the world personal computing.

San Francisco
December 2004

CONTENTS

1 | THE PROPHET AND THE TRUE BELIEVERS

In February of 1960, two young California engineers boarded a plane on their way to an annual electronics technical meeting in Philadelphia. The International Circuits Conference had until recently been focused on the world of radio, but that was changing as electronic systems began to find their way into a broader range of consumer, business, and military equipment.

It was, of course, a time of great hope. John Kennedy was campaigning for the presidency. California, caught in the throes of the post–World War II economic boom, was seen as the Promised Land. Santa Clara County, in particular, long before it became Silicon Valley, was known as the Valley of Heart's Delight, a term coined by the San Jose Chamber of Commerce to promote the region during the 1920s. In 1922, the county had eighty thousand acres of plum orchards, but by 1960 they and local cow pastures were giving way to tract homes for the waves of engineers and scientists who were arriving in the area. Sputnik had shocked the nation out of its complacency, and Santa Clara County was quickly becoming an important aerospace and technology center.

Despite the overall climate of optimism, it was a troubling time for both engineers, for in recent years they had been working at the Stanford Research Institute on research that now seemed to have rapidly diminishing prospects. The project, led by one of the young men, Hewitt Crane, explored developing magnetic solid-state circuits.

The idea of magnetic computing had been attractive to the project's military backers, concerned that warfare would increasingly move off the planet and into space, where the bulky and unreliable vacuum tubes then in use would be inappropriate. The hunt was on for a new generation of electronic switches that could be squeezed into the cockpits of rocket ships bound for the moon or the nose cones of the ballistic missiles aimed at the Soviet Union. But the previous year both Texas Instruments and Fairchild Semiconductor had perfected new techniques for etching transistors directly onto wafers of silicon and churning them out as easily as if they were photographic prints, an innovation that had seriously tarnished the prospects of the SRI effort.

Hew Crane had a remarkably curious and fertile mind and had been one of the first men to program and design computers. As a graduate student at Columbia University in the late 1940s, he had taken a night job programming IBM's Selective Sequence Electronic Calculator, a room-sized machine that had been installed in the company's Madison Avenue offices in New York City, where it was visible from the street, a powerful symbol of the company's high-tech panache. Composed of thirteen thousand mechanical relays, the SSEC, which could perform a lumbering twenty-five instructions per second (today an Intel Pentium microprocessor will easily surpass three billion instructions in the same second), was a computing machine that straddled the divide between calculators and modern computers. It didn't have a memory in the modern sense, and programs were entered via punched paper tape.

The skills Crane developed on the SSEC later proved useful when he was hired to work on a new computer being built by the legendary mathematician John Von Neumann at the Institute for Advanced Study in Princeton. Frustrated with the slow speed of getting data into and out of his machine, Von Neumann had persuaded IBM's founder, Tom Watson Sr., to donate a punch-card reader to help speed up the process. Since he was one of the few people who knew how card readers worked, Crane was enlisted in the project.

In Princeton, he was witness to one of the world's first artificial light shows when, late at night, he sat and watched the Johniac's one hundred thousand neon tubes dance on and off in rhythmic patterns. Before long, he learned to recognize which programs were running by watching the hypnotic sequences. The Johniac was one of the first computers to use a new type of storage known as magnetic-core memory. Shaped like tiny LifeSavers, each magnetic ring in its memory bank could store a one or a zero, and the technology came to dominate the world of computing for the next two decades.

After the Johniac project ended in 1955, Crane moved several miles down the road, where he continued to work on magnetic storage technology at Sarnoff Laboratories. He invented a quirky memory called a Multi-Aperture Device (MAD), which was capable of storing more than a single bit of information. He also began to muse about the possibility of building computers out of wires and magnets. It was an obvious train of thought, because the computers of that era could run for only an hour or so at a time before one of their tube-based switches failed.

His magnetic explorations were delayed, however, by an urgent call from Stanford Research Institute, inviting him to come west to help debug a new data processor that the research group's "whiz kids" were building for the Bank of America. In 1950, when the company had first approached SRI with the idea of automated check processing, it was customary for banks to close their doors at 2:00 P.M. every day so that armies of bookkeepers could manually process and update the day's accounts. In the midst of the postwar economic boom, Bank of America was adding twenty-three thousand accounts each month, and its check-processing system was groaning under the load. Now, five years later, the bank was getting edgy about whether the engineers could actually succeed in building a working machine capable of automatically handling its checks.

Since Crane had already been through the design of two major computing systems, he was considered a seasoned expert. He moved to California and for the next year spent virtually every day and night on his knees on the floor poring over the blueprints of the circuits for ERMA, which stood for Electronic Recording Machine Accounting.

After he completed his work on ERMA, Crane looked around for an interesting project, and his attention returned to the field of magnetics. The work in that area was fun, but everyone in the SRI group could see the writing on the wall: Magnetic computers simply weren't fast enough to meet the demands of the coming data-processing era. Still, Crane had found the challenge intellectually stimulating, and his MADs ultimately made their way into several commercial and military systems, including the New York City subway system, where they are still functioning nearly five decades later.

In the winter of 1960, Crane's group was working on a magnetic shift register, one of the key components of a computer. The previous year, he had introduced the idea of an all-magnetic computer at an industry technical conference and now was planning to deliver a report on the group's work at the Philadelphia meeting. His traveling companion, Douglas Engelbart, was a member of Crane's small team of engineers that was exploring magnetic storage and magnetic computing systems. The two men frequently socialized and were both devotees of Greek folk dancing, which they performed in their homes on the Midpeninsula.

Yet Engelbart presented special managerial headaches for Crane. A dreamy engineer with a mind of his own, Doug Engelbart was not an easy person to control. He had joined the group in 1957, and though he recognized that he had to earn his keep by working on SRI projects, he had arrived with his own agenda: a scheme for building a machine to "augment" human intelligence. It was not a popular idea, and one of the people he had interviewed with when he applied for a job at the institute had warned him to keep quiet about it. If the think tank discovered what he was planning, the interviewer said, it would never hire him.

Doug Engelbart had always understood he was a bit different. He had grown up on a farm in Portland, Oregon, without a father during his teenage years, in a family that was barely able to get by. He was aware early on that he could be oblivious to some basic social insights that were immediately obvious to most people. One day in his senior year of high school, he was sitting in class when he happened to look down the aisle at a row of his schoolmates. He was struck by the fact that his only pair of shoes were the old and battered high tops he was wearing. As he looked at the other students' carefully polished shoes, he also realized that his were the only ones that had milk stains and cow shit on them.[1]

Being a bit eccentric, however, was not considered a liability within the nerdy world of 1950s engineers. Engelbart quickly became a valuable member of the SRI magnetics laboratory, contributing a number of his own ideas and receiving a series of patents for his work. Still, there was no denying that Engelbart was quirky and from the outset was a handful. He had his own vision, and little else mattered. At one point, Crane threw up his hands and ended up going from one manager at SRI to another looking for help in coping with him. No one had much useful advice to offer, and so one day Crane finally walked into the office of one of the research center's top managers and said, "Jerry, I know you well enough. I have two things to say, and it will only take sixty seconds. Point number one is that you have to choose. You either have to risk it on this guy or you have to fire him. The second thing I have to say is that this is the brightest guy I have ever worked with." He then said good-bye and turned around and walked out the door.

Engelbart survived.

Moreover, he remained passionate about his ideas in a way that few men manage to be in the course of doing their jobs. He had been fortunate to stumble upon the defining purpose in his life more than a decade earlier while he had been waiting out the formal end of World War II, in the Philippines. He had been trained as a navy radar technician in 1944, and as his boat backed out of its berth on the San Francisco waterfront in August of 1945, headed for the Pacific, he stood on deck waving good-bye. Suddenly there was a burst of whistles, firecrackers, and cheers from the shoreline, and the sailors gathered on deck turned and asked one another if they did this for every ship that left port. Then the ship's PA speaker announced that the Japanese had surrendered—it was V-J Day![2] Engelbart had been struggling with his fears about combat, but now they vanished. On deck the shouts rang out, "Turn around! Turn around!"

Thirty-eight days later, the ship dropped the technicians off on the island of Samar in the Philippines. Although everyone was tremendously relieved that the war was over, it was to be a full, monotonous year before Engelbart returned to California. He amused himself during these long days by watching the towering, tropical cloud formations. The tops of the clouds would be bathed in white light and would pass through the spectrum of colors to their base, where they were dark purple. Engelbart frequently found himself stopped in his tracks with his head back, gazing at the sky. In the evenings, he made a habit of walking down to the gate of his base and asking the shore-patrol soldiers if he could go out and sit on the seawall and watch the sunset.[3]

During his stay, he was relocated with another group of sailors to the neighboring island of Laiti, where he stumbled across a Red Cross reading library in a native hut set on stilts, complete with a thatched roof and plentiful bamboo.

It was in that library that he found what would become his calling. On the bookshelves he discovered a pile of magazines, and while reading an issue of *Life* he came across a description of an article that had appeared in the *Atlantic Monthly* in July of 1945.[4] It contained a proposal by the physicist Vannevar Bush for the creation of a machine that could track and retrieve vast volumes of information. As director of the Pentagon's Office of Scientific Research and Development, Bush had overseen science and engineering during the war. Now he speculated on the application of these fields to the deluge of data that was threatening to overwhelm researchers.

The piece was a *Popular Mechanics*–style vision of tools for the scientist of the future, but toward its conclusion Bush briefly outlined his concept for a machine that startled Engelbart:

> Consider a future device for individual use, which is a sort of mechanized private file and library. It needs a name, and, to coin one at random, "Memex" will do. A Memex is a device in which an individual stores all his books, records, and communications, and which is mechanized so that it may be consulted with exceeding speed and flexibility. It is an enlarged intimate supplement to his memory.[5]

The idea of a device that could extend the power of the human mind left Engelbart awestruck, and he wandered around for days afterward telling people what he had read. But Bush's Memex vision was not the only idea that he came across on the beach in the Philippines. He also found an essay written by William James titled "What Makes a Life Significant," which also made a lasting impression. It may, in fact, have left a mark as enduring as Memex, inspiring the young man to pursue a head-down, dogged commitment to his goal.

When Engelbart returned to the United States after a year he went to Corvallis, Oregon, to finish the studies he had begun before joining the navy, obtaining his degree in electrical engineering at Oregon State University, graduating in 1948. Out of school, he was recruited to work at the Ames Research Center in Mountain View, California. The center was part of the National Advisory Committee for Aeronautics, or NACA, the forerunner to NASA. There, he served as an electrical engineer in the electrical section, a service and support group. The department was responsible for maintenance of the center's giant wind tunnels as well as for creating specialized electronic gadgets. The job didn't evoke any special enthusiasm in

Engelbart, but it exposed him to a number of new technologies and intriguing ideas.

Engelbart remained a bookworm, and he soon gravitated to Stanford's vast libraries. They were wonderful places for someone who was shy, and he roamed through the stacks after work. This was not, however, a great way to meet women or socialize, and after several years he was still very much a lone engineer and a bachelor.

One day, a colleague suggested that one way he could meet girls was to go folk dancing. Engelbart initially resisted, as the idea seemed silly to him. But his friend insisted, and eventually he was persuaded to attend an intermediate folk-dancing class at the Palo Alto Community Center. After briefly watching the lively scene, he plunged in, dancing with everyone. It was not long afterward that he met his wife-to-be, Ballard, at one of the classes.

Getting engaged precipitated a deep crisis for Doug Engelbart. The day he proposed, he was driving to work, feeling excited, when it suddenly struck him that he really had no idea what he was going to do with the rest of his life. He stopped the car and pulled over and thought for a while.

He was dumbstruck to realize that there was nothing that he was working on that was even vaguely exciting. He liked his colleagues, and Ames was in general a good place to work, but nothing there captured his spirit.

It was December 1950, and he was twenty-five years old. By the time he arrived at work, he realized that he was on the verge of accomplishing everything that he had set out to accomplish in his life, and it embarrassed him. "My God, this is ridiculous, no goals," he said to himself.[6]

That night when he went home, he began thinking systematically about finding an idea that would enable him to make a significant contribution in the world. He considered general approaches, from medicine to studying sociology or economics, but nothing resonated. Then, within an hour, he was struck in a series of connected flashes of insight by a vision of how people could cope with the challenges of complexity and urgency that faced all human endeavors. He decided that if he could create something to improve the human capability to deal with those challenges, he would have accomplished something fundamental.

In a single stroke, Engelbart experienced a complete vision of the information age. He saw himself sitting in front of a large computer screen full of different symbols. (Later, it occurred to him that the idea of the screen probably came into his mind as a result of his experience with the radar consoles he had worked on in the navy.) He would create a workstation for organizing all of the information and communications needed for any given project. In his mind, he saw streams of characters moving on the display. Although nothing of the sort existed, it seemed the engineering should be easy to do and that the machine could be harnessed with levers, knobs, or switches. It was nothing less than Vannevar Bush's Memex, translated into the world of electronic computing.

In order to create such a machine, he realized that he would need to learn more about computing, which led him to think again about the William James essay he had read in the Philippines. Every project has a first step, he remembered. And the first step in this case was to write to graduate schools. He was accepted at both Stanford and at the University of California at Berkeley, but after learning that Stanford offered nothing special in computing, he immediately enrolled in Berkeley when he discovered that a professor there was beginning to build an early computer.

School was a hectic period during which the Engelbarts had three children and the young researcher explored some esoteric ideas for gas-based computing devices, leading to his doctorate. Afterward, he taught for another year as an assistant professor at Berkeley, but the demands of teaching proved all-consuming, and it soon became clear that he would not be able to pursue his Augment vision at a university. He explored working for several corporate research laboratories, but none seemed a perfect match. In his interviews, he couldn't find anyone who shared his passion. General Electric Research Labs

tried to hire him, but when he broached the idea of digital computing, he came up against a stone wall.

He contacted Hewlett-Packard, which was then a successful man-
ufacturer of test equipment and analog oscilloscopes in a small
Palo Alto factory. Barney Oliver, the company's director of research,
considered some of Engelbart's technology ideas, and after deciding
that HP might be able to harness them for its products, introduced
him to both Hewlett and Packard. Bill Hewlett tried to sell him on
the idea of coming to work for the test equipment maker, while after
speaking with him Dave Packard suggested that the company simply hire him and pay him a royalty for any of his inventions that it
decided to use.

"Everything you can disclose in the first six months of your employ, whether you think about it during that time, or brought it in, is
yours, and everything after that is ours," said Packard.

The idea appealed to Engelbart as a simple and fair solution.
"Sold," he said.

He was preparing to go to work at HP when, while driving home
several nights later, it occurred to him that he hadn't asked the company's managers whether they planned to enter the market for digital computers. He had naturally taken it for granted that their
instrumentation business would take them in that direction.

He pulled over, found a phone booth, and immediately called
Oliver. It was a short and disappointing conversation.

"I am assuming you are going to go into digital technology, aren't
you?" he asked.

The research director replied that the company had no such
plans.

"Well, I should have found that out earlier, and I'm sorry to take
your time," a crestfallen Engelbart said, "because I just can't then go
ahead."[7]

Gradually, Engelbart came to the conclusion that he was going to
have to do it himself. He made the acquaintance of two wealthy
young San Francisco brothers, whose family owned a successful

store in the city. They seemed intrigued with his idea of using gas-discharge components for computing or possibly as display devices. He also met a patent attorney who told him he had a "fond place in his heart for two kinds of people: ministers and college professors,"[8] and that he would be interested in helping him. Engelbart finally created his company, Digital Techniques, in the summer of 1956.

The enterprise didn't last long. Engelbart's investors hired Stanford Research Institute to prepare a report on the technology, and it came back pessimistic. For a time, the business tried to soldier on, making a go of it with commercial ideas like outdoor electronic displays. Then one morning Engelbart woke up and realized he simply couldn't shake his original vision of building a machine to augment human intelligence. He called his three partners and told them he was backing out of the company. They drove over to his house, and everyone sat around the kitchen table feeling bad, but his mind was made up.

He approached Stanford University about a teaching position in computing again, but the school had not yet instituted a computer-science program and still saw computing as a service function rather than an academic discipline. Engelbart received a terse note thanking him for his interest, and he returned to the idea of finding a research laboratory where he might be able to sell his vision. That led him back to Stanford Research Institute. He had since come to the conclusion that, if he paid his dues by working on electrical-engineering research projects at the center, he might earn the freedom to fund his own project. Three months later, he was hired as an electrical engineer.

Stanford had created the institute as an interdisciplinary research center shortly after World War II on the grounds of what had once been the Hopkins estate, an early mansion in Menlo Park. During the war, the land had been occupied by the U.S. Army, which had built a hospital there in anticipation of a wave of wounded soldiers from the planned invasion of Japan. By the mid-fifties, SRI was still housed in its scattered Quonset huts and temporary buildings. The think tank was a collection of young engineers and Ph.D.s, most in their twenties, all eager to build careers and develop skills. Although the new world of digital systems was already on the horizon, analog versus digital computing was still a hotly debated topic. In the wake of the Bank of America ERMA project, SRI research efforts had spread out in a variety of directions, including computer logic, magnetic storage, and artificial intelligence. It was an environment in which a new idea would get others excited, and though Engelbart was at heart a loner, he thrived in it, not only developing concepts that extended the field of magnetic storage but discovering the fundamental principle underlying all of modern microelectronics.[9]

■■■

Much of what we take for granted in the modern world is the direct consequence of an industrial process known as photolithography, which is used to make silicon chips. The transistors, wires, resistors, capacitors, and other components of an integrated circuit are etched onto a thin silicon wafer using various steps involving exposure to light, heat, and chemicals, forming the circuitry in a laborious and precise layering and etching process. Although the integrated circuit was first demonstrated at the Institute of Radio Engineers show in early 1959 by Texas Instruments, the more significant "planar" process used in making silicon chips was developed independently at about the same time by a group of engineers in Mountain View, California, at Fairchild Semiconductor, a small start-up firm that had been founded in 1957 with a $1.5 million investment from Fairchild Camera and Instrument.

Six years later, Gordon Moore, one of the original Fairchild engineers, made an interesting prediction. Writing in the April 19, 1965, issue of *Electronics* magazine, Moore noted that the number of components that could be squeezed onto a single chip of silicon would continue to increase well into the future. At the time, the technology of the day dictated that no more than fifty transistors could be placed on one chip. Moore predicted that by 1975 a chip would be built with as many as sixty-five thousand transistors—a startling increase in density. The press seized on the assertion, which was dubbed "Moore's Law," though it wasn't a law in any formal sense of the word. What Moore had offered was a basic insight into a new industrial process that made it possible to continuously scale down the size of blueprints for the tiny geometric shapes that were used to make modern electronic components.

During the intervening three and a half decades, the significance of Moore's Law has become obvious. Today, it defines the microelectronics industry. Faster, denser computer processors and memory chips are introduced on a clockwork pace that shows no sign of slowing until the end of this decade at the earliest. Microelectronics-based systems have in turn transformed the world. Whether it is networks of ATMs, voice synthesis machines that answer questions via the telephone and displace jobs, or ubiquitous personal computers that have changed the way people communicate and learn, the world continues to be transformed at a hastening rate, driven by the silicon chip.

Gordon Moore has been widely credited with the insight underlying the revolution, but Doug Engelbart had arrived at the same conclusion six years earlier. His understanding of "scaling" and the resulting relentless increase in computing capacity shaped his own life, but those pioneering insights came too early and instead of jump-starting the computer revolution were lost in history.

In 1959, word of the arrival of solid-state electronics had set the insular world of laboratories like Stanford Research Institute abuzz. Led by Hew Crane, the researchers had been exploring solid-state magnetic computers. Now interest was rapidly shifting to silicon-based integrated circuits, and Engelbart seized on their potential. As he thought about them, his work at Ames Research Laboratory in the late 1940s and early 1950s came back into focus. Located at Moffett Field on the western shore of San Francisco Bay, the research center was based around a cluster of large and small wind tunnels. Aeronautical engineers made small models of airplane wings or even complete planes to explore how different designs functioned in simulated real-world conditions. Then they would scale their models up to full-size airplanes.

Engelbart's ruminations were affected by a chance visit to another laboratory at SRI, one that was just down the hall from the magnetics group where he was working. There, he found his first patron.

Charlie Rosen had arrived at the institute at about the same time as Engelbart. He had grown up in Canada and during World War II had worked in a manufacturing plant that churned out Helldiver dive-bombers. An expert in radio and navigation electronics, at times he wondered whether he would ever see the end of the war, even though he wasn't fighting on the front lines. Rosen would frequently have to go up to test the planes' electronics during their maiden voyages. Assembled by French-Canadian peasants, the aircraft were coming off the assembly line so quickly that on more than one occasion he was sure that a plane's first flight would be his last.

Luck was with him, though, and he survived the war. He studied electrical engineering and physics both in Canada and the United States and eventually became a computer designer at a General Electric research laboratory in Syracuse, New York. It was a good job, and he probably would have stayed there for his entire career had it not been for a long cross-country family vacation he took in 1956. The Rosens drove to the West Coast, and Charlie was stunned as they crossed the Sierra Nevada, drove to San Francisco, and then continued on down the Pacific Coast. California felt like paradise, and he immediately determined to get away from the frigid winters in the snowbelt of upstate New York.

A year later, he had job offers from IBM, Lockheed, and the Stanford Research Institute. Both IBM and Lockheed wanted him to take a position running pioneering projects building integrated circuits. SRI proposed a job doing anything he wanted to do, which proved to be too irresistible to refuse.

Soon after he arrived at Stanford, Rosen created an applied-physics laboratory, with the idea of pursuing a range of problems, including the new field of solid-state physics, which held out the promise of advancing the equally new field of microelectronics. In addition to having technical skills, Rosen was a consummate fundraiser and was the first SRI scientist to go routinely to Washington to begin selling government agencies on research projects. Soon, the laboratory was graced with a wide range of military contracts from the Army Signal Corps, the National Security Agency, the Office of Naval Research, and the Rome Air Development Center.

One day, an unusual character walked through the door. Ken Shoulders was the kind of unschooled scientific genius that Rosen loved. Later, he would say that in the early days there were no required skills, you just had to be smart. That described Shoulders, who bubbled with wild ideas at an astounding rate. Before coming to SRI, he had worked at MIT as a technician. Some time later, he was informally voted the SRI researcher most likely to build a perpetual-motion machine.

In 1958, a year before the invention of the integrated circuit, Shoulders told Rosen that he thought he could create a new class of electronic device: a machine that would exist in a vacuum and would be made of two materials, molybdenum and aluminum oxide. He had come west with a dream of making tiny triodes—microscopic switches—using the same processes that later became commonplace for making semiconductors. Shoulders's goal was to make triodes that would be no larger than one micron in size and make millions of them at a time using electron beams to etch patterns in exotic materials.

Rosen had had plenty of experience in electronics, and as he listened to Shoulders sketch out his dream he decided the idea wasn't a completely crackpot scheme, even though there were then no existing methods for making computer chips, or doing things in parallel, or using resists or acids to etch circuits. Rosen went to his own boss, Jerry Noe, who told him that everyone else Shoulders had talked to about the idea thought the technician was crazy.

"If you take him on, you've got to feed him, Charlie," Noe said.

So Rosen traveled east and met with the Office of Naval Research, which gave him $25,000 to get Shoulders started on his project. Gradually, he got money from other government agencies as well.

Engelbart and Rosen had met the previous year when Engelbart had been hired at SRI, and of course he had immediately told Rosen about his dream for building Bush's Memex information search and retrieval machine. It had sounded like an interesting idea to Rosen, but he hadn't thought much about it since. He had been immediately struck, however, by Engelbart's stubbornness and determination. The two men occasionally discussed scientific problems around the coffee machine, and Rosen's view was that Engelbart was remarkably systematic, even plodding, in his approach to tackling problems.

One day shortly after Shoulders had started working on his device, Engelbart wandered into the Applied Physics Laboratory. His initial reaction to Shoulders's idea was that it was too far in the future. But later he began thinking about the issues it raised, turning the concept over in his mind and considering the idea of scaling flat circuits down in size—shrinking them toward ever-more Lilliputian dimensions. It was like taking a telescope and turning it around and using it as a microscope. From his aeronautical-engineering days, he knew about constants like the Reynolds Number—a measure that allowed engineers to predict the behavior of an aircraft wing as they varied its size. It occurred to him that microelectronic components might exhibit the same qualities.

He wrote a short paper sketching out some of his ideas and circulated it among his colleagues. Rosen read the paper and thought it was interesting and took it with him on his next trip to Washington. At the Pentagon, he was talking to a high-ranking official at the air force's Office of Research who unexpectedly asked, "Do you know Doug Engelbart?"

"Sure, he works right next door to me," a surprised Rosen replied.

"Well, he's written a pretty good paper. Why don't you get him to come to see me?" the Pentagon man said.[10]

Shortly after Rosen returned to Menlo Park, Engelbart got his first $25,000 research grant, which permitted him to begin playing with scaling concepts in earnest. In May of 1959 he traveled to Austin with Hew Crane and discussed some of his ideas at an Institute of Radio Engineers subcommittee meeting.

The idea of shrinking circuitry was clearly in the air. That summer, he came across a paper that had been presented at the third national convention on military electronics in Washington, D.C., on June 30, 1959, that was pursuing the same line of reasoning as his own. Titled "Shrinking the Giant Brains for the Space Age" and presented by Jack J. Staller of the Missile Guidance Department of the ARMA division of the American Bosch ARMA Corporation, it began, "The problem is to compress a room full of digital computation equipment into the size of a suitcase, then a shoe box, and finally small enough to hold in the palm of the hand." It concluded optimistically: "Forming on the horizon are solid state circuits or the growing of the whole circuit on a single small solid-state wafer and molecular film techniques where films millionths of an inch thick and equally narrow conductors are built up layer over layer to form whole sections or perhaps complete computers in fractions of cubic inches."[11]

In October, Engelbart proposed a more formal presentation of his ideas to be delivered the following year at the International Circuits Conference in Philadelphia. That month, he mailed the abstract of his proposed paper to Tudor Finch, a manager at Bell Labs in Murray Hill, New Jersey, and chairman of the program committee for the 1960 Solid State Circuits Conference.

Engelbart noted in his cover letter that he wasn't directly working on the problem of miniaturization but that his thinking had been influenced by his basic research in magnetic logic. He was cautious and added that he was not in the position to judge the relative worth of the message that the paper would convey. He noted that when he had presented the same concepts in May in Austin, he had not come away with the impression that the ideas were "old hat."

In November, Engelbart sent a follow-up letter to Finch. It was a short note relaying the feelings of another member of the committee, who had told Engelbart that his title, "Microelectronics, and the Art of Similitude," would not be understandable by the average conference attendee.

"I assume that it is the word 'similitude' that makes the trouble, and so I offer the following substitution as a slightly less exact but perhaps more serviceable title: 'Microelectronics, and the Art of Dimensional Analysis.' . . . I hope that this serves to clear up the problem," he wrote.

It was pure Doug Engelbart: understated, polite, but persistent. Three days later, Finch wrote back and briefly said there was no reason for Engelbart to worry. The first title was fine.

The conference itself was held at the University of Pennsylvania Sheraton Hotel in Philadelphia on February 10–12, 1960. Engelbart had been thinking about how he could get the idea of scaling down into the microcosm across to the researchers in a dramatic fashion. He decided to engage his audience in a little storytelling.

"Suppose this building and this room were suddenly ten times bigger in every direction. Would you notice?" he asked. "This guy's ten times taller. But he's ten times farther away, so your visual field wouldn't change at all, would it?"

Engelbart paused, and the audience considered the question.

"Well, wait a minute, how much more do you weigh?" he asked. "You weigh a thousand times as much! How much stronger are you going to be?"

No one in the audience had an answer.

"Well, that depends on the cross-sectional area of bones and muscles, so you're only a hundred times as strong," he went on. "You have problems! It's as if you were just sitting there and suddenly you were ten times heavier, so if you weigh 150 pounds you suddenly weigh 1500, and the chair doesn't have a safety factor of ten. Boom!"

Next, he turned his attention to microelectronic components and explained to his audience that chip designers would have to be concerned about the same kinds of constraints as they thought about scaling down into a world that might one day require techniques of molecular engineering.

When he finished his talk, he was rewarded with a long and loud ovation.

On the flight home, Crane was enthusiastic. He told Engelbart he couldn't believe how lucky they both were to be at SRI at this moment in history. Unlike the academics who had just given papers, the two men were someplace where they could build things and turn them on and see them work.

Engelbart agreed, but his mind was already racing far ahead. More than anything else, the exercise in scaling had left him feeling relieved. Now he was certain the things he had been talking about weren't as crazy as many others thought. The idea that had stopped him dead in his tracks in December of 1950, the idea that it would be possible to augment human intelligence, was going to be real after all.

Now he was certain there would be enough computing capacity in the world, and not just for him but for everyone. He also realized that as scale changes, so do basic properties, and not in a simple linear fashion. The changes that were coming would be dramatic and disruptive, and they would keep happening faster and faster. And for Doug Engelbart, it didn't stop with the machines. He had also begun thinking about human systems and all of the organization and skills and knowledge and everything else you have to have when you seamlessly blend people with new technology. Engelbart saw it all first. As he told his audience in Philadelphia, "Boy, are there going to be surprises over there."

■ ■ ■

It was the dawn of the sixties. The United States hadn't gone to the moon, the country hadn't yet become trapped in Southeast Asia, and the civil rights, free speech, and antiwar movements hadn't formed. The United States had become an economic miracle, but a small minority of its citizens was feeling increasingly suffocated by a homogeneous fifties society that was overwhelmingly materialistic. In the world of the man in the gray flannel suit, people were starting to look for ways out. And while Engelbart was shaping his augmentation ideas in terms of computer technology and the principle of scaling, a similar search to extend the power of the human mind was arising in other disciplines.

In France, the Second World War had touched off a search for meaning that led to existentialism. Now in the United States, people were likewise exploring religion, spiritualism, and mysticism in a similar quest for understanding.

Myron Stolaroff had grown up in a Jewish household in Roswell, New Mexico, in the 1920s and 1930s. His father was a local merchant, and the family was prominent locally. Myron graduated first in his class both from his high school and from the local military junior college. At Stanford University, he received a Phi Beta Kappa key and a Tau Beta Pi key in recognition of his scholarship. He was a student at Stanford when David Packard and Bill Hewlett came back to campus to show off their first commercial oscillator. Near the end of the Second World War, he received an engineering degree and took a job working as the first employee of Alexander M. Poniatoff at a small electric-motor company in Belmont, California.

He began as a design engineer and later helped Poniatoff prototype the first magnetic reel-to-reel tape recorder, which launched the company that took its name from Poniatoff's initials plus "ex" for excellence. Ampex Electric and Manufacturing had been founded in San Carlos after Poniatoff had begun looking for new applications for his high-quality motors. Ampex is no longer a factor in Silicon Valley and today is remembered largely because its corporate logo is still prominently visible on Highway 101, the freeway that slices through the heart of the Valley. However, Ampex was as significant as Hewlett-Packard in the Valley's lineage, and many pioneering engineers still remember the company fondly.

Magnetic recording had made its way into the United States after the end of the Second World War, when a U.S. Army officer found German recorders at Radio Frankfurt and mailed two of the machines to the United States, where he was able to examine them carefully. The next year, he demonstrated the recorders at the San Francisco chapter of the Institute of Radio Engineers. When Poniatoff learned about them, he pushed Ampex into the development of tape recorders. The company's business took off after crooner Bing Crosby began using the recorders to help produce his radio shows, and ultimately Ampex became the standard for the broadcasting and recording industries.

Stolaroff's career blossomed with the tape-recording business. He moved quickly from being a design engineer, to application engineer, to director of instrumentation sales, to assistant to the president for long-range planning. Trained as an engineer, Stolaroff was also a humanist and a bit of a dreamer and early on gained Poniatoff's trust. The founder of Ampex knew that Stolaroff wasn't the kind of person who would challenge him as a potential CEO. Stolaroff was the analyst, the guy who stood a little bit off to the side and could offer another perspective on the company's strategy.[12]

As a humanist and as a not particularly religious Jew in a largely Christian community, Stolaroff also felt at something of a loss in terms of his spiritual life. One day, he received a phone call from another Ampex engineer with whom he was friendly. The two men enjoyed each other's company and often talked about issues that were far beyond the normal boundaries of an engineering company.[13] It was a phone call that would completely change Stolaroff's life and ultimately have a remarkable impact on America, playing a role in the creation of the sixties counterculture.

Of course, none of that was apparent from what was nothing more than an invitation to attend a lecture being given by Harry Rathbun, a professor of business law at Stanford. Rathbun was a charismatic teacher who was tremendously popular on campus, where he lectured to overflow classes on subjects that included discussions of personal ethics and values.

Rathbun's presentation was given in a small library in South Palo Alto, and it struck Stolaroff "between the eyes."¹⁴ The themes the law professor addressed that evening included "Who are we?" and "Where are we going?" They were Big Questions About Life. Stolaroff was transported, realizing that his life had been hollow and that the questions Rathbun was asking and answering mesmerized him.

It was the first in a series of five lectures Rathbun delivered in Palo Alto in the early 1950s. As he attended each one, Stolaroff developed an increasingly deeper fascination with the issues that Rathbun was raising. He became excited by the idea that human beings had tremendous untapped potential and that it could be reached.

Then, during the final lecture, Rathbun sprung a trap that infuriated Stolaroff.

As it turned out, Rathbun's own life had been transformed when he and his wife, Emilia, attended a 1935 wilderness retreat led by Henry B. Sharman, a wealthy retired Canadian. Sharman had written a book entitled *Jesus as Teacher,* which probed the historical records surrounding the New Testament. After returning to Stanford, the Rathbuns began conducting study groups for Stanford students in their home on the teachings of Christ. The sessions were later expanded to include a two-week retreat at a center that was established in the mountains about forty miles southwest of campus near the sleepy beach town of Santa Cruz. They became known as the Sequoia Seminars and ultimately, in the 1970s, spun off a series of cultlike groups (including the Creative Initiative Foundation, Beyond War, and Women to Women Building the Earth for the Children's Sake) that attracted a broad, largely upper-middle-class following. In many cases, people who joined them sold their homes and personal belongings and dedicated their lives completely to these groups.

However, long before the 1970s, the Sequoia Seminars had a less well known but more dramatic and far-reaching consequence, in their immediate impact on Myron Stolaroff. Although he had been angered by Harry Rathbun's sneaky trick of guiding him to the philosophy of Jesus, Stolaroff remained intrigued by Rathbun's ideas. The following year, he decided to set aside his anti-Jesus bias and his concern about what was happening to Jews around the world in the name of Jesus and attend a longer set of discussion groups led by the Rathbuns.

At the seminar, Stolaroff became a convert. By the time it was over, he felt that he had experienced true love for others for the first time in his life and become a believer in "the power of the message" of Jesus.[15] He decided that the most important thing that he could do with his life was to commit himself to the will of God.

Perhaps not surprisingly, it was at the Rathbuns' retreat that Stolaroff, the Jewish engineer, had his first mystical experience. One night, he was lying on the floor of the lodge where the group met, meditating and looking up through a glass skylight at a grove of moonlit redwood trees while listening to Gregorian chants, when he felt a deep pain in his chest, which left him in an ecstatic state. He concluded that the experience was evidence that God had touched him, and the moment left him convinced that God was real.[16]

At a Sequoia Seminar, Stolaroff first met a close friend of Rathbun named Gerald Heard, an Anglo-Irish writer who had begun his career at Cambridge and Oxford as an academic. In the 1930s, he had become a committed pacifist and had immigrated to Los Angeles at the same time as Aldous Huxley, the author of *Brave New World*. In California, Heard became a devotee of a Hindu religious order and wrote books on subjects ranging from spiritual essays to science fiction novels on UFOs. He also developed a reputation as a mystic, and he introduced Huxley to eastern thought. He led a wide-ranging discussion group at one of the Sequoia Seminar retreats, and later Stolaroff, who by then was in charge of instrumentation marketing at Ampex, became a regular visitor at Heard's home in the Pacific Palisades when he was on business trips to Los Angeles.

It was during one of his visits in 1956 that Heard spoke enthusiastically to Stolaroff about a new drug called LSD. The very idea shocked the young engineer, who couldn't figure out why a world-famous mystic would need to take a drug. Nevertheless, Heard was fervent and told Stolaroff about an unusual man who would occasionally come from Canada and administer the substance to both him and Aldous Huxley.

With two passports and with a murky history of connections to both law enforcement and intelligence agencies, Al Hubbard was without question one of the most curious characters in America during the 1950s and 1960s. There are conflicting accounts of Hubbard's life, but the best summary of his early years appears in Jay Stevens's *Storming Heaven: LSD and the American Dream*. Born in Kentucky, Hubbard surfaced publicly in Seattle in 1919 with the invention of a perpetual-motion machine.[17] Later, there were tales of his running war materials by boat up the West Coast, where they were then shipped by land through Canada to Great Britain. And there was an intimation that he had had some loose affiliation with the Manhattan Project as a black-market supplier of uranium. Even after Stolaroff had come to know Hubbard well, he wasn't certain where the truth lay. But he soon fell under Hubbard's spell, viewing him as an especially powerful and articulate individual.

Hubbard is intriguing in part because while most popular accounts of the introduction of LSD in America focus on the roles played by author Ken Kesey and psychologist Timothy Leary, Hubbard was an earlier proponent, and an important influence in the use of psychedelics by a number of Silicon Valley's pioneering engineers. Hubbard, while he was the president of a Canadian uranium mine, had discovered psychedelics in the early 1950s when he participated in mescaline experiments at the University of Vancouver. He found LSD in 1955, and in addition to Huxley, Heard, and perhaps more than one thousand others during the 1950s, he introduced the drug to Stolaroff and indirectly to a small group of engineers who formed a splinter group from the Rathbuns' Sequoia Seminar.

After learning of Hubbard from Heard, Stolaroff had forgotten about him until Alexander Poniatoff mentioned having met this remarkable character in Canada who claimed he had been able to use LSD to cure a variety of diseases, including alcoholism. Hearing about him a second time persuaded Stolaroff to sit down and write Hubbard a long letter about his spiritual journey in the Sequoia Seminar and his interest in LSD. Shortly afterward, Hubbard called him and then soon visited his Ampex office. That meeting turned Stolaroff's life upside down and eventually wrenched him out of his position as a respected engineer and corporate planner.

A small, heavyset man with a perpetual smile and an uncanny ability to read people and discern their weaknesses, Hubbard led Stolaroff off on a remarkably wild trip. On the day he arrived at Ampex's San Carlos office, he took Stolaroff to a motel, where Hubbard and his wife were staying with a traveling companion. He gave Stolaroff a tablet of Methedrine and then had him inhale a mixture of oxygen and carbon dioxide, which is known as Meduna's mixture, or Carbogen. It induces a mild psychedelic effect, which disappears quickly. Carbogen was used frequently in the 1960s as a precursor to psychedelic therapy, an introductory experience to give a subject a brief preview of what a psychedelic experience would feel like. Stolaroff took several breaths and was plunged instantly into a euphoric, magical state that was prolonged by the Methedrine. He was now certain that he wanted to try LSD.

In April of 1956, Stolaroff took LSD at Hubbard's apartment in Vancouver. Because Hubbard had been able to build a relationship with the Catholic Church in Canada to support his experiments, Stolaroff even received a blessing for his journey from the archbishop of the local diocese. The priest not only blessed him but also promised to remember him the next day at the noon Mass, when Stolaroff would be on his trip.[18]

His first encounter with LSD involved taking sixty-six micrograms of the drug, which had been manufactured by Sandoz Pharmaceuticals, the Swiss firm that had pioneered the chemical. Hubbard, his wife, Rita, and another man served as his guides for the experience, which left Stolaroff shaken. He considered it a deeply religious event, and at the same time he felt that he had plunged deeply into his own unconscious mind.

He returned to California a zealot, a convert to the new LSD faith. He had decided that experiences like the one he had had in Canada were the answer to the world's problems. LSD would give society a new set of powerful tools to advance human development. Like Engelbart, Stolaroff set off on his own grand quest to augment the human mind.

His first stop was his closest friends at the Sequoia Seminar, where he had become a member of the group's planning committee. He introduced them to LSD in turn and created an informal research group composed of five fellow engineers and their wives. The group included a young Ampex engineer, Don Allen; Stanford electrical engineering professor Willis Harman; and several others from both Hewlett-Packard and SRI. Stolaroff's study group set in motion an unheralded but significant train of events, plunging a small group of technologists into the world of psychedelics almost a decade before LSD became a standard recreational drug on American college campuses.

The group was not focused on drugs per se but became a forum for wide-ranging discussions on all kinds of topics in philosophy and life in general. During their evenings, they would talk about what it was possible to learn about the universe, about life, about what it meant to be human. They brought up subjects such as past lives and considered whether such a thing was possible, and if it could be investigated. The group met on Monday nights at the home of one of its members, and one person would take LSD while the others assisted. The following Monday, that person would describe his experience, and then the subsequent week the group would move on to the next experimenter.[19]

Stolaroff invited Hubbard to address the group. The Canadian evangelist with twinkling eyes and a cherubic face exuded a whiff of danger, as if he might be a government agent, but he charmed his listeners with striking charisma that came with a hint of vulnerability. Hubbard was deeply emotional, and his eyes occasionally teared up when he was describing something extremely meaningful.

The familiarity he gained with LSD from hearing the engineers' experiences made Stolaroff confident that he understood the drug, and he became increasingly skeptical about the medical reports he had read that described its effects as hallucinations, delusions, or other symptoms of a psychosis. He decided that in an LSD-induced state it was possible to attain moments in which the mind was both sharp and clear and where a flow of new ideas would emerge. It struck him that, if used as part of the Ampex product-design process, the drug could be a perfect tool for improving a company's business. That insight set Stolaroff off on an even more curious quest, as he became convinced that psychedelic drugs could open new vistas of creativity in both engineers and artists. Even before LSD was in widespread use, this was a controversial notion, and remains so today, as an angry debate continues over whether enhancing creativity is possible with chemical substances. The most celebrated scientist to have explored the effect of psychedelic drug use has been Kerry Mullis, the winner of the 1993 Nobel Prize in chemistry for his discovery of the process known as polymerase chain reaction (PCR), a crucial technique underlying much of modern biotechnology.[20] Possibly the question is so cloudy because the psychic costs are potentially so high: Despite intriguing evidence of positive effects in the first years of LSD experimentation, there were also incidents of psychotic outcomes as well.

Stolaroff brushed off the critical reports, confident that, armed with Hubbard's familiarity with the drug, he could avoid any of its negative consequences. At the time, he had become assistant to the president in charge of long-range planning at Ampex and was a member of the company's management committee. He proposed the idea of an LSD-based research project to the executive group, but it was immediately rejected. Stolaroff argued that his own experience with the substance and that of Hubbard suggested that it was well worth exploring in a business context, but the notion of tampering with the brains of the company's most valuable resource was too much for the executive committee to entertain.

Stolaroff, however, was not to be put off. Informed that the company was unwilling to approve his experiments, he went ahead with them anyway, gathering eight Ampex engineers as his subjects. With the help of Hubbard and a friend who was a physician, the group drove into the Sierra Nevada to a small cabin, where LSD was administered to the engineers. Unfortunately, Stolaroff's vision of LSD as an unprecedented design tool was undone when one member of the group, Bob Sackman, had a bad trip.

Sackman later founded US Venture Partners, one of Silicon Valley's most prestigious venture-capital firms, and also became a major force behind the founding of Sun Microsystems. However, he wasn't prepared for the impact of an LSD experience, and it "scared the hell out of him."[21] It also scared the hell out of Ampex's board of directors, and so in 1961 Stolaroff, who had become independently wealthy, gracefully agreed to leave the company to carry out his research independently. Largely with his own financial support, he set up the grandly titled International Foundation for Advanced Study on a quiet side street in Menlo Park. During the next four years, initially charging subjects five hundred dollars to participate in a study of LSD and creativity, the foundation ultimately led more than 350 people, including some of the Valley's best engineers, through their first psychedelic experiences.

■ ■ ■

On the San Francisco Midpeninsula, the late fifties and the early sixties were a bucolic time. Kepler's bookstore on El Camino Real, just two miles north of the Stanford University campus, served as a beacon for an eclectic group of intellectuals who were outsiders in a community that was largely split in its economic dependence among Stanford, a fledgling electronics industry, and large military contractors like Lockheed.

Woodside, a forested town just northwest of Stanford, was already a bedroom community and retreat, but for an earlier San Francisco financial elite with roots in the California Gold Rush. The Silicon Valley technology magnates hadn't yet taken over the mansions and estates set among the redwoods.

There was a small bohemia tucked away in nooks and crannies on the Peninsula, like the Perry Lane writers' community, in a rustic cluster of cabins adjacent to the Stanford Golf Course. Some of the houses were tiny cottages, no more than four hundred square feet in size. Although it was partially torn down in 1963 by developers, it was for many years the center of the Midpeninsula intellectual underground in the fifties, home to an eclectic group of artists, authors, communists, and other ne'er-do-wells. The Lane and the surrounding neighborhood had once been known as "Sin Hollow," and the community traced its roots all the way back to the early days of Stanford itself.[22]

Perry Lane's alumni included Thorstein Veblen, a radical economist and author of *The Theory of the Leisure Class,* a biting indictment of the upper crust of American society. Veblen taught at Stanford for only three years at the turn of the century, but he left a lasting impression. The economist arrived at one faculty tea with a young woman who was warily introduced by his host as Professor Veblen's "daughter."

Veblen interjected tersely, "Madam, she is not my daughter!" leaving his host flustered.

The bohemian tradition continued for half a century, and in 1959 a Stanford graduate student named Vic Lovell convinced young writer and fellow student Ken Kesey to take part in a series of experiments with psychedelic drugs being conducted at the Menlo Park Veterans' Administration Hospital. Lovell later became the first coordinator of the Palo Alto Free University, and Kesey introduced the world at large to LSD through a series of ecstatic gatherings called Acid Tests, which were a harbinger for the making of a counterculture that was to explode on the national scene at Woodstock in 1969. Indeed, Perry Lane disappeared in front of a bulldozer's blade only a few years before an unlikely band that first called itself the Warlocks and then the Grateful Dead became the house band for the Acid Tests.

But in the early part of the decade, the counterculture was still bubbling out of Perry Lane. At the same time, the New Left was emerging, deeply influenced by the counterculture. In the fifties, the politics of dissent around Stanford had been subterranean. There was a Communist Party, but it met secretly in the Palo Alto home of a high-ranking executive of a multinational corporation. There were even some party members who lived on Perry Lane, but the fear of McCarthyism kept politics underground. Not surprisingly, it turned out that one Stanford professor who was a Perry Lane resident was later discovered to be an informer for the FBI.

Across the bay in Berkeley, events were already taking an edgier, more political and confrontational turn. Intermittent protests had taken place at the University of California against mandatory ROTC training ever since it was instituted under the aegis of the Morrill Land Grant Act of 1862. The State Organic Act of 1868 formalized the training as law.[23] At the end of 1956 the tenor of the opposition to the rule changed with the formation of the student Committee for Voluntary ROTC, calling for a referendum on mandatory service. It foreshadowed the tensions that would burst into flame in the Berkeley Free Speech Movement eight years later. In 1956, the student who was head of the new committee, Hank di Suvero, attempted to distribute leaflets on campus but was stopped by the dean of students, who first argued that they would "litter the campus and burden the janitorial staff" and then later declared the main campus organization, the Associated Students, had not endorsed the leaflets. Ultimately they were distributed off-campus while the Military Department distributed pro-compulsory ROTC literature in classes.

The dispute ended with the passage of the referendum opposing ROTC by 1,591 to 715.[24] The issue of mandatory ROTC was complicated by the fact that military training was tied to the requirement of a loyalty oath, and freshmen who refused to sign the oath were barred from entering the university. However, the administration referred the results of the referendum to a Regents' committee, where the matter lay dormant until the fall of 1959. It might have stayed that way indefinitely were it not for the arrival on campus of a serious young freshman named Fred Moore.

As a high school student, Fred Moore had climbed aboard his German NSU motorcycle toward the end of the summer of 1958 and roared away from his family's Arlington, Virginia, home. The Moores were an all-American family. Fred Sr. was a military man who raced sports cars, winning a national title in his Austin-Healey just two years earlier. Fred's brother, Keith, was a straight arrow, home from his first year in college, where he was studying to be an electrical engineer. A sister, Peggy, was six years younger. The two brothers loved to accompany their father on weekend racing expeditions, serving as his pit crew.

Fred was short and skinny, but in his motorcycle gear he looked a little like Marlon Brando in *The Wild One*. It was a hint of what was to come. For even with his middle-class upbringing, he was always something of an outsider, prone to deep, unshakable convictions.

The morning he vanished, his father found a terse note left behind on a piece of plain stationery closed with sealing wax:

Dear Mom, Dad, Keith, Peggy + Friends + Foes

I have gone to try to live the way I believe.
  I love you all.

  Fred (Larry) Moore Jr.[25]

When Fred failed to return the next day, his father was frantic. He called the police, and an all-points bulletin was put out for the missing sixteen-year-old. But there was no sign of either Fred or his motorcycle.

His father's notes from his phone call to the police read:

Dark Brown eyes
Brown hair
Pink cheeks
Small nose
2 upper front teeth are broken
About 5 ft. 7 about 120–135 lbs.
28" waist
Wears men's size small in shirts
About a man's size 36
Has small brown leather bag
Small green tent
Yellow slicker
Dark brown dress suit
Black shoes—tennis shoes
2 prs. grey slacks—old pr. of khakis
Bright blue T shirt
No warm clothes or jackets—
NSU motorcycle—new back tire Arlington & Va. tags[26]

The search proved fruitless; the Virginia police found no clues.

Then, as dramatically as he had left, Fred returned. On a Sunday evening a week later, Fred's older brother heard the familiar bleat of the two-stroke motorcycle heading back up the driveway.

His father was furious. Where had he gone, and why had he refused to tell anyone what he was doing? Grudgingly, he told his family that he had hidden his motorbike in the bushes next to a nearby highway and hitchhiked to the bus station, where, with the savings from a summer job, he purchased a Greyhound bus ticket for a trip to Miami. His intent, he admitted, had been to rent a boat and motor to Cuba.

Yet he refused all of his family's entreaties to reveal why. More than six months later, he decided one afternoon to confide in his high school classmate Sam Kingsley. The two were bright students who shared a number of advanced-placement courses and membership in the school philosophy club. Kingsley promised to keep the secret, and he honored that promise until thirty-nine years later when, at the age of fifty-five, Fred Moore died in an automobile accident.

During the summer of 1958, Moore had decided that he was a pacifist. Years later, no one was ever completely certain about the origins of his pacifism. His daughter, Irene, believed Moore had developed his faith in nonviolence when he was eight or nine years old, while his family was based in Tokyo, where his father served as part of the American occupation force. On his father's tour of duty, in 1952, the younger Fred came in contact with the consequences of Hiroshima and Nagasaki. Seven years after the end of the Second World War, the wounds of the war hadn't yet healed, and Fred had told his daughter about seeing Japanese sick with radiation burns and watching dogs crawl into the gutters to die. It is conceivable that something scared into the memory of a nine-year-old boy in a way that few others who grew up in America during the 1950 experienced.

Entirely without outside influence from adults or high school friends and with only a limited amount of reading, he acted on his convictions and decided to go to Cuba, where he had learned a civil war was taking place.

Once he had arrived in Miami, he had rented a small, open aluminum motorboat, which he had supplied with orange juice and food. When night fell, he set out for Cuba. His plan had been to land his boat on the Caribbean island and approach both the rebels and government soldiers in an effort to persuade them to put down their arms.

He never got there.

The waters around Florida can be treacherous. Not long after setting out, his boat scraped a hidden sandbar, shearing off the propeller. Without power, he drifted for more than a day until a sport fisherman spotted him and hauled him back to shore.

Yet as unsuccessful as his Cuban journey may have been, Fred Moore was destined to have a dramatic impact on the world. Intent on bringing about change simply by putting his body on the line, in the mold of Mahatma Gandhi, Moore ultimately was to alter both the world's politics and technology.

A year after his Cuban misadventure, Fred Moore came to Berkeley to study science. He had an obvious talent for math and engineering, interests that had been sparked in part by frequent weekend visits to the home of a maiden aunt, who always gave him a mental puzzle to work at. In an era when America was a conforming society outwardly, his appearance was like that of other entering freshmen. He wore tennis shoes and white socks and rolled his jeans into a cuff. He was clean-shaven, and his hair was cut short, coming down onto his forehead in a pronounced widow's peak. His crooked smile was bracketed with braces, still unusual even for children of middle-class families in the late 1950s, and he later joked about the irony that his braces were paid for by his father's Pentagon-funded medical plan.

He was thousands of miles away from his family's home in Virginia, but he hadn't forgotten his crusade from the previous summer. Like much of the rest of his life, it had been a solo campaign. Although he was new on campus and had made no friends, several students remember that he set up a card table during registration, soliciting support for a campaign against mandatory ROTC.

On October 1, from his rented room two blocks north of campus, he sat down and typed a letter to William P. Rogers, the U.S. attorney general:

Dear Sir:
This letter is to inform you that I, Frederick Lawrence Moore, Jr., will not register for the draft. Due to my religious beliefs I cannot comply with any law which opposes them.
    I follow a Higher Law—a law called "LOVE."
    I am opposed to war, and I will not participate in killing, whether

directly or indirectly. I will neither serve, nor support, any organization or action in which I do not believe.

My services are to all mankind.

Sincerely,

Frederick L. Moore, Jr.[27]

After sending the letter, Moore was summoned to the office of the dean of students, William Shepard, since he had requested an exemption from ROTC enrollment as a conscientious objector. The dean informed the young freshman that the only permitted exemptions from ROTC were physical disability, foreign citizenship, and previous military service. Moore must either take the course or withdraw from school.

He chose a third option. On the morning of October 19, he walked to campus and sat down on the steps of Sproul Hall, the university's administration building. He carried with him a two-page statement, a canvas mat, a pint bottle of water, a petition calling for the end of compulsory ROTC, and a hand-lettered sign resting on a tripod, which read:

NON-COMPULSORY ROTC

This seven-day fast is undertaken to express my beliefs that the University of California should respect conscience.

The protest created an immediate sensation on campus. It was one of the first times that students had actually gathered in Sproul Plaza, which until then many people had thought of as a no-man's-land to scurry across.

Fred Moore had fired the opening antiwar salvo of the 1960s. It was a bold first step that would change the nature of protest on American campuses. Although a growing number of students shared his views, none had used civil disobedience as a response to the military or the war.

Because Fred's father was a colonel stationed in the Pentagon, his action quickly became the subject of national attention, and reporters flocked to campus to interview the young protester. Moore told the *Oakland Tribune* that he had been raised a member of the Virginia Methodist Church but had more recently taken up the Christian existentialist views of the nineteenth-century Danish philosopher Søren Kierkegaard.[28] He had joined the philosophy club in his junior year of high school. The kids met after school and talked about existentialism, which was in vogue in the late 1950s. It had led Fred to think deeply about the draft, which he had decided was slavery and unconstitutional. How could anyone accept it? he asked the reporter. He added that he had become a mystic and was no longer a member of any organized religion. Another newspaper noted that Fred's brother, Keith, was a student at Virginia Polytechnic Institute and was currently in that school's ROTC program.

Students walked by in the morning and stole glances at the forlorn figure sitting on the steps. Several stopped to sign his petition, while others yelled insults. After several hours, the dean, claiming that Moore's presence was creating a commotion below his window, called the freshman's mother. Later that morning, he sent Moore a message asking him to come to his office. Fred left his seat on the steps and went upstairs to the dean's office to talk to his mother by phone. He was gone for forty-five minutes.

When he returned, he announced to the reporters that she had asked him to come home immediately. As he told the student paper, "If I am forced to leave my place on the Sproul Hall steps, it will be because of circumstances beyond my control, and not because my convictions have altered or changed." He said that he had already sent his parents a letter explaining what he intended to do and that on the phone he had tried to explain to his mother that his stand was the right position to take. He repeatedly assured her that his action was not intended to embarrass or hurt his father.

"We've always gotten along very well," he said, "but we disagreed on the method of insuring peace. My father feels the best way is for our country to be strong militarily, but I feel this is not the way to achieve peace."[29] The right way, he added, was to create more love and do things like offer more foreign aid.

By the second day, word had gotten out about his fast, and it began to attract visitors from around the Bay Area. Lee Swenson was a nineteen-year-old Stanford junior majoring in philosophy. On Tuesday morning, he learned about the lone protester while visiting Kepler's bookstore, as word had passed from the employees of Cody's Books, a Berkeley institution several blocks off campus, to its Midpeninsula counterpart. Roy Kepler had been a World War II conscientious objector, who in the early 1950s had founded the lively Menlo Park institution. Ira Sandperl, who would later be well-known as folksinger Joan Baez's mentor and a committed Gandhian, was a fixture there, where he could be found each evening, behind the cash register.

For Swenson, who was a working-class teenager from Richmond, California, and thus an oddity among the upper-middle-class Stanford students, Kepler and Sandperl were mentors. So in the afternoon he got permission to take time off from his parks-and-recreation job handing out basketballs to Palo Alto elementary school students, and drove his black 1951 Chevrolet to Berkeley, joining Moore on the steps. A crowd of students was sitting around talking about the philosophical issues related to the protest. Was there any philosophical justification for killing another? Was there a God? Swenson had been reading Heraclitus, a pre-Socratic philosopher, and the two young students exchanged ideas comparing ancient Greek philosophy to modern existentialism.

Every few minutes, angry students shouted that Moore was a coward or a traitor, interrupting the discussions.

"Commie, go home!" yelled one passerby.

Swenson stayed for several hours, dashing off once to feed the parking meter, before returning to Palo Alto, deeply moved by Moore's fast.

The freshman's protest lasted through two nights, until his father arrived by plane to take his son home to Virginia. It was a remark-able reunion, suggesting a great deal about where Moore's indepen-dence of conscience came from.

"My son is his own person," Colonel Moore told the reporters. "My son makes his own choices."

It may have been that the senior Fred Moore not only tolerated his son but took a small amount of pride in his iconoclastic behavior. He may have flown west to bring his son home not so much be-cause he was worried about his own career but rather because the young man had upset his mother so deeply.

In any case, although Fred Moore Jr.'s protest ended prematurely, some 1,300 students signed his petition. But his action had a far deeper impact. It was, in effect, a prelude to the Free Speech Move-ment, which would not take place for another five years. In fact, Fred Moore's solitary sit-in was in many ways the opening political act of the sixties.

"If you want to speak about courage, speak about Fred Moore. He stood alone," wrote David Horowitz, who was one of the Berkeley students who were moved by the protest and who later became a stu-dent leader during the 1960s. Michael Rossman, who later also be-came an FSM activist, walked across the Berkeley campus on the day that Fred Moore staged his protest and was stunned. He had never seen anything like it, and he was deeply affected by Moore's willing-ness to take such a strong-willed and independent stand.

The deep impression that this solitary figure made, professing an act of conscience, cannot be underestimated. The ripples spread off campus and around the Bay Area. At San Jose State College, where students were trying to form a peace movement, it was Fred Moore's action that gave a direct answer to their indecision about whether to stage a protest. His example was there for the students several months later, when San Jose State fired sympathetic faculty, leading to the first on-campus protest action at the school since the forties.

The *San Francisco Chronicle* editorialized against mandatory

ROTC, and by the end of the week California governor Edmund "Pat" Brown stated that he opposed it as well. Fred Moore returned to Berkeley in the fall of 1962 after the Regents had voted to end compulsory ROTC training, but the lesson from the events was clear and set the stage for the Free Speech Movement which followed: Direct action was an effective form of protest against large bureaucratic institutions, which would otherwise ignore students' demands.

Personally, Fred Moore had chosen a hard path. His solitary action became a factor in giving birth to the political protest movement that was to define the next decade. A decade and a half later, following that same inner sense of social justice, he was to have an equally significant impact on computing. It was Moore who would be the first to try to make the direct connection between computer hacking and the outside world. Indeed, his life was like a runaway billiard ball. He never intended to provide the spark that would create the personal-computer industry, but was merely attempting to extend his draft-resistance community-organizer politics with the help of an eclectic group of engineering misfits. It just got a little out of hand. Throughout it all, he remained remarkably unaffected, acting as a solitary individual and a wanderer with an uncompromising moral sense and an inability to comprehend why others were not able to see what he saw so clearly and take the same actions. It was to be almost a decade after dropping out of UC Berkeley before he returned to California. When he did come back, he found a very different world than the one he had left.

▪▪▪

As the sixties began, the three separate threads that each of the men profiled in this chapter represented came together. Doug Engelbart had a clear vision of using computing to help mankind by augmenting human intelligence; Myron Stolaroff was wandering around Johnny Appleseed–style with a new drug he believed would enhance engineering creativity as well as human spirituality; and Fred Moore had set out on a pacifist's crusade to end war by putting his body on the line.

Engelbart was the prophet, largely unsung until much later, and both Stolaroff and Moore became true believers who each in his own way touched off momentous events that still reverberate. Moore shared Engelbart's belief that computing could change the world, and Stolaroff shared the notion that it was possible to expand the power of the human mind.

How could such seemingly isolated endeavors contribute to setting the stage for the creation of an industry? It would be a decade and a half before personal computing would emerge, and when it finally did so, it would be unlike any other industry the world had ever seen. Started in large part by a ragtag army of hobbyists who shared a passion for their own universal machine, the PC was the product of a unique set of circumstances that went far beyond the confines of business.

Today (Gordon) Moore's Law, as well as the advertising hype machine that surrounds the computer and the consumer-electronics industries, has made technology innovation appear routine. Three decades ago, the direction of computing innovation was by no means certain.

2 | AUGMENTATION

Not long after Doug Engelbart arrived at the magnetics group, another young engineer, William English, joined Stanford Research Institute. The army had funded English's first job at SRI, but before long he was bored with building devices that required little of his creativity, and he began looking for something more interesting to work on.

English had come to SRI on a fluke. A natural tinkerer whose father had been an electrical engineer, English had grown up in Kentucky. He had gone to school to get an electrical engineering degree at the University of Kentucky, where he had been an engineer for the college radio station. Like many young men in the mid-1950s, he had joined the navy after college. After leaving the service in 1958, he had planned to go to graduate school at the University of California at Berkeley and showed up there looking for a research assistant position. He had been accepted into the graduate program in civil engineering, but he found the Berkeley campus to be remarkably inhospitable. A quiet man with an easy and open smile, English was stunned by the snobbery of professors and researchers. No one showed the slightest interest in the young engineer, and so on an impulse he decided to call SRI about the possibility of a job. On the Peninsula, he received a much warmer reception, and so he shelved the idea of graduate school and went to work in Menlo Park.

Although his new job working on a military training system was humdrum, he was soon able to enter a co-op education program and begin study for a master's degree in electrical engineering at Stanford, where he took classes from Bill Linville, a legendary professor at the time. When the military project was finished, English was introduced to the magnetics group and began working with the tiny magnetic-core memory devices that the military was funding for use in space and in high-radiation environments.

In the magnetics group, he met an eclectic group of young researchers who worked and socialized together. There was the folk-dancing scene, which frequently assembled at Doug Engelbart's home, and there was also a tight bunch of four friends, Hew Crane, Dave Bennion, Howie Zeidler, and from the neighboring physics laboratory, Charlie Rosen.

Rosen had bought some property high up in the Santa Cruz Mountains, behind Stanford, and discovered that it had twenty acres of grapes planted by one of the previous owners. He had planned to use the property as a camping retreat for his family, but Bennion in particular was enthusiastic about the grapes. A logic engineer like Crane, Bennion had come from a farming background and was looking for a way to get away from his engineering work and spend more time outside. In 1959, the four men and their families accordingly started Ridge Vineyards, which ultimately became one of America's most respected small wineries.

In the magnetics group, English also met Engelbart, and it didn't take long before he learned about the quiet engineer's passion for building a working version of Vannevar Bush's Memex machine. It was generally understood around the lab that Engelbart was simply putting in time at SRI in order to help pay the bills, as his real interest lay in building digital computers. Initially, the idea failed to captivate English. It was still very much an analog world, and he quickly learned that Engelbart was an inveterate dreamer.

What set Engelbart apart was that he was persistent enough to get money for his wild ideas. The first funding had come in the form of the small grant that Charlie Rosen had helped him get from the air force's Office of Scientific Research. That was a trickle, but eventually SRI pitched in some support from general funds to contribute $120,000 between 1960 and 1965.[1]

During the first two years of his contract, Doug Engelbart largely ruminated about his dream machine. He wrote several draft versions of papers exploring what he had come to call the concept of the "man-machine interface." Historically, machines had only handled materials or generated power, but now, by adding information, it became possible to control their actions by programming them. For the first time, it was possible to consider using computers as something other than mere calculators.

Engelbart's ideas stressed interaction between a machine and its user, an idea that was unheard-of at the time. As he wrote, the "computer world should see similar evolution. We are in the phase now of big machines, formally scheduled, but we will pass soon into new applications where a human directs the movement and manipulation of information under continuous control as he pursues his occupational goals."

Then he added these prophetic words: "Let's be sure that our concept of the man-machine interface problem doesn't get stuck on the big-installation, formal-scheduling picture. The interface problem . . . required adapting controls to suit human capabilities."[2]

Doug Engelbart was on the hunt for the personal computer. However, like the researchers at PARC who were to follow him a decade later, he was looking well beyond the idea of an isolated machine. He always couched his vision in terms of a work-group community and not the isolated individual. It was an idea that was to gather momentum toward the end of the decade when Engelbart's group was picked by the Pentagon's Advanced Research Projects Agency to become one of the first two nodes of the ARPAnet, what J. C. R. Licklider thought of as an "intergalactic computer network" that would weave together an expanding community of scientific researchers and engineers.

Shortly before he traveled to Philadelphia with Hew Crane to present his ideas on scaling in January 1960, Engelbart began organizing a series of informal seminars at SRI on the idea of augmenting the human intellect. Although they did not have computers with which to explore their ideas, members of the group had been fiddling with proto-PC applications. At the time, the most efficient simple sorting techniques were card-file systems. Data were entered by hand on cards, the outside edges of which were ringed with punched holes. Cutting notches to match various attributes made it possible to retrieve information by sliding a knitting needle through a stack of cards and shaking. The cards with the notched holes would fall out of the deck; it was thus possible to perform simple statistical operations this way.

On occasion, the group would invite outsiders to make presentations, and in February of 1961 Engelbart announced in a memo: "Mr. Paul Howerton has been invited for a give and take session." He "heads a large group within a government intelligence activity and is responsible for the management of a very large file of information. He is the widely read, widely traveled sort of person that is a good talker, and we should find the session very stimulating."[3]

The group also explored a range of techniques for improving the efficiency and productivity of meetings, an early indication that what Engelbart was interested in doing was as much about sociology and organizational theory as it was about technology. In his mind, augmentation was always a complete system, not just a box.

In the meetings, Engelbart pioneered an idea that two decades later became a staple of a new generation of "meeting facilitators" who would tease ideas from a group and then display them on whiteboards or large sheets of paper. Engelbart's early informal Augmentation groups assigned one person as "blackboarder" and thought of this process as a form of real-time feedback.

In what might be described as an early nod to the cartoonist Scott Adams, creator of Dilbert, in his early writing on the problems encountered in meetings, Engelbart assigned categories for the different personality styles, with a veritable rogue's gallery of titles including: hairsplitter, pigeonholer, eager beaver, explorer, fence-sitter, superior being, doubting Thomas, wisecracker, dominator, manipulator, belittler, distracter, and silent member. It was a typology of the behavior that has since become synonymous with the corporate staff meeting.

One possibility for improving the way a work group functioned was to use a vote-taking device that provided instant feedback. By April of 1961, the group had jury-rigged a voting system involving yes and no voting options and explored the idea of letting a speaker continue until his favorable rating fell below 50 percent. The group also came up with a "covert interrupt procedure," which involved multiple pushes of a button by each of the meeting participants. It was not a great success as it unfortunately relied on the leader's ability to guess the number of times the buttons had been pushed.

Through it all, Engelbart served as a quiet conductor with a single unshakable focus. He wasn't a dictator, and he had none of the enfant terrible qualities that would later become the stock-in-trade of some of Silicon Valley's most imposing figures. Instead, he evinced a kind of unpretentious determination, coupled with a slight sense of fatalism suggesting that the world might fall apart at any moment. Betraying that uncertainty, he noted in concluding the announcement of one of the early meetings: "One of the interesting features of this meeting is that yours truly, Doug C. Engelbart, will be absent. Have fun, and if you get anything accomplished, please be gentle about telling me that it was because I wasn't there."

■ ■ ■

The period from 1961 to 1962 served as a crucial time in the evolution of what Engelbart would come to call the Augmentation Framework. Still, early on much of it was hand waving, with nothing you could see or touch. To begin to build his system, Engelbart would need large research grants. For a while, he thought that the emergent field of artificial intelligence might provide him with some support, or at least meaningful overlap. But the AI researchers translated his ideas into their own, and the concept of Augmentation seemed pallid when viewed through their eyes, reduced to the more mundane idea of information retrieval, missing Engelbart's dream entirely.[4]

Gradually, he began to understand that the AI community was actually his philosophical enemy. After all, their vision was to replace humans with machines, while he wanted to extend and empower people. Engelbart would later say that he had nothing against the vision of AI but just believed that it would be decades and decades before it could be realized. He thought his idea was the one that was more practical.

He frequently ran up against a wall of intellectual prejudice, which continued to plague him throughout his career. In 1960, Engelbart presented a paper at the annual meeting of the American Documentation Institute, outlining how computer systems of the future might change the role of information-retrieval specialists. The idea didn't sit at all well with his audience, which gave his paper a blasé reception. He also got into an argument with a researcher who asserted that Engelbart was proposing nothing that was any different from any of the other information-retrieval efforts that were already under way.

It was a long and lonely two years. The state of the art of computer science was moving quickly toward mathematical algorithms, and the computer scientists looked down their nose at his work, belittling it as mere office automation and hence beneath their notice.

Moreover, his support from the air force was slightly suspect as well. The Office of Scientific Research had a reputation for funding way-out ideas, or in some cases outright kooks. Engelbart's research was in danger of being thrown in with the work of somebody who was studying the clustering behavior of gnats. Even his colleagues had their doubts. A friend told him at one point, "You know, if people really get to know you, it's one thing. But otherwise, you sound just like all the other charlatans."

He had difficulties getting his ideas across to people throughout his career, but Engelbart persisted. By October 1962, he had sketched out his vision in a summary report for the air force entitled "Augmenting Human Intellect: A Conceptual Framework," and the following year he condensed his ideas into a chapter in a collection titled *Vistas in Information Handling*. His "framework" was both a technological and organizational prescription for creating computer-equipped teams of people who could more efficiently work on a broad range of human problems. Augment was thus the personal computer and the Internet rolled into one.

In an effort to communicate the power of augmentation to his audiences, Engelbart occasionally relied on the concept of deaugmentation, an approach that was inspired by the same insight that underlay the original scaling ideas that he had come across in his days working around the NACA wind tunnels. To convey the idea of deaugmentation, he would attach a pencil to a brick and ask someone to write with it while he measured the subject's performance, comparing it both to a typewriter and to normal cursive script. Of course, it was possible to enter text rapidly with a typewriter, and it was laborious with an awkward pencil that was ponderous to move.

In his first comprehensive outline of his broader vision, Engelbart employed the idea of a computer-assisted architect. "Let us consider an 'augmented' architect at work," he wrote. "He sits at a working station [the term "workstation" would achieve popularity in Silicon Valley twenty-five years later] that has a visual display screen some three feet on a side; this is his working surface, and is controlled by a computer (his 'clerk') with which he can communicate by means of a small keyboard and various other devices."[5]

Then, after describing the new relationship between the human problem solver and his computer "clerk," Engelbart briefly sketched out his broader vision: The computer was not just a number cruncher, he wrote. Computers have many capabilities in nonmathematical processes for planning, organizing, and studying: "Every person who does his thinking with symbolized concepts . . . should be able to benefit significantly."[6]

Buried in his dry prose was a description of computing far broader and more comprehensive than anyone else had envisioned. Computers until then were hulking behemoths deemed useful for large organizational tasks, ranging from check processing to calculating missile trajectories. Doug Engelbart realized that computing could be more than data processing. Previously, teams of humans had served a single computer; now, the computer would become a personal assistant. The notion flowed directly from Vannevar Bush's Memex, and Xerox researcher Alan Kay's Dynabook—a fantasy concept of a powerful, wirelessly networked portable computer—was to embody the idea a decade later. Indeed, it has become one of the enduring touchstones of Silicon Valley, and it was born in Doug Engelbart's search for ways to elevate the power of the human mind.

In the 1962 report, he also described a writing machine that would dramatically alter the process of working with ideas. He hadn't yet conceived of a mouse pointing device as an editing tool, but he could clearly see that his computerized mechanism would fundamentally change the way people worked with information.

He offered his readers a quick tour of Vannevar Bush's Memex system and spent several pages discussing "associative linking" possibilities, a notion that was to serve as the forerunner of hypertext and led three decades later to the World Wide Web. In a significant aside discussing related work, he mentioned the ideas of J. C. R. Licklider—the two men had met at a technical conference earlier that year—and noted that Licklider had provided the clearest case for the modern computer, coining the expression "man-computer symbiosis." It was soon to prove to be a fateful connection.

Summarizing his augmentation idea, Engelbart turned to the example of a friendly fellow he called Joe, who worked in front of an imposing system with two display screens and a keyboard flanked by rows of command keys organized into sets. The pointing and editing device was a conveniently placed light pen that hung in front of him in midair.

Most of Joe's time, Engelbart noted, is spent with one hand on the key set and the other on the light pen. He is manipulating symbols on his screens.

Joe was the earliest extrapolation of Engelbart's notion of a human augmentation system that implemented some of the ideas he had first stumbled upon in the grass hut library in the Philippines. The first outline of Augment also came a little more than a decade before the creation of the Xerox Alto, the first modern office personal computer. Ultimately, the Xerox group and not Engelbart got much of the credit for pioneering the personal computer. But the group of researchers at Xerox who created the Alto were intimately familiar with Engelbart's ideas.

With his framework proposal in hand, Engelbart had already begun hunting for support for his project. He had learned some things from Charlie Rosen, and he approached both military and nonmilitary government agencies with copies of his report. One of these agencies was the National Institute of Mental Health, which was beginning to support various kinds of computer research.

He seemed to be on the verge of a breakthrough. After receiving his proposal, NIMH sent a site-review committee composed of four computer experts to SRI. However, after assessing his project, the committee notified him that they had decided it would require sophisticated computer programming resources that, because of his location on the West Coast, he would not have easy access to. As a result, they did not feel justified in investing in the program.[7]

But scattering his proposal around to many potential sponsors eventually paid off. One of the people with whom Engelbart had left a copy was a young NASA program manager named Robert Taylor. He didn't know it at the time, but in approaching Taylor Engelbart was taking his ideas to one of the few people in the country who could understand them and who was in the right place to do something about them.

Taylor was a psychologist who had received his master's degree at the University of Texas studying psychoacoustics, the study of the perception of sound. In the early sixties, he was running a research program on computing at NASA headquarters. Although he was not a computer scientist, Taylor had read widely in the literature about the interaction of humans and computers. He had also been intrigued by Vannevar Bush's *Atlantic* article when he was in college and had read the work of cyberneticist Norbert Wiener. Most important, however, was that he knew J. C. R. Licklider, who was a leading researcher in the area of psychoacoustics and a close friend of Taylor's thesis adviser at Texas.

Beginning in 1960, Licklider had sketched out a vision that closely paralleled Engelbart's in a paper entitled "Man-Computer Symbiosis." His ideas were rooted in research done by a small group that Licklider had headed at Bolt, Beranek and Newman, a Cambridge, Massachusetts, engineering and military contractor. The group had purchased the first PDP-1 minicomputer built by Digital Equipment Corporation, and on it they had designed and then implemented one of the first computer time-sharing systems based on John McCarthy's pioneering research. Like Engelbart, Licklider's vision was to use computers to facilitate thinking on a much broader scale than numerical computing, coupled with interactive computing, which he viewed as being more flexible than the batch mainframe computers of the 1950s that were programmed with decks of cards.

Perhaps Doug Engelbart's greatest piece of luck was that Taylor and Licklider had become close friends in 1962. Licklider had shown up in Washington that year with the intent of remaking the Information Processing Technology Office of ARPA in pursuit of his man-machine symbiosis ideas. His immediate goal was to push the military computing-research arm forward by focusing on the problem of using computers in command-and-control applications. To get the project under way, Licklider had called together everyone in Washington who had anything to do with computer research for a meeting of the minds.

Taylor showed up early for the event, which was being attended by

representatives from NASA, the air force, the navy, the National In-
stitutes of Health, the Atomic Energy Commission, and about half a
dozen other agencies. He walked into Licklider's office, and the
older researcher immediately began asking a surprised Taylor about
his master's thesis. Sharing the same intellectual passion, the two
men quickly became friendly, and the friendship was cemented
later that year when both scientists traveled to a NATO meeting in
Athens.

Taylor had begun funding Engelbart with small amounts of
money from his NASA budget in 1961, and the following year, out of
the blue, he called the SRI researcher and told him he had finagled a
grant from NASA's Langley Research Center, which directed eighty
thousand dollars to help launch the Augment project. Taylor soon
told Licklider about Engelbart, and shortly afterward, ARPA kicked
in a nearly matching sum—enough to permit Engelbart to purchase
a Control Data Corporation minicomputer as well as to begin hiring
engineers.

It was not a simple project, however, and the early problems it encountered foretold the struggles Engelbart was to have with his
backers over the next decade and a half. Unfortunately, the first
money from ARPA came with strings attached. Licklider had come
from Cambridge, where at MIT John McCarthy had recently invented time-shared computing. Licklider was determined to push
the research efforts of the government in that direction, and so he
went to System Development Corporation in Santa Monica, California, and instructed it to begin development of a time-sharing system
in order to make the technology widely available.

In order to make his time-sharing vision real, Licklider then
told Engelbart to begin developing his Augment ideas on the SDC
machine.

Engelbart was aghast at the prospect. "But it's not time-sharing
yet," he protested.

"It will be," Licklider responded.[8]

The SDC contingency marked the start of a tempestuous relationship between the two men. At times, Engelbart would say that Lick (as he was known) was the first one to believe in him and that he was like his big brother.[9] But there was a darker side to their interaction. Engelbart later stated that he learned that Licklider's faith had been only grudgingly given, that the money had been offered more out of embarrassment after Licklider had discovered that there was someone out on the West Coast who had similar ideas about computing. He also discovered that Licklider felt that it was highly unlikely that anything significant would come from the funding.[10] And in the end, it was Licklider who betrayed Engelbart when he needed help most.

But in 1963, Engelbart had found credibility, and he set out to demonstrate his concept, which he dubbed NLS, for oNLine System. Doing so by long distance was a laborious process, but he tried. He had one programmer at the time, who wrote code in Menlo Park and then traveled to Santa Monica to run and debug it, and sometimes Engelbart himself flew down to work on the machines. But SDC had set up only a tiny display with a keyboard to provide access to the SRI programmers, and to make matters worse, the terminal was a long way from the computer itself, which was kept in a secure area. The machine was in time-sharing mode for only several hours each day, and it was so unstable that it crashed repeatedly. A frustrated Engelbart began to explore the idea of remotely connecting to the SDC computer from the Control Data minicomputer in Menlo Park using an early modem. Unfortunately his engineers were never able to make the system communicate reliably. As a result, for the next two years Engelbart's fledgling Augmented Human Intellect Research Center began to build his system on a computer that had far less processing power than an Apple II of a decade and a half later.

The Menlo Park computer used the magnetic-core memory that Engelbart, Crane, and English had all worked on improving in the fifties. It had a capacity of eight thousand twelve-bit characters—a little more than three pages of typed text—in its main memory. Instead of on a disk drive, it stored information permanently on a rotating drum that could hold thirty-two thousand characters. It also had a magnetic-tape storage system for backup and a paper tape and typewriter for entering programs. One other oddity about Engelbart's machine was that it came with a sixteen-inch circular monitor that could display sixteen lines of sixty-four characters, in uppercase only.

In 1964, Engelbart began to look around for help. He had an anemic minicomputer to get started on, but he still needed someone to help program it and develop it into a complete system. He had come to know Bill English in the SRI magnetics laboratory, and the two men had begun talking about some of the Augment ideas after Engelbart had approached English to present a magnetics paper on his behalf at a technical conference. Shortly afterward, he asked English to join the project as chief engineer.

Bill English became the perfect sidekick. For the next six years, while Engelbart struggled to describe his broader and sometimes cloudy notions of where his technology was heading, it was English who had the skills and the patience to actually implement his ideas. He didn't immediately connect with Engelbart's larger vision, but by the early sixties he had come to love computers and programming and so jumped at the chance of being involved in a hands-on project, even if it didn't involve a big computer. And if the larger vision of augmenting human intelligence initially eluded him, he quickly decided that Engelbart was doing the neatest stuff at SRI. He immediately took to the idea of manipulating text on a computer screen, and the experiments with pointing devices gave him the opportunity to build things. And building things is what Bill English loved most. Although he looked the part of an engineer with his white shirt, dark tie, and horn-rimmed glasses, he had a computer hacker's sensibility. His work wasn't a job; it was a passion.

In early 1964, SRI still didn't have its modern buildings in place, and the tiny group had sought refuge in one of the ramshackle World War II barracks that dotted the grounds of the Menlo Park campus. The buildings had open crawl spaces beneath their wooden floors, and the Augment team soon gave new meaning to the concept of a raised computer floor. One day while he was stringing cables, English brought his Skil saw from home and simply cut a hole in the floor where he could drop the cables and then cut another where he wanted the cables to come up again.

While the other programmer working for Engelbart at the time kept business hours, English considered himself more of an oddball.[11] Although he had a family and two young children, his attitude was that the job required that he do whatever it took, which made his hours unpredictable. It was a big and exciting challenge in just getting the computer up and functioning in order to begin the experiments with pointing devices.

Later, it was English, as Augment's quiet engineering leader, who would inspire the deepest loyalty from the hardware designers and programmers. He had his own agenda, but it was based on the success of the group as a whole, and through times of crisis he pulled the team together. He communicated a sense that he "just wanted to build the best damn system there is," and people rallied behind him.[12]

Engelbart had almost—but not quite—hit upon the concept of the mouse in his original 1962 paper. With his NASA funding, he began exploring pointing devices and became interested in the problem of selecting text or graphics objects that were displayed on his screen. The goal of the study was to discover which device would allow a user to get to a given point on the screen most quickly as well as repeatedly with the fewest errors.

English was anxiously looking for a project to get into, and so Engelbart told him to begin organizing pointer experiments. Other kinds of pointing devices were already in use, including light pens, trackballs, and tablets with styli. The RAND Corporation had invented the latter, and though Engelbart hoped for a while that he could persuade them to lend him one for their research, the company told him it didn't have any available.

The actual idea of a rolling, handheld pointing device came to Engelbart one day when he was at a computer-graphics conference. As he often did, he was feeling like an outsider, because everyone was talking, and he was uncomfortable and having trouble making himself heard. At times like this, he frequently tuned out and dropped into his own reverie.

On this particular occasion, he thought to himself, *How would you control a cursor in different ways?*[13] His mind drifted off and focused on a device called a planimeter—a simple mechanical device that allows the user to trace the edge of a two-dimensional image and instantly calculate its area. He remembered seeing one in high school and being fascinated by it. His teacher had explained its inner workings. He thought about the two wheels he remembered the planimeter used for tracking, and as he did everything magically came into form.

Pulling a small notepad from his shirt pocket, he made a quick sketch of a device that would track movement across a desktop. The idea was to use the two wheels to drive two potentiometers— devices that would register varying voltages as they were turned. Each one would move depending on the degree to which the wheels turned, and the resulting voltage could then be translated into the position of a cursor—they originally called it a "bug"—on the screen.

Of all the issues facing the researchers who were trying to build a man-machine interface at the time—keyboards and commands and everything else—pointing at something on the screen was one of the most difficult. People had pointed at blips on a radar screen in the SAGE early-warning system using light guns, Ivan Sutherland had designed a remarkable graphics program that worked with a light pen, but a pointing device that would let the computer user easily specify where he wanted to do something on the screen had rarely been used with text before.[14]

When he returned to SRI, Engelbart gave English a copy of the sketch. They turned to an SRI draftsman to carve an elegant, hand-sized lacquered pine case large enough to contain the two wheels and two potentiometers, and then gave the case to a crafts-man at the SRI machine shop to manufacture the other mechanical components. The original mouse that the team assembled was large and bulky, in part because of the size of the available potentiome-ters. English had also figured that he would need a device that would roll about five inches, a distance that could be translated into the width of the screen. That, in turn, required large wheels, which would rotate only once in five inches of travel.

Although it is commonly believed that the story of how the mouse got its name has been lost in history, Roger Bates, who was a young hardware designer working for Bill English, has a clear recollection of how the name was chosen. Bates had initially been hired as a lab technician for a summer job after his sophomore year of college, and English quickly became his mentor. His first official position at the laboratory was building an electronic circuit called a shift regis-ter to convert parallel data to serial data, for the small one-handed keyboard that English was testing. He remembers that what today is called the cursor on the screen was at the time called a "CAT." Bates has forgotten what CAT stood for, and no one else seems to remem-ber either, but in hindsight it seems obvious that the CAT would chase the tailed mouse on the desktop.

Engelbart's idea had been to get a collection of devices, including the mouse, together and then perform an experiment that would give the researchers some idea of which one was the best in terms of selecting text. The screen that had been rigged to work with the minicomputer that would serve as a test machine was set into a frame that sat on the computer desktop, and looked very much like the round screens that are still used today by air-traffic controllers. The challenge for the volunteers they brought in as part of the ex-periments was to see how quickly and accurately they could get to a particular character on the display. A subject would tap the space bar, grab the pointing device, find the character on the screen, and then push a selection button. In a sense, they were all playing one of the world's first video games. The mouse won the contest hands down, but there were some surprising results. Pedals were thrown out immediately, as were cursor keys, but the knee control actually provided good results, in some cases ranked second behind the mouse.

After they completed the tests using the first mouse, English began to refine the concept and made a key design decision that was revealing. He had wondered how many buttons were appropriate to place on the mouse, and it quickly became obvious that the right number would be three, not because of any detailed study but because there was room for only three switches inside the early wooden mouse case.

The number was a disappointment to Engelbart, who was passionate about the need for a complex control device. Using it would require training, he argued, but once the user mastered the contraption it would give him far more power over the system. In his mind it was like the scaling lesson of the pencil tied to the brick.

The conflict between ease of use and expert power was one that would plague the inventor throughout his life and years later lead him to say that he had failed in his mission. Eventually, ease versus power became a divisive issue in the computing world. It was an example of a range of issues where he was both ahead and slightly out of touch with the reality of the world that surrounded him. Engelbart had a complete vision, but as he evolved it, his best ideas were cherry-picked by others and used to create one of the world's most vibrant industries. Within a decade, Engelbart came to feel that he was rejected, misunderstood, and ultimately betrayed by those he had trusted most closely.

Ultimately, Doug Engelbart lost control of both his vision and his technology. When that happened, it was not just as the result of developments within the insular world of computer design. It was the mid-sixties, and the outside world was both closing in and coming asunder in ways that shook the very foundations of American society. Engelbart's project was to become a casualty of the chaos.

•••

It wasn't until 1968 that Stewart Brand and Jim Fadiman made a very public appearance together, in a cameo in the opening pages of Tom Wolfe's *The Electric Kool-Aid Acid Test*. Brand is introduced as the "enamorado" of a half-Ottawa Native American, Lois Jennings, as the two bounce along in a truck Brand is driving through the San Francisco hills as they wait for Ken Kesey to get out of jail. Fadiman is described as the nephew of Clifton Fadiman, the writer and editor who was known for the encyclopedic knowledge he displayed on the *Information Please* radio programs of the 1930s and 1940s. He and his wife, Dorothy, had met Wolfe while they were busy stuffing I Ching coins into the lining of a dense volume on mysticism they were preparing to give Kesey in his jail cell, and they had asked Wolfe to let Kesey know the coins were there.

By the end of the decade, both Fadiman and Brand were to play roles in Doug Engelbart's quest to augment human intelligence, but in 1962 the two had only just become friends when Fadiman, who was a young graduate student in psychology at Stanford, became Brand's guide on his first LSD trip.

Fadiman had gone to Harvard and studied social relations. He soon came to consider the field as psychology without rats, and he had instead focused his energy on being an actor. After graduating in 1960, he spent a year in Paris, and while he was there Timothy Leary and Richard Alpert along with Aldous Huxley passed through on their way to deliver an academic paper on psychedelics in Copenhagen. In Paris, Alpert, who had been Fadiman's professor at Harvard, told him, "The greatest thing in the world has happened to me, and I want to share it with you." He proceeded to pull a small bottle out of his pocket, introducing his former student to LSD.

Forced back to America by the threat of the draft, Fadiman moved to California a year later and arrived at Stanford as a distinctly unhappy graduate student in 1961. He was feeling that school was a waste of his life, which he would have rather spent in more cultured

Europe. Moreover, having recently been introduced to psychedelic drugs, the world suddenly seemed like a much different place. Full of self-pity, he began leafing through the Stanford class catalog looking for something that might be interesting to study. He found a small section of cross-disciplinary classes, including one being taught by an electrical engineering professor, Willis Harman, called "The Human Potential." The class was to be a discussion of what was the highest and the best to which human beings could aspire.

In his new, more highly attuned state, Fadiman thought to himself, *There's something here.* That morning, he walked across campus to visit Harman. The man to whom he introduced himself looked like a totally straight and conservative engineering professor, and when Fadiman asked if he could take the interdisciplinary course, Harman replied that it was already full for the quarter, and perhaps he should think about it for the next quarter.

"I've taken psilocybin three times," Fadiman said quietly.

The professor walked across the room, shut his office door, and said, "We'd better talk."

In the end, Fadiman became Harman's teaching assistant. He was able to talk to the students about things that Harman felt he couldn't. He also soon became the youngest researcher at the newly founded International Foundation for Advanced Study, Myron Stolaroff's project for continuing his research on the uses of LSD.

When Stolaroff and Harman set up shop in Menlo Park in March 1961, they weren't the only ones on the Midpeninsula exploring the therapeutic uses of LSD. Experiments were already being conducted at the Veterans' Administration Hospital in Menlo Park, and the Palo Alto Mental Research Institute had also begun introducing local psychiatrists and psychologists, and even writers such as Allen Ginsberg, to psychedelic drugs.[15] But the foundation was something new. Engineers rather than medical professionals led the project, and the clinic was intent on charging a five-hundred-dollar fee for each experience. An early local newspaper report described the foundation's goals as being "partly medical, partly scientific, partly philosophical, partly mystical."[16] Stolaroff, with the help of Willis Harman, largely funded the foundation, the real purpose of which was to conduct the research needed to make LSD credible in the medical profession. They worked with several psychologists, including Fadiman, as well as the mysterious Al Hubbard, who was a mentor to both Harman and Stolaroff and who became a member of the board of directors. Fadiman, who soon was teaching at San Francisco State, finished his Ph.D. in psychology at Stanford, and his research at the foundation focused on the changes in beliefs, attitude, and behavior that resulted from taking LSD.

Before long, the group published a glowing research report based on a survey of its first 153 subjects. The results were in the realm of the kind of advertisements typically found on late-night TV. Fully 83 percent of those who had taken LSD found that they had lasting benefits from the experience. The behavioral changes cited included: increase in ability to love, 78 percent; to handle hostility, 69 percent; to communicate, 69 percent; to understand self and others, 88 percent; improved interpersonal relations, 72 percent; decreased anxiety, 66 percent; increased self-esteem, 71 percent; a new way of looking at the world, 83 percent. The researchers found a high correlation between "greater awareness of a higher power, or ultimate reality," and claims of permanent benefit. They also noted that only one patient in the experiment felt he had been harmed mentally, but that a year later that person had revised his opinion.

Among the first 153 subjects was Stewart Brand. In general, Brand was a hard man to label. Unlike many in the sixties and seventies generation he later deeply influenced with the *Whole Earth Catalog,* he saw the world from a perspective that in some ways was much more conservative and traditional. A Midwesterner who had come to Stanford via prep school at Exeter, Brand had taken training as a paratrooper in the late 1950s and served in the army in Europe. Toward the end of his tour of duty, he had worked at the Pentagon as a photographer, and in 1961 he had asked to go to Vietnam. He decided that since he had trained as an infantryman he wanted to participate in a real war. The military's response was that certainly he could go, but he would have to re-up for another three years. To underscore the point, they told him that if he didn't re-up he would be sent to Fort Dix for menial duties.

Brand declined the invitation and went to Fort Dix, receiving his discharge in 1962. He settled in Menlo Park and began studying to become a professional photographer. Not long afterward, he visited the Stanford computer center with Jim Fadiman and saw a number of the researchers playing with an odd program, a video game called Spacewar. He filed the program and the group who were playing it away in his mind. It was to be six years before he returned to them.

What he did remember of the visit was telling. What stuck in his mind was an image of computer-obsessed young men in the thrall of the game, locked in an out-of-body experience. It was the second of two insights that came to Brand in short order. The first had been photographing the Warm Springs Indian reservation with a family friend, Dick Raymond. Now, in the computer center, the same feeling came over him: Here was a whole other world, one that was perhaps more compelling than his own. He had happened on the first inklings of what years later would come to be known as cyberspace.

He also stumbled around the same time upon Stolaroff's foundation. The psychedelic underground was then small, and everyone knew everyone else. In the fifties, as a Stanford student, Brand had read Huxley's *Doors of Perception* and later met the author. With a number of his friends who were traveling on the edge of the bohemian scene, he had already explored peyote, and while he was in the army he had made frequent trips to New York City, where he hung out on the fringes of the Beat scene. There, he befriended Gerd Stern, a Beat poet who had known Allen Ginsberg since the two men had met in a mental hospital in 1949. With Stern and a group of friends, he had taken mescaline at a converted church up the Hudson.

At the end of 1962, Brand signed up to take the foundation's guided LSD experience. The clinical exposure to LSD was a very different process from what would become commonplace several years later when acid was a recreational drug. For Brand, it began with an introduction to Carbogen, much in the same way that Al Hubbard had introduced Myron Stolaroff to its temporary effects before taking LSD. To Brand, however, it seemed as if they were forcing his brain to take in too much oxygen and "flame out." He went to a "very interesting" other universe for what he thought must have been "seven eternities." When he came back, everyone who had been watching him was still sitting there, and their cigarettes were just a little shorter. He thought Carbogen was just great and later concluded that, in comparison, LSD was a bit of a disappointment.

He showed up for his daylong LSD session on December 10, 1962. Outside of the office was a large oak tree with gnarled, baroque branches that would during the next four years attract the attention of many of the experimenters. The foundation was not far from Roy Kepler's bookstore and a short walk from the hole-in-the-wall store where the Midpeninsula Free University store and print shop were to locate in the mid-sixties. In another building a block away, Brand later established the Whole Earth Truck Store and the *Whole Earth Catalog*. About a mile away from the truck store, the original People's Computer Company settled and in turn was the catalyst for the Homebrew Computer Club in the mid-1970s. The club itself served to ignite the personal-computer industry.

Brand was one of the first to explore what millions would pursue during the next decade. It was a wrenching experience that pulled him out of his middle-class upbringing and gave him a new way of looking at the world. In a report that he wrote several days afterward, he noted that he took a goblet containing the drug at 8:41 A.M. He then lay in a quiet room listening to classical music through headphones. He was then given a second goblet of LSD at 10:00 A.M., and a final dose by injection at 2:00 P.M.

In his journal, he broke the session down into different periods, which he described as "purple attics," "purple helixes," "vacuum cleaners," and "cement."

First, there were the cartoonlike pictures that played through his mind to the sound of the music. "I recall the notion of gaily pursuing cobwebs through a succession of angular attics, of feeling the music was too spectacular and superficial, and of intimations that Being was large and take-able for granted but out of my then range of vision," he wrote. "Bodily sensations were pleasant chills and a neck-ache. I recall chuckling with feelings of things which had no humor."[17]

After the second goblet of LSD, the experience changed and became more "Daliesque." He asked for simpler music. He looked at a rose and found it enjoyable but not profound. He became talkative. He began to race through various "scopes of being" and imagined various scales of his location on earth.

In the afternoon, he was asked to sit up, a change that made him very uncomfortable. He began to feel he could separate people from their faces, which appeared to him like masks. The foundation's psychologist—Mary Allen, the wife of Don Allen, the Ampex employee—appeared to be a woman of great beauty. His own visage in the mirror revealed a person who was battered and tough.

He was asked to look at murals and yin-yang symbols, but he found nothing interesting in them. He walked to the bathroom and found the experience dizzying and humiliating. It appeared to him that he was holding a child's penis.

After he was given the injection of LSD, everything was transformed into what he called vacuum cleaners and cement. "Vacuum cleaners" described a roiling series of images that now passed through his head. Soon he began to feel as if he could barely move.

He was asked how he felt, and he replied, "very 'thing.' " He was shown a picture of Christ and began to feel manipulated.

Jim Fadiman asked Stewart to look deeply into his eyes, and when he did, he vomited. He looked at his vomit, and it was purple.

Later, when the session ended, he was taken to Fadiman's house, which he greeted with pleasure and a feeling of escape. Brand was still very much in the throes of his LSD experience, and after he sat down Fadiman gently continued the experiment. He was shown a series of pictures: an indistinct woman's picture on a record album, a statue, and a transparent picture that reminded him of himself, which in his head he turned into a mask made of two stones and a carrot. Then came several more pictures, including one he had seen earlier at the foundation office depicting clouds moving like smoke and a darkened, hellish scene with a satanic child silhouetted against the backdrop. As Brand peered at it, it dissolved into a Valley scene.

Dinner turned out to be a bizarre experience of chewing and swallowing. Brand found that he was traveling down into the plate, among the potatoes. He watched as a potato piece, lit by the candle on the table, became a heroic version of himself.

Later that night, after he thought the effects of the drug had worn off, he walked outside and looked up at a full moon. He stood frozen as it receded, transforming itself into three separate dancing images.

The next morning, he was in an odd mood that turned to depression when he returned to the clinic. He stayed deeply depressed for several days until he accompanied Fadiman to a Japanese dinner prepared by a friend for a small group. Over the meal, he said to Fadiman that he wished he had tried to look into his eyes again after he had vomited.

"Try it right now," Fadiman said.

He stared at Fadiman over the single candle that was set on the table. He had no idea what might happen, but he found that tears were forming in his eyes. Fadiman told him to let them come. Finally, he told Brand to close his eyes and to "stay with it." He continued to focus on his feelings and then realized that Fadiman, drenched in emotion, was crying, too. Their eyes locked for a few more moments, and when Brand rejoined the party he felt rejuvenated.

At the end of the evening, with the other guests watching, Brand took off his clothes and dived into the spooky underwater light of a backyard swimming pool.

■ ■ ■

Most of the Bay Area was comfortably oblivious. Beginning in 1961, for a period of more than four years, the International Foundation for Advanced Study led more than 350 people through LSD experiences.

The sessions took place on Tuesdays and Thursdays, and they lasted the entire day in two specially prepared rooms where the music and lighting were controlled. Although initially the subjects were expected to pay for the session, the government soon began to add new restrictions limiting experiments with individuals. Ultimately, the researchers began work on a project where they specifically chose scientists, researchers, engineers, and architects as their test cases. Their theory was that psychedelics were mind-expanding drugs, but they were not sure they could be used in a directed way. The drug seemed to make people feel better, but could LSD improve rational cognitive abilities as well?

Volunteers were not hard to find. Among the participants were Dr. Charles Savage, a physician who had conducted medical experiments for the U.S. Navy in the early 1950s, exploring the use of psychedelics as a truth serum, and Robert Mogar, a psychologist at San Francisco State College, who helped design and administer psychological tests. Toward the end of the studies, Robert McKim, a professor of industrial design at Stanford University, joined the project to help explore the relation between creativity and psychedelic-drug use. Don Allen and another man worked as "counselors." Since LSD has such a powerful effect, the group would joke about what they called "Midwest engineer's syndrome," in which the drug experience would entirely open up people who had once been very uptight.

From the SRI group, the first to try LSD was Hew Crane, who was followed by a number of other scientists from the research laboratory, including Doug Engelbart and Bill English.

It is easy to understand why Engelbart would find the idea of enhancing creativity with psychedelic drugs so intriguing. After all, the aims of the early LSD community closely paralleled his own passionate quest to augment human intelligence. Drug-induced creativity was not part of his original vision, but if it would make a difference it certainly might be a welcome addition to the process, which he referred to as bootstrapping: working in an iterative fashion in which each improvement would in turn accelerate the pursuit of further advances. In a way, bootstrapping was simply a restatement of the concept of exponential change, in this case applied to a human organization. The results of Engelbart's own psychedelic-drug experience, however, proved disappointing.

His first LSD session was with a group and was held under Jim Fadiman's guidance. Engelbart was given a "modest" dose of twenty-five micrograms and then spent four hours meditating, listening to music, and relaxing. The night before the experiment, each of the subjects in the creativity study went through an extensive psychological preparation aimed at infusing them with the idea that under the influence of the drug they would be able to solve their problems, for the premise underlying the experiments was to motivate a group of people who had spent at least three months working on a difficult technical or creative issue and were not making progress. The problems were supposed to be ones the scientists had a high emotional need to solve. After lunch, and after the LSD had taken effect, they would be put to work, while the researchers observed.

In the group setting, everyone was making progress. Electrical engineers were designing circuits; Hewlett-Packard mechanical designers were improving their lighting designs; architects were designing buildings. But not Doug Engelbart. His reaction to his first trip was to become virtually catatonic. He simply stared at the wall for the duration of the experiment.

Even so, Engelbart remained intrigued, for he had been totally captivated by the experience. He therefore suggested to Fadiman that they try a group session to employ the bootstrapping idea: "If you really believe we can be more creative, why don't we try this as a group and see if we can actually invent something?"

A second meeting was accordingly scheduled, this time a group of eight computer researchers in the young psychologist's living room. Fadiman entered the room carrying a tray of small cups containing the dose for the evening's experiment. Based on his conversations with Fadiman, Engelbart sensed that he was about to be given a lower dose than the others because of his reaction to his first drug trip. He unobtrusively shifted his position in the group about three places and continued talking as if nothing had changed. Sure enough, when Fadiman finally approached Engelbart, he had to rotate the tray so that he would receive the cup with a half dose.

In the end, the second drug experience aided Doug Engelbart's creativity, but its ability to augment human intelligence was less clear. Engelbart's contribution to the creativity session was a toy he conceived under the influence of LSD. He called it a "tinkle toy," and it was a little waterwheel that would float in a toilet bowl and spin when water (or urine) was run over it. It would serve as a potty-training teaching aid for a little boy, offering him an incentive to pee in the toilet.

Eventually LSD began to escape from its niche in the Midpeninsula's tiny intellectual bohemian community and threaten to break like a huge wave on American society. One of the first signals alerting the country to the arrival of the psychedelic onslaught was a special issue of an influential magazine.

In his hunt for subjects for the foundation's creativity studies, Fadiman called George Leonard, a California-based editor for *Look*. The magazine was at work on a special issue entitled "California: A New Game with New Rules." Leonard and a colleague came to the foundation and took part in an LSD session in an attempt to help them think through the design of the issue. In the end, Leonard, who wrote about his trip in his autobiography, *Walking on the Edge of the World*, wasn't sure if the experience made a difference. However, the June 28, 1966, edition of *Look* introduced the rest of the world to the social and cultural changes that were ripping through California. Something radically different was going on in the state, *Look* told its readers. There were new politics, and there was a counterculture that was busy throwing off America's uptight fifties values. On the cover was a photo of Jim and Dorothy Fadiman, locked in a deep embrace amid a field of California poppies.

A backlash was inevitable. Fadiman continued to oversee the LSD creativity research with scientists and engineers, until one day, while he was at the office with a group of four scientists lying on the floor listening to music in preparation for work on their technical problems while under a low dose of LSD, he opened an official-looking letter from the Food and Drug Administration. He knew what was coming. It was July 1966, and the government was looking for ways to show that it was acting to stop teenage drug use. The letter was an order to immediately stop the foundation's research. Fadiman turned to his colleagues and said, "I think we opened this letter tomorrow."

The formal experiments ended, but the secret was out. In 1966 and 1967, LSD was seeping out of an isolated bohemian niche and into the mainstream of America. It would even permeate SRI, the largely military funded research center that sat just blocks away from offices of the foundation and the Whole Earth Truck Store.

■ ■ ■

Doug Engelbart began to develop a magnetic effect in the halls of Stanford Research Institute as it became increasingly apparent that his group was doing something unusual with computing. Bright— and sometimes quirky—people found their way to his project, and one who quickly fell into his orbit was a young technical writer named David Casseres, who had been working at SRI for a year when he began hearing about Augment. Casseres had spent two years at the California Institute of Technology studying aeronautical engineering, physics, and biology before shifting gears and completing a degree in literature at Reed College, a Portland school legendary for its hyperintellectual and bohemian students.

One day, Casseres, who had been composing his reports about military projects using typewriters and paste pots, walked past Engelbart's laboratory. He peeked in and was transported into the future.

His first memory of Doug Engelbart was seeing the researcher seated before an imposing workstation with a screen that was embedded in a custom-built desk. In front of the screen was a bulky keyboard—unusual in its own right in 1967. On one side of it was an odd-shaped rolling device with a wire tail, while on the other was a second device shaped like a piano keyboard with just five keys.

Casseres introduced himself, and they were soon talking about the engineer's need for assistance in preparing the technical reports required by the project's various sponsors. He left the room with his head spinning with the idea that it might be possible to "augment" human intelligence with the futuristic computer system that Engelbart had assembled.

David Evans was a blustery Stanford Ph.D. student from Australia who discovered Engelbart one day on his way to a class lecture in the electrical engineering building. Posted on a bulletin board was a notice about a seminar, "Augmenting Human Intellect."[18] Intrigued, he skipped his class, went in, sat down, and was, as he said, "gobsmacked."

One of the things that Evans prided himself at doing well was listening to out-of-the-ordinary stories told by inventors, and Engelbart entirely seduced him. He audited the rest of the seminar and as a class project wrote a short essay. The piece caught Engelbart's eye, and he invited Evans to come to work for him part-time while he was finishing his Ph.D. in electrical engineering.

The young researcher was immediately caught up in what he referred to as the "big vision." When he arrived at the SRI laboratory, one of his first conversations was about similitude, the scaling idea that had first captured Engelbart's attention in 1959. They initially talked about it in the strictly technical sense as it applied to micro-electronics, but Engelbart's aims were much broader. He was also interested in the idea of "scaling up" his Augment tools, in trying to expand his community of users. It was the problem that Engelbart struggled with—unsuccessfully for the most part—throughout his career.

Since he wasn't a programmer, Evans had some difficulty fitting in with the software wizards who were busy coding the NLS system. But he soon found his strength in helping to communicate the big vision, expressed as Engelbart's desire to build a "bootstrap community" of technical people who would learn to work together as a "high-performance" team.

Sometimes Engelbart himself found these acolytes, and other times it was Bill English who did. Often, people heard about what Engelbart was doing from the growing buzz in the nation's tiny computer-research community. With backing from Licklider and then from his protégé Bob Taylor, who would eventually succeed Licklider at ARPA, the Augment Group grew steadily through the mid-sixties.

A group of four young University of Washington students had all spent long hours together at the computer center there and had become friends, and they all came to graduate school at Stanford, where, one after another, they found their way to the Augment project. Jeff Rulifson, Elton Hey, Don Andrews, and Chuck Kirkley came to work during 1966 as the first NLS was being created. Kirkley did not stay long, having quarreled with Engelbart over whether it was possible to program a particularly difficult software function the researcher wanted built into the system. The young graduate student insisted, "You can't do that!"

Engelbart's answer was, "I don't care, do it!"

As a leader, Engelbart was soft-spoken, but he was remarkably focused and sometimes even fiery about what he was trying to accomplish. His strength was that he saw things from the point of view of the user and then challenged his programmers to figure out how to make his ideas work as part of the overall design.

In 1966, a more powerful CDC 3100, a twenty-four-bit computer, replaced the CDC minicomputer, the 160A, that the project had begun with. Initially, the system was used in the noninteractive batch mode, but then Jeff Rulifson created a real-time graphics display for the new CDC, and a text editor was also written from scratch.

In 1966, the Augmented Human Intellect Research Center also relocated to one of SRI's new buildings. Visitors entered first into a large bullpen ringed with private offices, which were fairly spartan, with metal furniture. That changed quickly as large Persian carpets were added, offering a striking contrast with the rest of the institute. The Augment Group then began working with the Herman Miller furniture company on innovative office work systems. One of them, called a "yoga workstation," consisted of a low, four-legged coffee table with a keyboard extension. The mouse and the piano-style, one-handed chord-key system could sit on either side of a notepad or work document. The monitor was a bulky TV that sat on a flexible, four-wheeled stand. The programmer sat on two comfortable pillows.

The Augment offices were on the second floor of a three-story SRI building, and as you came in from the parking lot you could see into the windows facing the lot. It soon became clear that one of Engelbart's programmers had decided that he would take up residence in his office. Among the consequences of sharing a single underpowered computer was that access to the machine was a scarce commodity, and so computer hackers naturally gravitated to late nights and early-morning hours, when the demand was minimal. When you had the computer all to yourself, you could get decent response times, so living in the laboratory seemed a natural solution. That worked fine until the live-in hacker decided to put some of his clothes on hangers and air them outside of his office window. That was the end of the programmer's cost-effective live-work strategy.

The Augment researchers initially focused on projects that required only a single workstation. In addition to the pointing device, text editors and programming tools were created. Once again,

Engelbart's intuitive understanding of the falling costs of microelectronics played a crucial role in his early research. He didn't worry
about the remarkably high expense of the systems he was developing because he knew that by the time they were really mastered,
prices would have plunged.[19] However, in the boom and bust research world that relied on military and NASA contracting dollars,
Engelbart's research projects were invariably at risk, often at the
mercy of visionary backers like Taylor and Licklider.

The Augment experiment went through a shaky review with
NASA in 1967, and the entire project was in danger of losing its
funding until Bob Taylor came to Engelbart's aid again. Taylor had
replaced Ivan Sutherland as director of the ARPA Information Processing Technology Office in 1966 and soon discovered that Engelbart's project was having financial problems. During this period,
Engelbart was barnstorming the country with a film that showed
some of the possibilities of editing on a computer screen instead of
on paper-based typewriter terminals. With film in hand, he appeared
at one of the annual ARPA investigators' meetings, held at different
locations around the country, this time at MIT. Taylor began the
meeting by turning to Engelbart and saying, "Well, Doug, why don't
you start by telling us what you are doing?"[20] Ever insecure, Engelbart had been feeling he was invited almost as comic relief. The general consensus at the time was still that the artificial intelligence and
time-sharing researchers were doing the "important" work. He figured that Taylor was asking him to go first just to warm the group up.

So he ran his movie, which among other things demonstrated a
faster interaction with a computer than most of the researchers had
ever seen. He was surprised to find that his film made an impact.
The idea of using a display screen was an instant hit.

That evening, when the group was sitting around the lounge so-
cializing, Taylor turned to Engelbart and said, "The trouble with you,
Doug, is that you don't think big enough."

Engelbart was stunned. He was simply trying to keep his tiny
group afloat.

"What would you really want to do?" Taylor asked.

"Get a time-sharing system so that we can have a lab, or we could build it and use it ourselves and evolve it from there," he immediately responded.

"Well, let's write a proposal," Taylor instructed.

The following year, Taylor gave the Augment laboratory $535,000 to purchase an SDS-940 from Scientific Data Systems in El Segundo, California. The computer, a time-sharing machine, had originally been developed by Project Genie, an interactive computing and time-sharing research effort at the University of California at Berkeley that had been funded by ARPA.

After arriving at the Pentagon, Taylor had decided that the Project Genie work should be turned into a product, so he invited Max Palevsky, the head of Scientific Data Systems, to pay him a visit. It seemed obvious to Taylor that the development of the operating-system software had already been paid for by the taxpayers' money and that it would be a great thing to get time-sharing computing out into the commercial world.

Palevsky showed up with a number of his staff, and Taylor laid out his idea. The executive—who several years later sold his company to Xerox to pave the way for the copier maker's abortive foray into the computing world—did not see the commercial possibilities.

"No," he said, after hearing Taylor's pitch.

"Why not?" Taylor asked.

"Because it won't sell," Palevsky responded.

Taylor argued for a while, but Palevsky was unmoved.

"This is just some crazy, wild idea about some university people," he said. "They don't know what they're doing. You know, I'm a businessman. This is silly."

That infuriated Taylor, who shouted, "You're wasting my time," and asked the group to leave.

A few moments later, one of Palevsky's staff poked his head around Taylor's door and asked if he could speak to him. He said he thought that Palevsky was wrong and asked what he could do to help. Taylor suggested that he bring potential customers to his office at the Pentagon, where he would demonstrate remote use from the terminal connected to the Berkeley computer.[21]

Within a couple of months, they had more than twenty interested buyers, and Palevsky caved in and agreed to market the new computer as the SDS-940.

Following Licklider's lead, Taylor was instrumental in pursuing technologies that enhanced human-computer interaction, and he remained Engelbart's single most significant backer throughout the sixties. He was emblematic of a small group of scientists at the Pentagon at the height of the Vietnam War who had a very different worldview than much of the military organization that employed them. The people working with Taylor in the Defense Department who supported the computer-research activities of the 1960s were largely uncoupled from the military. Not only did they keep their distance from the soldiers in uniform, but they also had a set of values more in common with those in the universities and the corporate laboratories than with the bureaucratic system that was waging war in Southeast Asia.

Like many of his peers, Taylor had been a moderate supporter of the war. He thought there were bad people in South Vietnam who were taking advantage of good citizens, killing innocent people. However, over a period of four years he made a number of trips to Vietnam in an effort to straighten out the information systems that were being used to report the progress of the military effort to Lyndon Johnson in the White House. Johnson was upset that he was getting bad data from the front, and he demanded that Secretary of Defense Robert McNamara fix the problem. McNamara in turn called the director of ARPA and said, "Don't you have a computer guy or somebody that can go out there and find out what the hell's going on?"

McNamara had been one of the original "whiz kids," who applied modern statistical methods to the management of the Army Air Corps, the forerunner of the U.S. Air Force, during World War II.

After the war, a group of ten of the whiz kids went on to help turn around an ailing Ford Motor Company. Their success had a wide impact on a generation of American business management, which increasingly adopted numerically driven strategies. McNamara later brought that philosophy to the Pentagon, first under John Kennedy and then under Lyndon Johnson. Critics subsequently argued that the American failure in Vietnam was due in large part to the overreliance on a body-count algorithm, which ignored the real-world politics of the civil war.

It fell to Taylor to rationalize the body count.

In a matter of weeks, he was on his way to Vietnam. On his first trip, he took three staff officers of the Joint Chiefs of Staff, including an air force colonel, an army major, and a navy commander. When three officers representing the Joint Chiefs show up, the military pays attention.

By the end of his second trip, he was convinced the U.S. military had no business being in Southeast Asia, but his job was to fix the flaws in the Pentagon's information-reporting system. He quickly discovered that the three different services had different definitions for each of the objects they were supposed to be reporting, as well as different methods for accounting for the data. Taylor had a new set of logistics definitions and reporting formats created and a new computer center built at an air force base outside of Saigon. In the end, a single report was sent to the White House. The report, he concluded, was probably still full of lies, but at least it was a consistent set of lies.

His life in the military became increasingly intolerable, and Vietnam and his visceral dislike for Richard Nixon eventually led Taylor to leave the Pentagon. After a brief stay at the University of Utah, he moved to Palo Alto to become a manager at a new computer laboratory that was being established by Xerox. There, he would harvest the seeds he had sown in computing research during the 1960s. Like J. C. R. Licklider and Engelbart, Taylor had perceived early on that the computer had the potential to be more than an arithmetic machine. He foresaw instead its use as a communications medium, and it was that insight that had put him in a position to fund the ARPAnet, the research computer network that would ultimately become today's Internet.

The computer network came into being because Licklider had begun the funding of interactive computing research around the country—at MIT, at the Systems Development Corporation in Santa Monica, and at Berkeley—and when Taylor arrived at the Pentagon he assumed that task. Yet he found himself with separate terminals connected to all three projects. It made no sense, and it also made the logic of a single computer network inescapable.

In retrospect, Taylor's influence was remarkable, not because he was looking for an immediate application for the computing needs of the military but because he was most interested in funding what he thought of as the avant-garde or even the lunatic fringe. In a crucial period during the 1960s, it was Taylor who made sure that the envelope was pushed.

■■■

The arrival of the SDS-940 at SRI enabled Doug Engelbart to finally embark on his original vision: a community of researchers working with a shared computing system to experiment with the idea of extending the power of human intelligence.

Previously, the CDC minicomputers that the Augment project had been using were single-user systems of limited interactivity. They now referred to them as FLS (for oFf Line System) and began work on a new version of NLS. The FLS required loading a paper tape and from the terminal typing a series of commands. It was then possible to load a second tape, and the computer would edit the document for you according to the commands you had typed in. It was a remarkably cumbersome process.

It is impossible to overestimate the significance of the role that the revised NLS played in the development of personal computing. In 1968, Doug Engelbart started "living" in the future. A display was installed in his office that was connected to a jury-rigged video system that ultimately made it possible to harness as many as ten similar television monitors simultaneously to the SDS-940. Because the cost of the existing computer-display monitors available during the 1960s was astronomically high, Engelbart's hardware designers had to figure out a less expensive alternative for displaying black text on a white screen. What they arrived at was a kluge—an inelegant but clever solution.

Because of the prohibitive cost of computer memory and large cathode-ray tubes, the researchers set up an array of five-inch high-resolution monitors. A video camera was then pointed at each one, with the space between each monitor and camera shrouded so that the camera signal could be carried clearly to a remote, larger, and relatively less expensive television screen that functioned as a desktop display. It took one-and-a-half full-time technicians just to keep the system functioning, but it made it possible to create individual video workstations that could display both text and graphics, for roughly around five thousand dollars—inexpensive at the time.

It also made it possible for several monitors to share the same information display, paving the way for work-group computing. In the new NLS system, each workstation consisted of a keyboard for entering data and alongside it a mouse with three buttons and a five-key keyboard. The small keyboard, which looked a bit like a short piano without sharps and flats, could be used either for entering text or for sending commands to the system, making it possible to edit rapidly with two hands without being forced to move a hand between the keyboard and mouse.

For those who had been trained to use a standard qwerty keyboard, the Augment system took a while to get used to, and Engelbart glued one of the five-key keyboards to the dashboard of his car so he could practice using it while driving.

The Augment researchers tested the system and found that it was easy for the programmers to master and that it enabled blindingly fast and efficient editing. Some of the team even mastered the art of typing using the chord-key set exclusively—one young programmer was able to type more than fifty words per minute. To a world that would not see the introduction of the IBM Correcting Selectric II typewriter until 1973, it made for a stunning display of text editing at hyperspeed.

The Augment system eventually offered word processing, outline editing, hypertext linking, teleconferencing, electronic mail, a windowing display, online help, and a consistent user interface. In trying to convey its significance, some have attempted to draw parallels between it and integrated software packages such as Microsoft Office, which appeared in the 1980s. However, the scope and vision of Engelbart's system was vastly broader, and it was created as part of a project that would eventually blend with the ARPAnet as a community of technical researchers.

Much of the breadth of Engelbart's original Augmentation Framework idea would be lost until the early 1990s, when the commercial computing world finally discovered the power of the Internet. There was an abyss between the original work done by Engelbart's group in the sixties and the motley crew of hobbyists that would create the personal-computer industry beginning in 1975. In their hunger to possess their own computers, the PC hobbyists would miss the crux of the original idea: communications as an integral part of the design. That was at the heart of the epiphanies that Engelbart had years earlier, which led to the realization of Vannevar Bush's Memex information-retrieval system of the 1940s.

During the period from the early 1960s until 1969, when most of the development of the NLS system was completed, Engelbart and his band of researchers remained in a comfortable bubble. They were largely Pentagon funded, but unlike many of the engineering and computing groups that surrounded them at SRI, they weren't doing work that directly contributed to the Vietnam War. Still, there were constant hints that the larger world outside was about to intrude, and occasionally it did.

There was, for example, the "Man with No Name."

During the sixties, most of the funding for the laboratory came from either NASA or ARPA's Information Processing Technology Office. Later, when NLS was functioning, there were customers such as the Rome Air Development Center. On occasion, there were also shadowy organizations that took an active interest in the Augment technology. In August 1966, Engelbart and English had paid a visit to the headquarters of the CIA in Langley, Virginia, and there had been sporadic contacts after that.

The "Man with No Name" arrived one day from what was referred to as the Army Special Operations Group, which was assumed to be a front for the Central Intelligence Agency. He held a series of meetings at which the members of the Augment laboratory described their technology, but the meetings could not be recorded or photographed. A contract had been quietly awarded the lab to make it possible for their visitor to have an occasional presence. He stayed for a while and then vanished, and the younger Augment programmers assumed that the purpose had been simply to look around, in case the agency ever wanted to make real contact. There was a fair amount of muttering and whispering about the "SOG [Special Operations Group] contract," but the Man with No Name had vanished.

It was just a hint of what was to come. Spurred on by Bob Taylor, at the end of 1968 the Augment Group decided it needed to raise its profile and invite the outside world to see what they had done. Opening the door would change everything.

3 | RED-DIAPER BABY

B ill Pitts was a loner, in that typical math-science-nerd way.
Growing up during the sixties in Palo Alto, he had top grades
in high school and was accepted as a freshman at Stanford University in 1965. It was in that year that the school had finally established
a computer-science department, and Pitts's first course was, fittingly,
"Introduction to Computer Science," taught by the founder of the department, George Forsythe.

Pitts quickly developed a hacker's love for computing and even
managed to postpone Stanford's mandatory "Introduction to Western Civilization" course so that he could take additional computer-
science courses during his freshman year. He found computing fun
and easy—easy, because it was all very logical. And although he was
a loner, he managed on his own to pick up a habit that is characteristic of computer hackers of every era: the love of cracking locks, in
part for the intellectual challenge, and in part because of the thrill of
pursuing illicit and hidden information.

Pitts took up this extracurricular hobby during his freshman year.
Late at night, after he finished studying, he began breaking into
buildings all over the Stanford campus. It was a great challenge, and
he bagged his targets in much the same way a stamp collector ex-
pands his holdings or a climber scales peaks. By the middle of his
sophomore year, he had been inside virtually every building at the
school, as well as the catacombs—the steam tunnels that ran under-

neath the campus. His trophy prize was the nipple atop Hoover Tower, the library that commemorated the conservative president. He got into the tiny cupola through a trapdoor, which he discovered was made of copper. He also saw that it was covered with the initials of those who had come before him, so he added his own.

Pitts was almost out of challenges when one day he decided to drive out to Rossotti's, a funky beer house and favorite hangout of students, bikers, and bicyclists, located on Alpine Road in Portola Valley, a couple of miles west of the Stanford campus. As he headed out Arastradero Road in the rolling foothills behind Stanford, he noticed a driveway running up a hill. What caught his eye was a sign next to the driveway that identified the site as the Donald C. Power Laboratory. He could tell by its lettering that it was a Stanford facility; thinking that he had found a new potential conquest, he made a mental note to come back later that night.

He showed up at 11:00 P.M. in a parking lot in front of an impressive-looking semicircular building that sat on top of the hill. He was initially disappointed to find that the doors were all unlocked, the parking lot was crowded, the lights were on, and thirty to forty people were inside, hard at work. However, his curiosity won out over his disappointment, and he went inside to figure out what all of the people were doing there so late at night. He was astounded to find a computer room that housed a Digital PDP-6 computer and John McCarthy's Stanford Artificial Intelligence Laboratory.

Pitts had found his new home. Moreover, the irony of his situation was not lost on him: He had just tried to hack his way into one of the world's two or three bastions of top-flight computer hackers.

The light of day revealed that the laboratory was tucked away in a remarkably beautiful hillside retreat next to a small reservoir named Felt Lake, with views of San Francisco, the bay, Yerba Buena Island, Mount Tamalpais to the north, Mount Diablo to the east, and Mount Hamilton and Mount Umunhum to the south. Visitors were greeted in a small lobby that over time had spawned an ungainly "You Are Here" mural. It had a bit of the flavor of the famous Saul Steinberg

New Yorker cover depicting a New Yorker's relativistic map of the United States. The SAIL version began with a simple view of the laboratory and the Stanford campus, but then creative souls had continuously appended alternative perspectives, ranging from the center of the human brain to that near an obscure star somewhere out on the arm of a medium-sized spiral galaxy.

Computer scientist and mathematician John McCarthy had created the Stanford Artificial Intelligence Project in 1964. Before arriving at Stanford in 1962, McCarthy had already made several towering contributions to the world of computing. He had invented the LISP programming language, a highly flexible tool that during the sixties became the standard for artificial-intelligence researchers, and he had pioneered the modern time-shared operating systems that would become the foundation of interactive computing.

McCarthy had been born a "Red-Diaper Baby" in Boston in 1927, with both his parents active in the Communist Party. His father, John Patrick McCarthy, was an Irish immigrant who later became business manager of the Communist Party organ *The Daily Worker* after the family moved to Los Angeles because of their young son's health problems. His mother, Ida Glatt, was a Lithuanian Jew who had been active in the women's suffrage movement. Young McCarthy, when he moved to Princeton to study mathematics in graduate school in 1949, joined the local party cell, which consisted of two other members: an elderly African-American woman who cleaned homes and an Italian immigrant who worked as a gardener. Such was the Red Menace. He watched the Moscow show trials of the early fifties, hoping that the abuses of the Soviets would moderate. In the end, because he had left home, he was able to quit the party without being embarrassed or embarrassing his family.

At Princeton, McCarthy was a contemporary of John Nash, who later won a Nobel Prize in economics for his work in game theory, and whose life was chronicled by Sylvia Nasar in *A Beautiful Mind.* As graduate students, McCarthy, Nash, and several of the other students enjoyed constantly scheming and playing practical jokes on one another, justifying their antics in terms of their game-theory explorations.

McCarthy arrived at Stanford for the second time (he had taught math there briefly in the early fifties) as a thirty-five-year-old former wunderkind who had invented the term "artificial intelligence." While teaching math at Dartmouth during the summer of 1956, he had been the principal organizer of the first conference on modeling intelligence in computers and coined the term as part of the conference proposal. At the time, he was working on a chess-playing computer program, and throughout his career he remained an optimist regarding the possibility of creating intelligent machines. However, after the heady period of the sixties and seventies, when it seemed that thinking machines were truly within reach, he adopted a healthy respect for the challenge, saying that creating artificial intelligence would require "1.8 Einsteins and one tenth the resources of the Manhattan Project."[1]

Indeed, from the beginning there were hints that progress in the field might be slower than forecast. An embarrassing incident occurred just three months after the PDP-6 computer was installed at the lab in 1966. At an open house held to introduce the facility, a prototype robot arm was programmed to pour punch for the visitors. For a while the arm did a reasonably good job. However, when the system had been set up the night before, the PDP-6 had been only lightly loaded. Now, with lots of demonstrations taking place in different parts of the lab, the arm began to malfunction. It dipped the cup in the punch, lifted it, but it failed to halt at the proper level, continuing instead on its vertical axis until it poured the punch all over itself. This was considered hilarious by the assembled crowd, who made the machine repeat the errant motions endlessly.[2] Although the progress in robotics was slow and halting, it ultimately did have consequences. The SAIL hand-eye robotics group surpassed its rivals at MIT, and its work later led directly to the robotic arms used extensively today in industrial assembly.

A time of open scientific and technical experimentation, the period 1963 to 1969 was considered the "golden years" of AI. Rapid progress was made in a range of areas, including vision, robotics, expert systems, speech, and language understanding. The AI world was then largely split into two camps. One group believed that it would be feasible to successfully model the neural functions of the human brain, making it possible to synthesize human capabilities like vision and speech. A competing view was held by a group who thought that it was conceivable to build a "superbrain" and that AI machines could exceed human capabilities.

From the very beginning, McCarthy believed that artificial intelligence should be interactive with the user, but he never dreamed of having his own machine. Instead, computers had become fast enough so that by slicing the computer's programming resources into tiny time slots and allocating them to different users, each user would have the illusion that he had a single large computer all to himself. Since computers did things at lightning speed, and since in the days before graphical displays most user interaction with the machine consisted of merely entering text and data at a keyboard, the vast majority of the computer's time was being wasted while it waited for user input. To be sure, there had been an earlier time-sharing machine invented at the RAND Corporation known as JOSS, but it consisted of lights on top of terminals—the computer's time was allocated to the terminal whose light was switched on at the moment!

In the late 1950s, however, McCarthy's notion was prescient and similar to Doug Engelbart's vision for the Augmentation machine. However, they remained fundamentally different concepts. At the deepest level, the question was whether humans would remain in the loop. Brilliant machines that could both mimic and surpass human capabilities were not what Engelbart foresaw, and although the two camps didn't directly quarrel they did pursue opposite agendas, representing humanist and mechanist ideas about the future of computing and technology. Yet ultimately, despite the fact that they were philosophical opponents, together the work of the Augmentation laboratory at SRI and the Stanford Artificial Intelligence Laboratory came to define a vision for "personal computing," predating the personal computer itself.

When inexpensive personal computers finally came on the scene a decade later in the mid-1970s, they were viewed in opposition to time-sharing minicomputers. However, McCarthy's original notion of interactivity—a computer that made possible a virtual personal computer for each user—is the more important one. McCarthy himself didn't grasp the implication of Engelbart's insight into scaling ever-more-powerful microchips. Still, he was interested in the possibility of getting dramatic increases in personal productivity, and since individual computers were prohibitively expensive, time-sharing was an effective alternative.

In 1962, McCarthy was seduced by sixties California, which, with its political and cultural freedom, stood in stark contrast to the more stifling and buttoned-down East Coast. Although the MIT hackers grimaced at the combination of computing and California, McCarthy eagerly embraced the Golden State. He was also bitterly disappointed that MIT had decreed that before the university embarked on a big, new time-sharing project it had to conduct a market survey. McCarthy likened this to the idea of "taking a market survey among ditchdiggers over whether steam shovels were a good thing."[3]

When he came west, McCarthy brought with him a young computer hacker named Stephen Russell. "Slug," as he was known, had been one of McCarthy's programmers since his days as a math student at Dartmouth in the fifties. He had done the heavy lifting in the design of the LISP programming language. Friendly and open, Russell had an infectious way of smiling with his head tilted back and his chin up whenever he said something particularly clever and funny.

In many ways, Russell was the quintessential hacker. Although he had never been to California before, he thought nothing of picking up and following McCarthy cross-country. In many respects, he didn't even notice the change of coasts, for his existence still revolved around the care and feeding of a Digital PDP-1 computer. A science fiction fan, with a small group of other MIT hackers he had also programmed the world's first video game in 1961 and 1962.[4]

Russell and his friends had something very ambitious in mind. They were all devotees of the E. E. "Doc" Smith "Lensman" pulp science fiction novels, a series of shoot-'em-up space operas that seemed the perfect model for an interactive software game. Russell, who was a bit of a procrastinator, had put off writing the foundation code, pleading that he didn't have a necessary subroutine and that he didn't know how to write it. That excuse was undone after another MIT hacker, Alan Kotok, traveled all the way to Digital Equipment Corporation's headquarters in Maynard, Massachusetts, to obtain the necessary code, stored on a paper tape. He gave Russell the programs and told him, "All right, Russell, here's a sine-cosine routine; now what's your excuse?"[5]

By January 1962, Russell had a rudimentary object-in-motion worked out on the screen. Spacewar, as the game came to be called, pitted two two-dimensional spaceships against each other on a background of stars. Pressing keys on the keyboard would move the ships on the display, and they could shoot tiny projectiles at each other. Spacewar was significant in that it was the classic collaborative hacking exercise, which would be cited as an early example of how open-source shared programs could be continuously improved by a group of volunteer programmers. For although Russell did the initial yeoman's work of creating the basic program, others had soon added lifelike constellations and a gravitational effect generated by a star placed in the center of the screen. Initially, the PDP-1 had enough power to compute the gravitational effect on the ships accurately but not enough to compute the trajectories of multiple torpedoes. The hackers defined away that problem by decreeing the projectiles were actually "photon" torpedoes and were thus beyond the gravitational pull of the star.

After Russell left MIT Spacewar soon gained a cult following wherever there were Digital Equipment Corporation computers. It also became a magnet for a generation of mostly young men who were not programmers. A decade later, a commercial version of Spacewar, designed by Bill Pitts and a friend, was installed at Stanford's Tresidder Union coffeehouse. Called Galaxy Game, it first appeared several months before a similar game, Computer Space, was developed by a young entrepreneur named Nolan Bushnell. Bushnell had come across Spacewar while he was a graduate student at the University of Utah. Although Computer Space was a commercial flop, it was followed by Pong and the explosive growth of Bushnell's company, Atari.

■ ■ ■

Initially, the AI programmers were housed in cramped quarters in several makeshift buildings that had been erected to house the early Stanford campus computers. Moreover, before McCarthy's first ARPA-funded computer arrived, they were forced to share a bulky IBM 7090 mainframe with other scientists—in particular, with two mathematicians who were not even Stanford faculty members who monopolized the computer for hours or even days. When Russell needed to run a program, he would politely ask them to stop their calculation, at which point the number theorists would output an interim result onto a single punch card and hand over the computer. When Russell had completed his program, they reinserted the card and continued their calculations.

Eventually, they acquired the PDP-1, which was jury-rigged with twelve displays, shared equally between the artificial-intelligence researchers and Patrick Suppes, a Stanford philosophy professor who was beginning research on computer-aided instruction. The machine was remarkable for several attributes: It was the first display-oriented general purpose time-sharing system created anywhere in the world. Moreover, its keyboard used two "control" keys, used to modify the function of the standard typewriter keys.

The design had been influenced by a visiting professor, Niklaus Wirth, a Swiss mathematician and computer scientist. With the particularly dogmatic style of a European academic, Wirth had insisted that the keyboard needed an additional two extra modifier keys

besides the principal control key. Russell and McCarthy began referring to the keys as "Bucky bits," named affectionately after Wirth,
whom they had taken to calling "Bucky Beaver," behind his back.
Today, vestigial remains of the Bucky bits of the early PDP-1 can be
found in the "alt" and "option" keys on modern keyboards.

At SAIL, McCarthy and his researchers pursued a diverse set of
interests in the field of computer science and beyond. Early on, he
attempted to root AI research in the context of philosophy. He sided
in that respect with the community of researchers who were more
interested in modeling human intelligence in an attempt to understand it as a necessary first step toward achieving artificial intelligence.[6] In another sense, however, McCarthy was also interested in
the idea of the AI superbrain. His fascination with chess-playing
machines had taken root at MIT, where he had begun developing a
chess program soon after he began teaching the first undergraduate
course in computer science. McCarthy took the program, which had
been designed by several MIT undergraduates, with him on his first
trip to the Soviet Union in 1965.

On that visit, he gave a lecture about the program and discovered
that Soviet computer scientists had their own chess-playing computer. Alexander Kronrod was a mathematician and the leader of the
group that had designed its program at the Institute of Theoretical
and Experimental Physics in Moscow. Kronrod challenged the Stanford group to a match, and since there was no computer network
available in either country, the moves were communicated each day
by telegraph.

The match consisted of four games and lasted for the better part of
a year. McCarthy's program ran on an IBM mainframe and did not
consume a great deal of computer time, while the Russian program
was much slower, and its algorithm was much more elaborate. In the
end, the Soviet program, in both weaker and stronger versions, was
superior to the American one, and it won all of the four games.

It was his first and a series of later trips to the Soviet Union that
soured McCarthy on the idea of socialism. Although he had long

since quit the Communist Party, he had remained hopeful about the prospects for socialism, even in the early 1960s. By 1968 and the Soviet invasion of Prague, however, he had come to believe that Russia would not become more democratic under socialism during his lifetime.[7]

On campus, McCarthy's political disaffection from leftist politics took form in an odd incident that was to solidify his credentials as an irascible crank in the years to come. The episode in question took place one morning in White Plaza, a sprawling asphalt-and-grass-covered space that served as the gathering spot for most campus political activities. The Stanford Students for a Democratic Society had organized a colorful fair on the lawn that separated the old student union from the student bookstore. They had erected a geodesic dome and a humorous display that asserted that the Stanford faculty members were the lackeys of the board of trustees, who in turn were the lackeys of the military-industrial complex. The montage included a goofy wheel of fortune, which attacked the faculty's integrity. Walking across campus, McCarthy spied the display and stopped and examined it. He was so enraged at its insinuations that he stepped up to the wheel and tore it down. The SDSers were equally outraged. If he was so angry at the Soviets and the student left, hadn't he heard of the idea of freedom of speech? McCarthy would have none of it. In fact, the incident only whetted his appetite for baiting the activists.[8] Despite his disaffection from the left, McCarthy remained deeply immersed in the sixties counterculture, to the point that, during the late sixties, he affected a headband, long hair, and a beard.

In the computer-science world, there were different styles of research leadership: Doug Engelbart at Augment and David Evans, the founder of the University of Utah Computer Science department, inspired fanatical devotion; several years later, at Xerox PARC, Robert Taylor proved remarkable at getting the best work out of the brightest people.

McCarthy had none of these qualities. He was an iconoclast, prone to being brusque and abrupt. He could be standoffish, and he had little interest in taking the role of charismatic leader. However, although it frequently seemed that way, he wasn't so much arrogant as overwhelmingly shy. He was also brutally honest, even about his own shortcomings. But even with those limitations, he created a laboratory that afforded a remarkable amount of freedom and that attracted an eclectic band of scientists interested in gaining access to computing power. Years later, lost in the glare of publicity surrounding PARC's accomplishments, the SAIL researchers failed to receive the credit that should have been given to their system. Work on the PDP-6 computer time-sharing and multiterminal-display technology was done under a contract for artificial-intelligence research and, as a result, went largely unnoticed. Yet for a period of several years, SAIL had the only system in the world in which the entire staff had a display terminal on his or her desk, including secretaries.

For a while, there was some concern over whether "mere" secretaries would be able to master such a complicated system. Then one day McCarthy came to work and found a new woman sitting at one of the terminals typing away quite comfortably. "Who's that?" he asked. And when he was told that it was a temp who had been hired to replace someone who was absent, he realized his fears had been misplaced.

■■■

As a professor at Stanford, McCarthy had felt as if he had been given a hunting license for money, and he turned to J. C. R. Licklider, who was already ensconced at the Pentagon, where he was passionately pursuing his own vision of interactive computing. McCarthy had previously gotten Licklider interested in time-sharing, and years later McCarthy said that if he had known that Licklider was going to underwrite the MIT work, he would never have come to Stanford.

Initially, McCarthy had been successful in getting a small amount of funding for AI research from Licklider, and the Digital Equipment Corporation had donated the PDP-1 to the young professor. McCarthy had meanwhile become interested in some vexing issues in computer vision that would need to be solved if robots were to recognize and manipulate blocks successfully. In 1964, he had applied for a larger grant, which he received, and he even had the audacity to ask ARPA to allow him to hire an executive officer. By that time, Ivan Sutherland, the designer of the brilliant Sketchpad drawing system, had succeeded Licklider. He told McCarthy he thought the notion of an executive officer was a great idea.

"You're the only one of our investigators with a perfect record," Sutherland said. "You have never turned in a quarterly progress report."[9]

Sutherland had quickly realized that McCarthy had little interest in the management side of the SAIL project. The computer scientist and ARPA manager was at the same time trying to figure out what to do with Les Earnest, an iconoclastic engineer who was growing increasingly frustrated working for MITRE Corporation. "The less I do that's interesting the more they pay me," he had told Sutherland. By bringing Earnest, a creative engineer who had been educated at Cal Tech and MIT and who would also soon dabble in the sixties counterculture scene, to SAIL, ARPA inadvertently created an extremely informal research laboratory that served as a magnet for both straight computer scientists as well as brilliant misfits.

When Earnest arrived at the school, Stanford had only recently instructed the group of about thirty researchers and graduate students to move off campus to occupy the then-unfinished Donald C. Power Laboratory, which had been given to the University by General Telephone and Electronics. The company had almost finished building its new research center on a piece of land adjacent to the campus when a quiet corporate scandal and a management change led to the decision to relocate to New Jersey. Although it would ultimately be a blessing for SAIL to be tucked away in the hills, at first it proved a hardship.

When Earnest asked who would be the architect for the interior of the ramshackle, half-donut-shaped building, the Stanford administrators replied, "You are." So even though he had no architectural experience, the young engineer created the plans for a computer room and an office layout. There was even an attic space large enough for several of the researchers to eventually take up full-time residence.

The SAIL researchers first occupied the building in May 1966, and an ARPA-funded PDP-6 computer showed up in June. It became a magnet for an unruly group of researchers, graduate students, and hangers-on. Many of them were, like Bill Pitts, the really bright kids who never quite fit in. They came from all over the country and from around the world, and they shared a passionate belief in an unbounded future, coupled with a slightly dark and sardonic worldview that only people with a truly deep understanding of the way things work could have. It was a late-night crowd. After the interminable Chinese meals that hackers tend to prefer often came the lab's unofficial rallying cry: "Back to the lab, Igor!" The Frankensteinian possibilities of artificial intelligence were obvious to all.

Hints of living in the future led some of the astonished researchers to shake their heads in wonder. One day, after a late-afternoon volleyball match, everyone rushed into the lab to watch *Star Trek.* Shortly thereafter, the SAIL robot rolled in as well and perched near one of the couches while training its robotic lens on the screen. Everybody did a double take. Had the dawn of robot AI arrived? No. It turned out that one of the robot researchers needed to complete some work in his office and didn't want to miss the episode.

Dozens of the world's best computer scientists began their careers at SAIL. More than half a dozen companies including Foonly, Imagen, Xidex, Vicarm, Valid Logic, Sun Microsystems, Xerox PARC, and Cisco Systems can trace their technology either directly or indirectly to SAIL. Moreover, other important companies such as Digital, Lucasfilm, and Intel received important technological boosts from SAIL innovations. SAIL research also led to a wave of AI startups in the late seventies and early eighties.

Ultimately, the dream of AI went unrealized, but SAIL nurtured an eclectic group of computer hackers who passed through before going on in a computing diaspora that eventually was every bit as influential as the later scattering from Xerox PARC.

During the evenings, Donald Knuth, a Stanford computer scientist who invented several of the field's most important algorithms, would show up to use the SAIL computer along with other hackers. Knuth eventually wrote *The Art of Computer Programming*, the definitive text in the field. Years later, after becoming annoyed with the declining quality of the typesetting in the production of math books, he designed an advanced text-formatting language called TeX. Decades after the SAIL computer was surplus, someone cataloged all of the files and discovered that Knuth had created more data and files on the system than any of the other 1,700 users. But Knuth wasn't all work during his evenings at SAIL. He would take advantage of the fact that each terminal could double as a TV display and would frequently ask one of the SAIL hackers to tune in television programs while he was programming in the evenings.

SAIL was such an open and inviting place that it also became a magnet for a group of bright and disaffected high school students who much preferred hanging out with the hackers than attending classes. One of the regulars was a Woodside dropout named Marc Le-Brun. LeBrun lived in a neighborhood that was only a mile away from SAIL. His father was a Hewlett-Packard engineer who had early experience with transistors, and LeBrun had grown up in a comfortable, upper-middle-class home. He had acquired his first taste of computing when he stole his father's time-sharing account at HP to write math and music-composition programs. Bored with school, he had an unusual ability to learn on his own. At age ten, he had contracted pneumonia and spent much of one summer at home reading anything he could lay his hands on. One book he found was an early account of LSD experiences. His mother was horrified, but LeBrun was fascinated. The collision of psychedelic drugs, antiwar protests, and easy access to the world of SAIL led him to leave high school in 1969. He was interested in math and had started composing music.

By now, his parents were at their wits' end, and so one day his father drove the boy over to SAIL and apologetically asked John Chowning, a pioneer in computer music whose research group had taken space at SAIL, if there might be any way for him to become involved in the laboratory. As SAIL was a complete meritocracy, Chowning grabbed a handful of manuals and said, "Take these and read them." LeBrun did, came back, and eventually became a fixture around SAIL.

He also studied calculus and then began reading Knuth's book on programming, doing the exercises on his own. How much better it was to actually be able to talk to Knuth, instead of being trapped in a stultifying high school classroom! In the end, he contributed an important algorithm for music synthesis called wave shaping.

LeBrun wasn't the only high school kid to find his way to SAIL. Geoff Goodfellow, a hypercybernetic Menlo Park teenager, had found a job working at SRI and the Network Information Center after the computing manager realized that it was better to have him hacking inside than hacking in from outside. Goodfellow dropped out of school and took to living at SRI around the clock. On the weekends, he would come hang out at SAIL. Early on, he discovered Zen wisdom in the SAIL computer room. Someone had pasted a prize from a Cracker Jack box on the computer that read, "Try to divide your time equally to keep everyone happy." It was the obvious credo of the time-sharing world.

Two other occasional visitors were high school students Steven Jobs and Stephen Wozniak, who hung out at SAIL with an older friend, Allen Baum, who was working at the laboratory during the fall of 1970. Jobs later said that the "vibrations" he felt at SAIL would stay with him his entire life. The bewitched Wozniak rode his bike up to the laboratory from his home in Los Altos, and he later said that his experiences there contributed to his hunger for his own computer.

●●●

Despite being tucked away in the foothills behind Stanford, SAIL wasn't politically or culturally isolated. The politics of the sixties flowed into every aspect of the research center. Years later, Les

Earnest described his political trajectory during the sixties as being from right to left, in contrast with John McCarthy's move in the opposite direction. There was certainly no party line at SAIL. Indeed, what was most remarkable about the institution that McCarthy and Earnest created was that the surprisingly eclectic and intensely effective gathering came not only from all kinds of academic disciplines but from every imaginable political and cultural background as well.

As in any self-possessed subculture, the SAIL hackers created their own expressive jargon. Many of the terms were imported by the first generation of hackers from MIT, but others were added as well. By 1975, a jargon file had been created by Raphael Finkel, a SAIL systems programmer. Shortly thereafter, a duplicate was kept at MIT, with periodic resynchronizations between the two. The jargon captured the spirit of the hacker culture with adjectives like "moby" and nouns like "frob" and descriptive terms like "phase-wrapping," a synonym for the noun "wraparound." The latter was an artifact of the reality that because computers were more lightly loaded late at night, the hacker community tuned its sleep cycles to work accordingly, with varying degrees of success. Online calculators were even designed to compute sleep cycles so that hackers who were working around the clock could compute their individual cycles to be functional for an upcoming test.

SAIL was a hacker's paradise, but far different from the engineering-centric world of MIT. To be sure, it was the two MIT refugees, McCarthy and Earnest, who had been responsible for creating it. Because McCarthy, an intense intellectual, had little interest in or tolerance for the necessities of management, Earnest was responsible for controlling a menagerie of computer hackers, yet even in that role he came to represent the anarchic spirit of the laboratory.

Earnest had the endearing quality of thoughtfully musing about the perplexing events that inevitably seemed to emerge from his pool of creative talents. He was soon known for wandering the halls of SAIL and, when confronted with a problem or question, putting his hand to his chin, furrowing his brow, and saying "hmmmm." It became such a trademark expression that he later obtained a license plate that read "MUMBLE," the hacker's ambiguous response to statements or questions that he would rather not answer.

Musicologist John Chowning, who at SAIL invented the technology that underlies modern music synthesizers, called it a "Socratean abode." SAIL embodied what University of California computer scientist and former SAIL systems programmer Brian Harvey called the "hacker aesthetic." Harvey's description was a reaction to what Steven Levy in *Hackers: Heroes of the Computer Revolution* had described as a "hacker ethic," which he characterized as the unspoken manifesto of the MIT hackers:

- Access to computers—and anything which might teach you something about the way the world works—should be unlimited and total. Always yield to the Hands-On Imperative!
- All information should be free.
- Mistrust Authority—Promote Decentralization.
- Hackers should be judged by their hacking, not bogus criteria such as degrees, age, race, or position.
- You can create art and beauty on a computer.
- Computers can change your life for the better.[10]

In contrast, Harvey, who had been one of the hard-core programmers at the MIT AI lab and later was one at SAIL, argued that computer hacking wasn't an ethical stance at all; it was an aesthetic one. "A hack can be anything from a practical joke to a brilliant new computer program," he wrote. "(VisiCalc was a great hack. Its imitators are not hacks.) But whatever it is, a good hack must be aesthetically perfect. If it's a joke, it must be a complete one. If you decide to turn someone's dorm room upside-down, it's not enough to epoxy the furniture to the ceiling. You must also epoxy the pieces of paper to the desk."[11]

And yet, he demurred that when Richard Stallman, one of MIT's best-known hackers, stated that information should be free, Stall-man's ideal wasn't based on the idea of property as theft—an ethical position—but instead on the understanding that keeping infor-mation secret is inefficient: "it leads to unaesthetic duplication of effort."[12] Anyone who has spent time around the computer commu-nity, particularly as it evolved, will recognize that both writers are correct. Points were given for style, but there was a deeper sub-stance, an ethical stance that has become a formidable force in the modern world of computing.

Perhaps no one better represented both the hacker ethic and its aesthetic than Les Earnest. He had worked for the MITRE Corpora-tion. In 1962, he was "loaned" to the CIA and several other intelli-gence agencies to help integrate various military computer systems. Not surprisingly, an individual with a deeply rooted hacker sensibil-ity was never a perfect fit with a military-intelligence bureaucracy. Early on, he had been asked to fill out a form as part of an applica-tion for some new security clearance. When he reached the line that inquired about his "race," he considered the question for a while and then entered "mongrel." Earnest's impish intellectual honesty rang all the alarm bells in the corridors of power, and he was called on the carpet, where he refused to back down. After great gnashing of teeth, the intelligence officials gave in after he agreed to sign an affi-davit affirming that his race was indeed mongrel.

Possibly if the agency had scrutinized its computer expert's early years, it might have realized that Earnest had a predilection for wan-dering into Kafka-esque straits. As a teenager growing up in South-ern California during World War II, he and a close friend responded to an invitation proffered during the Jack Armstrong radio program and mailed in Wheaties boxtops to get a decoder ring to decipher the secret messages that were given near the end of the radio broad-casts.[13] The two boys subsequently developed a fascination with cryptography, and Earnest's friend purchased a book on the subject. They decided they needed their own secret code, and Earnest began carrying his version inside his glasses case. One day while on an outing to go bodysurfing at a beach in San Diego, he lost the case and his mother reported it missing to the streetcar company.

Unfortunately, a self-styled patriot found the case, and the hidden coding scheme was turned over to the FBI. The finder had concluded the code must belong to a Japanese spy. About ten weeks later, Earnest's mother received a call at work from an FBI agent, who insisted that she return home immediately to meet him.

Two agents showed up at the Earnest front door, demanding an explanation for the secret code. Fortunately, his mother was able to convince them—more or less—that her son wasn't an enemy spy. However, one of the agents insisted that the government keep the code.

Earnest thought that he had put the episode behind him, but it continued to haunt him for many years, thanks to his tendency to fill out government forms with unnecessary accuracy.

In 1949, he took a summer job at the Naval Electronics Laboratory in San Diego as a test subject for an acoustics experiment designed by J. C. R. Licklider, the scientist who would later become the DARPA manager. As part of the research project the group was to listen to sonar recordings, which required a security clearance. On the application form one of the questions was "Have you ever been investigated by the FBI?" True to character, Earnest checked "yes," and then in the small space where he was asked to describe the purpose of the investigation, he noted that he was suspected of being a Japanese spy.[14]

When he handed in the application, the security officer looked at the sheet and asked him to explain his answer. As he attempted to recount the cryptography episode, the officer became increasingly upset. Finally he tore up the sheet and instructed Earnest never to mention the incident again.

Earnest was an iconoclast even by the quirky standards of Cal Tech. Annoyed by the nerdy conformity of the twelve-inch slide rules that all of his compatriots carried from their belts, he found an abacus and did the same, irritating other students with its audible clicking during exams.[15]

■ ■ ■

Initially, there were about thirty researchers in the roughly hewn facilities in the half-finished building in the foothills behind campus.
Earnest soon invited John Chowning's computer-music group to locate at the laboratory as well, even though they came without research support.

Chowning's arrival was an early hint of what was to come: Computing was on the verge of becoming a medium, and John Chowning was one of the first to see the potential. He had initially been
exposed to electronic music while studying in Paris, where he attended live performances by Karlheinz Stockhausen and Pierre
Boulez. He arrived at Stanford as a graduate student in music in
1962, never having had any contact with computers.

Chowning had already been intrigued by the idea of using loud-
speakers as instruments, but nothing would have come of his interest had he not met Dave Poole in the Stanford student orchestra;
Poole was also one of the young computer hackers hanging around
SAIL. Poole handed him a *Science* magazine article written by Max
Matthews, a Bell Laboratories researcher. The article speculated that
the computer would soon emerge as the ultimate musical instrument, and it made the bold statement that in theory you might produce any perceivable sound with one. Knowing nothing about
computers, Chowning traveled to visit Matthews and returned to
campus with a deck of punch cards containing a program that
Matthews had designed.

Although Poole, who was still an undergraduate, was ten years
Chowning's junior, he took him under his wing and introduced him
to the world of computing. The classic hacker, he frequently became
impatient and shouted at Chowning when he was slow to pick up
some idea that Poole deemed obvious. Eventually, however, the
hacker came to understand that the musician's background had not
equipped him for the rapid acquisition of knowledge, and a great
deal of affection grew between the two men.

In 1967, Chowning made his breakthrough while experimenting with vibratos in an effort to add realism to electronic sounds. He had been playing with a pair of oscillators, modulating one sine wave with the output of another. The result was a richly harmonic tone from which he could approximate the sound of clarinets, bassoons, and similar instruments, and the discovery became known as frequency modulation synthesis. Four years later, he handed the technology to Stanford's Office of Technology Licensing, which in turn approached a number of American instrument makers. None of them was interested, and it was Yamaha that ultimately licensed Chowning's invention.

SAIL was also home to eccentric hackers who took on any number of curious projects. Hans Moravec was born in Austria shortly before his family immigrated to Canada in 1953. He developed a boyhood passion for robotics that he never outgrew. After getting a master's degree at the University of Ontario, he came to Stanford with the fantasy of building a robot that could independently make its way through the world. Since John McCarthy's own goal was to build a reasoning machine, he was willing to tolerate the idea that such a machine might also have eyes, arms, and wheels.

The SAIL hackers had salvaged a mobile cart that had been built in the Mechanical Engineering Department for a lunar-lander experiment. Soon after he appeared, Moravec took responsibility for the robot, which was known as the SAIL Cart. It wasn't fast, but it had the ability to navigate both indoors and out. Before long, the driveway leading up to the lab was sporting a yellow traffic sign that read "CAUTION ROBOT VEHICLE."

The robotic cart was an ungainly machine on four small bicycle wheels, with motors, electronics for steering, radio gear, and a video camera. It was still quite flaky. For example, when you commanded it to move forward, about a quarter of the time it actually traveled backward. Command it to go right, and about a quarter of the time it went left. Artificial intelligence clearly had a way to go.

As Moravec worked on it, the SAIL Cart soon seemed to develop a mind of its own. One day, the robot's display screen showed that the machine's camera was staring at a series of white lines. A second later, a programmer realized that the cart had escaped and was methodically working its way down the middle of Arastradero Road, in traffic. An all-hands alarm was sounded, programmers jumped on their bicycles, and eventually a pickup truck was sent out to bring back the errant robot.

Moravec spent years working on the cart, largely without funding. He had a stipend, but he frequently had to beg for equipment. He wrote a program that enabled the robot to travel in a straight line by tracking objects on the horizon, without following a line on the ground. It was a painstaking process, for it took about fifteen seconds for the SAIL computer to process each image; then the cart would move a few meters and take another sighting.

Within several years Earnest changed the site's name from Stanford Artificial Intelligence Project to Stanford Artificial Intelligence Laboratory, reflecting the fact that the center was actually a collection of wide-ranging projects, all of them representing some facet of artificial intelligence.

Ken Colby, a Stanford computer scientist and psychiatrist who had worked with Joseph Weizenbaum, who would later become a well-known MIT computer scientist, on his Eliza conversational program, brought his research group to the laboratory early on. One of the enduring hurdles facing artificial-intelligence research projects has been the Turing test, an experiment first proposed by the British mathematician Alan Turing in 1950. Turing identified a simple way of cutting through the philosophical debate about whether a machine could ever be built to mimic the human mind. If, in a blind test, a person could not tell whether he was communicating with a computer or a human, Turing reasoned, the question would be resolved. Weizenbaum had developed the Eliza program to explore the Turing problem, but it was Colby who wrote the machine's responses, which simulated a Rogerian psychiatrist, a program that responds to statements with questions. Colby was interested in producing a scientific theory of psychiatry instead of relying on Freud's "revealed religion." He had worked on a program called the Mad Doctor. His goal was to help psychiatrists work with their patients. He knew that in large mental hospitals at that time, there would frequently be a single professional available for five hundred or more patients, which meant there was almost no professional contact or help for many of them. It occurred to him that by creating a simulation he might be able to provide mental patients meaningful and helpful interactions.[16]

Once he was at SAIL, Colby began working on Parry, an interactive AI program that duplicated the behavior of a paranoid personality. The program ultimately became far more powerful than Eliza, which had begun with a limited set of fifty interactive patterns. Parry had about twenty thousand patterns and was eventually able to pass a rudimentary Turing test.[17]

Although Colby and Weizenbaum were friendly rivals for a period, Weizenbaum eventually became a harsh critic of AI research and attacked Colby for the idea of using machines to treat human beings. And while many of the AI researchers remained technological optimists, Weizenbaum challenged those who worshiped computers uncritically in a collection of essays titled *Computer Power and Human Reason*. The SAIL community, however, had no such philosophical objections.

•••

Both McCarthy and Earnest were world-class gadgeteers, and they created a remarkable computer system that ultimately featured text editing, windowing, and audio/video displays long before such capabilities were available elsewhere.

Earnest helped realize McCarthy's vision of a terminal on every desk by discovering a company that made a disk system that could support thirty-two terminals simultaneously, for which he subsequently fashioned a switch that doubled the number of terminals the system could host. Earnest also designed a custom keyboard for the SAIL computing system that had an extended character set with a lot of mathematical and Greek characters as well as special command keys. One was called "top," which gave access to an additional character set that was displayed on the top of each key. In addition to a traditional control key there was also a "meta" key to give even more command combinations. It was a keyboard that Doug Engelbart on the other side of the campus would have loved. Ultimately, by using inexpensive television monitors, the SAIL group was able to push the cost of each desktop display and keyboard down to as low as seventy dollars per station, an unheard-of price at the time.

One of the first programs to run on SAIL's PDP-6 computer was Stephen Russell's Spacewar. In the venerable hacker tradition, the SAIL researchers decided that it was necessary to create an embellished West Coast version of the MIT creation. One problem they encountered right away was in running the program in a time-sharing environment. When dozens of separate programs were competing for the central processor's attention, the tiny spaceships would freeze on the display as the Spacewar program became starved for computing cycles.

The SAIL researchers responded by adding a hack to the operating system that made it possible for a program to "Run me any given multiple of a sixtieth of a second," to set the amount of computer resources allocated to an individual program. If you abused the feature, it was possible to bring the computer to its knees, but in practice it was rarely a problem. The real-time mode turned out to be useful for all kinds of programming applications, including work being done by the computer musicians. It was called "Spacewar mode" and was one of the earliest examples of how gaming advanced the state of computing.

The general belief among the SAIL researchers was that software was a resource to be shared freely. When Earnest first arrived at Stanford, he had brought with him—stored on paper tape—a computer dictionary that he had written years earlier, while he was a graduate student at MIT, in connection with a cursive writing–recognition program. In effect, he had accidentally invented the spell-checker. When he began writing memos and letters on the SAIL computer, he loaded the ten-thousand-word dictionary into the computer and persuaded a graduate student to write a program in LISP to deal with the problem of suffixes. (It wasn't a perfect spell-check, because it would first attempt to strip away all recognizable suffixes, and then it would attempt to match the remaining letters.) Occasionally, there were matches with nonsense words. Also, it "clanked" a bit—in other words, it ran slowly. Whatever its limitations, though, the program was "freeware"—although that term wouldn't be invented for another two decades.

In the sixties, the idea of patenting software had not gained currency, and several years later, as SAIL became connected to other research labs via the ARPAnet, a spell-checking program written by a SAIL graduate student at Earnest's suggestion was quickly shared by an even wider community. Since it was possible to poke around freely in the computer directories of others across the early ARPAnet using a program called ftp (for file-transfer protocol), it took only a short time for the program to be borrowed and it spread across the country in a matter of weeks without prompting or advertising. It was the dawn of the file-sharing era.

Earnest largely gave up his research on character recognition as he assumed responsibility for managing SAIL. However, in 1971, he did make one other lasting contribution to the role of community in the early ARPAnet by inventing the idea of electronic "presence."

In a world where work went on around the clock, it was often hard to locate people with unpredictable schedules. Earnest had noticed that to determine who was around before making one of the researchers' regular runs for Chinese food or to recruit volunteers for a pickup volleyball game, users of the SAIL computer would run their fingers down the listing of the "who" command, which showed

IDs and terminal line numbers for people who were logged in. They might say things like "There's Don and that's Pattie but I don't know when Tom was last seen," or "Who in the hell is VVK and where does line 63 go?"[18]

Since Earnest liked talking to people face-to-face, he decided to create a program that put a human name on each computer user, and he added a bit of information that would make it possible to determine if a particular user was sitting in front of his terminal. He called his command "finger." A little while later, he added the capability to create a "Plan" file, which would make it possible for people to explain their absences or give instructions about being reached at odd hours. The program was an instant hit and quickly propagated from Digital Equipment Corporation computers to Unix machines throughout the growing ARPAnet world.

Even more popular was a program called NS (for news service), which was written by a young SAIL system programmer named Martin Frost. NS was the first computer-network news service, made possible by loading newswires from the Associated Press and *The New York Times* into the SAIL computer. Using NS, it was possible to watch the wires directly or to find stories based on a keyword search and even to create filters that would save copies of stories on particular subjects. Word of the wonderful online newspaper soon spread, and before long an elite underground emerged to take advantage of NS from all over the country.

Everything at SAIL was done with this characteristic openness. A volleyball court (for which McCarthy quietly found funds to pave) in front of the D. C. Power building was crowded every day at lunch. The building backed up against Felt Lake—a favorite skinny-dipping spot—and in addition a sauna was built in the offices, initiating what would become a grand Silicon Valley pastime. The SAIL sauna reflected not only the culture but the technology of the era. Computing power was so scarce and valuable in the sixties and seventies that people were forced to wait around the clock to get access to the

SAIL computer, and many researchers enjoyed spending this down-time hanging out in the sauna.

Although SAIL was not the only Stanford project using the build-ing, Earnest had been remarkably effective at expanding the AI lab's territory. As the computing population grew, when another group had not used its offices for a period of time, he would invariably point its absence out and then take the space over in an eminent-domain fashion. When he was finally able to add a large basement area to the laboratory, he decided that this new space might be a good place to build showers. He went to the university planning of-fice to ask that they be installed. The administration refused but sug-gested that the lab might build them anyway, if it was able to with its own funds.

Although Earnest didn't have any overhead money, he thought he might be able to come up with the funding by offering subscrip-tions. It occurred to him that such a proposition would be signifi-cantly enhanced by a sauna. After all, it was the height of the hippie era, and saunas had become the rage. Earnest knew that "everyone was looking for excuses to take their clothes off in social situations, whether in hot tubs or saunas or in Midpeninsula Free University classes on massage or advanced group loving."[19]

Earnest put together his proposal, sold shares at fifty dollars apiece, and quickly raised the two thousand dollars required for the project from his staff—mostly for materials, since he was counting heavily on volunteer labor. He put together a plan for four showers, a dressing room, and a sauna, and then he went back to the plan-ning office. Predictably enough the bureaucracy responded with a set of requirements spelled out in a memo that was intended to kill the idea. Luckily, Earnest found help from an unexpected quarter. A newly hired construction worker had recently been relocated to "Siberia"—the D. C. Power building—by the university in response to his union-organizing activities, and he volunteered to do the framing and plumbing.

Despite the fact that the population of the D. C. Power building was overwhelmingly male, the sauna was coed from day one. Girl-friends were frequently invited on weekends and evenings, and one of them happened to be a nanny for the university provost, Bill Miller. When she returned home one evening with wet hair, the provost asked her where she had been, and he learned about the sauna, which had never been formally approved.

His response was, "Who let them do that?"

Earnest had the memo from the planning office outlining the building requirements, which had been met, and so the fuss quickly blew over.

The sauna, in turn, led to the need for live-work amenities. Besides makeshift apartments in the attic, the laboratory offered the world's first computer-controlled vending machine, which kept a credit record, generated monthly electronic bills, and offered a double-or-nothing option. The vending machine—which was known as "The Prancing Pony," a reference to an inn in J. R. R. Tolkien's *The Fellowship of the Ring*—even awarded a prize: Approximately one out of every 128 purchases was free. The original vending-machine soft ware was written by Earnest, and some suspected that he may have added some special extensions; few remembered ever seeing him pay. For a while, even beer was available, and if the customer was underage the display read "Sorry Kid!"

Tolkien had a wide following among the lab's hackers, and there were many fantasy-world touches around the building. The first character alphabet created for the SAIL printer was in Elvish, a language devised by Tolkien. The university administration required that all rooms in the facility be numbered, but the SAIL researchers supplied the school with a detailed map in which each office was named after a place in Tolkien's Middle Earth. The whimsy was lost on the university's bureaucrats, who came out and placed conventional numbers throughout the building.

Computer hackers had a legendary enthusiasm for spicy Chinese food, and one of the closest restaurants to SAIL was a hole-in-the-wall Szechwan restaurant called Hsi-Nan, which for many years was located in a shopping center just across from the Stanford campus in Palo Alto. (Hsi-Nan was also known as Louie's after its chef and owner, Louis Kao.) Bill Gosper, who had been an MIT AI hacker before arriving at SAIL, ate dinner at Hsi-Nan every evening for an entire decade. For years, a bulletin board on the wall at Hsi-Nan was covered with business cards from the Valley's most secretive start-up companies, allowing the digerati to track the comings and goings of friends and colleagues.

Hsi-Nan was the source of one of SAIL's most frequently recounted legends. Jeff Rubin, a systems programmer at the Stanford AI lab, worked briefly for Kao as a waiter, in exchange for Chinese lessons. One day, a manager from SAIL came to lunch with a Digital Equipment Corporation salesman. At one point, the two were arguing about a technical detail, and the manager called a halt to the debate.

"There is no point in arguing," he said. "We can settle this very easily. Let's ask the waiter."

"Can you tell us about the cache on the KL 10?" the manager asked Rubin.

"It's a 32k two-way set associative cache," he replied and then walked away, leaving the salesman's mouth hanging open.

Not surprisingly, many people at SAIL were busy exploring psychedelics and other drugs while creating cyberspace. Graduate students generally shared large offices, with a number of students in each room. On one occasion, a student came to Earnest to complain that the guy at the next desk was smoking a joint, a problem he solved by asking the offending party to smoke outside. He just didn't see it as that big of a deal.

But it was a bit like herding cats. One of the systems programmers gained the nickname "Johnny Potseed," because he spread marijuana seeds everywhere he went. At one point, he discovered that the grass growing over the building's septic-tank drain field was particularly green. So it seemed only natural to sprinkle his seeds over the area. Later he came to Earnest and complained that deer were eating the sprouting plants.

It was only a matter of time before word filtered back to campus that things were generally getting out of control up in the hills at the D. C. Power building. A come-to-Jesus meeting was accordingly held between the university's administrators and the laboratory's managers. Drug use around SAIL had to be stopped!

Although it is now an article of faith that each new medium, whether the video camera or the VCR, finds early mass acceptance via pornography, SAIL achieved another less well-known first, the details of which have long been shrouded in mystery. In 1971 or 1972, Stanford students, using ARPAnet accounts at SAIL, engaged in a commercial transaction with their counterparts at MIT. Before Amazon, before eBay, the seminal act of e-commerce was a drug deal. The students used the network to quietly arrange the sale of an undetermined amount of marijuana.[20]

Even in the hedonistic California of the sixties and seventies, however, Raj Reddy, an earnest young Indian graduate student who was to become McCarthy's first Ph.D. candidate at Stanford, agonized for weeks over the idea of trying marijuana, which appeared to be all around him. Finally, his older office mate turned to him one day and said, "You might be interested in what it is like to murder someone, but you wouldn't feel the need to try it." That cured Reddy of his interest in illicit drugs.

Nevertheless, how could the laboratory crack down on the outrageous behavior of its students and researchers when the people running the lab were living the same lifestyle? At a Grateful Dead concert one evening, Andy Moorer, another former MIT AI lab hacker who had taken a job as a systems programmer at SAIL, watched as a senior SAIL computer scientist pulled a vial of LSD out of his shirt pocket and then accidentally spilled its contents. The computer scientist was unfazed; his only comment, Moorer remembered, was "I guess we'll have to use the mescaline instead."

What had been on the fringe was now center stage.

Until the mid-sixties, the Midpeninsula bohemian subculture had been for the most part hidden. Allen Ginsberg had come to Palo Alto to take LSD in the fifties; there was a tiny folk music scene; and the political left was largely a curiosity. A small group of radical social scientists, frustrated with the conservative politics of Stanford, had set up a "free university" called the Graduate Coordinating Committee in late 1964. Modeled after the Freie Universität of Berlin and echoing the aims of the Free Speech Movement in Berkeley earlier that year, it served as an umbrella organization for a diverse group of people interested in Marxism, pacifism, and educational reform. The course list was contained on a single mimeographed sheet, and the school's organizers frequently met at the home of Len and Lee Herzenberg, two university geneticists.

But on December 4, 1965, something happened on the Midpeninsula that shook the whole culture. That evening, the Rolling Stones were playing at the Cow Palace in south San Francisco, and author Ken Kesey suggested to a young guitarist named Jerry Garcia that he bring his band to Big Nig's, a club in San Jose, to play at one of the early Acid Tests. The Acid Tests turned out to be something else again, extending the impact of the drug a thousandfold, involving electric instruments and light shows and copious amounts of LSD. The Acid Tests—which were also held at Muir Beach; Palo

Alto; Portland, Oregon, and elsewhere—culminated early the following year in San Francisco with Stewart Brand's Trips Festival. That gave rise to the Grateful Dead and helped create the San Francisco music scene, which in turn contributed to the creation of a national counterculture. The counterculture converged with the growing tumult of political unrest that was escalating on campuses in the wake of the Free Speech Movement.

This all swirled around the Stanford campus in the sixties and early seventies, and it ultimately transformed the lives of many of the young men who were to pioneer the ideas underlying the personal computer.

■■■

Vic Lovell had lived on Perry Lane from 1957 until the developers bulldozed part of the neighborhood in 1963—an event so traumatic for the residents of the enclave that Faye Kesey, Ken's wife, took an ax to a piano in frustration.[1] Lovell had received his doctorate from Stanford in 1964 and had been working part-time at the Stanford counseling and testing center and part-time at San Francisco State University until he quit both jobs and stepped in to help run the Free University, largely because no one else was willing to do it. His partner in the effort was Rob Christ, a former philosophy graduate student at Stanford, who was an extraordinarily enthusiastic and effective organizer. Christ walked around in downtown Palo Alto and engaged people in conversation in order to find out what kinds of courses they might want to take. If the Free U didn't offer such a course, he looked for someone to create it.

The Free U was politicized from its inception. At first, the focus was on the current student political debates—whether to organize on campus or off campus. The off-campus faction won the debate, and the Free U located itself in a house in East Palo Alto, an impoverished community located across the Bayshore Freeway from affluent Palo Alto. At first they offered two courses, one on the American ruling class and the power elite and the other on yoga. Although

East Palo Alto was largely a black community, all of the students were white, and it wasn't long before the neighbors came and suggested—not so politely—that the Free U organize its own people on the other side of the freeway. The school returned to Palo Alto proper and split into two groups, one a Stanford program called the Experiment, and the other the Palo Alto Free University.

Then, in 1967, the Free U erupted. It went from being a tiny group made up of fewer than one hundred members and several factions that wouldn't talk to one another, to become almost overnight a vibrant organization with a catalog of more than one hundred courses, a newsletter, one thousand members, and a fifty-thousand-dollar annual budget. For the next three years, it became the heart of the Midpeninsula's thriving counterculture. It spun off a medical center, a law commune, a tenant union, a grocery store, and a machine shop. The main office was moved to El Camino Real in Menlo Park, just up the street from Kepler's, and doubled as an arts-and-crafts store and a print shop.

The Free U attracted people from the entire community, ranging from the professors at SAIL to Palo Alto High School students. One of the first to join was a young Israeli named Marc Porat, whose father had been a refugee from the Nazis and had come to Stanford to get his Ph.D. Although his father had arranged for him to get into a good college after he graduated, Porat had already been radicalized. In high school, he realized that something was wrong about the Vietnam War after a group of his classmates who were star athletes joined the Marines and were all killed within a year.

After graduating from high school, he left Palo Alto with his girlfriend to join the civil rights movement in the South. One night, they stopped at a gas station shortly after the murders of James Chaney, Andrew Goodman, and Michael Schwerner. As he pumped gas, he saw a group of five or six men start walking toward him. Without even taking the hose out of the tank, he jumped into the car and drove off. He ended up in Charleston, South Carolina, where he attempted to do political organizing work, until the Congress of Racial Equality asked whites to leave.

When Porat returned to Palo Alto the following year, he became a full-time organizer and activist. He had arrived in time for one of the Palo Alto Acid Tests over New Year's, where he took LSD for the first time. He became one of the organizers of the Free U as well as of a set of "be-ins" that were held in an open plaza in downtown Palo Alto and in a city park across the street from Stanford. Porat called San Francisco bands such as the Grateful Dead, Jefferson Airplane, and Sopwith Camel and asked them to come down to play for free for an antiwar benefit in the park. The bands almost invariably showed up.

He was emblematic of the New Left, which wasn't just about politics, but also about culture and community. For a while, he lived in a mansion on University Avenue in Palo Alto that was owned by a successful real-estate attorney named John Montgomery. A rambling house with a swimming pool, the mansion became notorious for several years in the late sixties as a site of wild parties that were attended by many of the Valley's more liberated techies. During the summer, something would happen there every weekend. There were nude sunbathers, peacocks strolling in the backyard, a PA system playing rock-and-roll music, and a light organ, an electronic device that projected colored lights to accompany music. Inside, the floors were covered with Asian rugs of the finest quality, and there were orgy rooms and a room where everyone could try laughing gas. The wife of one of Silicon Valley's best-known computer researchers later said that it was at John Montgomery's parties that she learned who in the Valley was circumcised and who wasn't.

Porat also became a member of Vic Lovell's psychodrama workshops. While encounter groups quickly became part of mainstream psychology in the sixties, psychodrama remained stronger, more emotionally challenging stuff, more confrontational and intense. Psychodrama became a significant activity in the Free U, and John McCarthy on occasion opened his home to these workshops.

Even though he had moved to the right politically, McCarthy retained his allegiance to the spirit of the Free U until a local Maoist group called Venceremos took over the school in 1971. McCarthy had just persuaded his friend, computer scientist Ed Fredkin, to donate six thousand dollars to the Free U magazine, but with the Maoists in power the money vanished. Outraged, he attended a meeting at the Tangent, a coffeehouse that was run by the school in downtown Palo Alto. There were about forty people in the room, and McCarthy stood up and made a motion that the Free University should reaffirm its policy of nonviolence. The motion died for lack of a second, and to make matters worse one of the militants stood up and threatened to kill McCarthy. The experience only served to confirm his belief that if the student radicals ever ran the country, they would be no different than the Stalinist bureaucrats in the Soviet Union.

The white-hot period of radicalism didn't last long. The same divisive forces at work within the American antiwar movement soon led Porat to burn out as well. He concluded that he had tried making change from the outside without a lot of success, so why not try from the inside? He entered Columbia University after deciding the goal of the political demonstrations he had been in was to get on Walter Cronkite's evening news. It seemed only logical to him that it was all about media coverage, and he was determined to become a top executive at CBS, which would enable him to make the changes from the inside.

It didn't work out that way, however, and two years later he was back at Stanford, where he received a graduate degree in economics. He coined the term "information economy," went to work for Apple Computer, and later became the cofounder of General Magic, one of Silicon Valley's ill-starred start-up companies.

The West Coast counterculture acted like a magnet for thousands of young people around the country. Dorothy Bender picked the Summer of Love to leave Washington, D.C., and come to California.

She was a rarity in the computer world of the 1960s: a woman and a programmer.

Her interest in computing came from her father, who had escaped Buchenwald in the late 1930s and come to New York, where he found work in a factory. He was passionate about the stock market, and in the evenings he turned to the stock tables, making endless lists of companies to consider. From over his shoulder, Dorothy watched him work with his lists and became fascinated by the idea of systematically organizing information. She grew up in Manhattan and studied math at the City College of New York. She married a lawyer and followed him to Washington, but within two years the marriage was a shambles, and desperate for a change, she was drawn to the West Coast by the excitement of politics and culture. When Stanford University offered her a programming job in their computer center, she jumped at the chance.

Although she was a skilled programmer, she didn't share the same hacker enthusiasm for the machines of the era as the men with whom she found herself working. One of those men was Larry Tesler, a twenty-three-year-old computer-science graduate student who ended up being around Polya Hall, where she worked much of the time. Tesler was a rarity—the first man she met who was a single father. Not long after meeting Bender, Tesler was without a place to live, and so with his young daughter, Lisa, he moved into Bender's cramped apartment several miles from campus. A thin man with aquiline features, a shock of curly red hair, and a beard, Tesler also blended several worlds in a way that Bender hadn't previously encountered. Not only was he immersed in computing, he was fully engaged in the emerging Bay Area counterculture and antiwar scene.

Tesler took Bender to her first meeting of the Free University. A remarkable transformation was taking place around the Stanford campus during 1967 and into 1968. The Human Be-in in Golden Gate Park in January 1967 had touched off a cascade of events all over the Bay Area. During the summer of 1967 and on through the summer of 1968, there was a dramatic new kind of music being played in the dance halls and the parks, and open talk of revolution was everywhere. Caught up in the political and cultural commotion around Stanford, Bender and Tesler became close friends. They turned on together and went to Free U classes together and even taught there together.

PL 28　IT'S A BEAUTIFUL DAY!!!　Dorothy and Larry

Driftwood, seaweed, sand rocks, mountain, Highway 1, San Gregorio, California USA . . . Let's enjoy and feel ourselves and each other. Introductory sensory awareness! Verbal encounter groups! Picnic! Kids! A one day happening.

Sunday June 8, 11:00am, leaving from Postal Unit, Macy's Parking Lot, Stanford Shopping Center[2]

Tesler eventually became a leader of the Free University, and occasionally, when the volunteers putting the school's course catalog together found that there was extra space on the pages, he would make up a course on the spot:

PL 1　TAURUS PARTY: Larry Tesler

People born with Sun in Taurus only. We'll overeat, overdrink, overdance, oversex, oversleep, and hangover in true Taurian fashion. Please bring food and drink, but no non-bulls. The Full Moon will be in Taurus and the Sun in Opposition.

Saturday, October 25, 8pm.[3]

Tesler also taught courses with a political edge. His first, offered at the end of 1968, was called How to End the I.B.M. Monopoly. Among computer hackers of the era, IBM engendered some of the same emotions reserved today for Microsoft. At the time, the Justice Department was preparing to file suit against IBM, and Tesler soon realized that most of the people taking his class actually worked for

IBM. At first none of them would admit it, but there was soon a series of confessions, and ultimately his students began freely discussing the giant computer maker's behavior.

Like Bender, Tesler had grown up in New York City, where he had developed an early passion for computing. In 1960, while he was at the Bronx High School of Science, he had on his own developed a new method of generating prime numbers. He showed it to one of his teachers, who was quite impressed. When Tesler told him that it was a formula, his teacher responded, "No, it's not really a formula, it's an algorithm, and it can be implemented on a computer."

"Where do you find a computer?" Tesler asked.

The teacher said he would get him a programming manual first and then figure out where to find a computer.

One day, Tesler was sitting in the school cafeteria reading the manual, which offered instructions on how to program an IBM 650 at the lowest, most arcane, level, machine-programming language. Across the room, Stokely Carmichael, who later became a leading black activist, was surrounded by a group talking politics. A student walked up to Tesler and said, "What are you doing with that?"

"I'm learning about programming," Tesler responded.

"I program the 650, but I don't use machine language, I use Fortran," the other student said. He then began telling Tesler about the wonders of the language that let a programmer control a computer using English-like instructions.

Tesler, who still hadn't even *seen* a computer, thought this was great. The obvious question was, Where could you go to actually use this language? The other student told him he had free computer time on a machine at Columbia University as part of the science honors program. He promised to ask the director of the computer center if Tesler could have his own time on the computer.

Soon thereafter, Tesler had a half hour every Saturday morning on a mainframe computer. He punched his cards and then laboriously ran them through a program called a compiler, which created a set of instructions that could be directly executed by the computer.

In the entire half hour, if he moved quickly, he theoretically could get the computer to attempt to run his program once.

Of course, it would inevitably contain a bug, and so he would have to go back a week later and start the process again. In the end, his program never ran successfully. To make matters worse, before he was able to finish his project he made a costly novice error and was banned from the college computer center. The IBM 650 had a ponderous magnetic-drum memory that was capable of storing two thousand words of information. The drum was driven by a rubber belt and required several minutes to slow down after it was turned off. One day, Tesler shut the system off by mistake, realized he'd made an error, quickly switched it back on, and heard the drum belt snap.

He went home and told his parents he wanted his own computer. "That's ridiculous," they told him, such machines cost tens of thousands or millions of dollars. Tesler, however, was not to be dissuaded. "Someday they're going to be cheaper," he told them. "Someday I'll have my own computer."

His parents rolled their eyes, but an important seed had been planted, for years later Tesler became the carrier of a gospel, which—while it was in certain ways antithetical to Doug Engelbart's vision of powerful, complex machines—would ultimately be the crucial factor in translating Engelbart's augmentation ideas to a much wider audience. That gospel was simplicity.

In the following year, 1961, Tesler entered Stanford, and on his first day he was introduced to several faculty members who gave him access to the school's computers. One of them was a vacuum tube–based IBM 650. No one was using it, so he now had all the time he wanted. But when he realized he continued to be the only one using it, he became curious about the other school computer, which was a transistor-based Burroughs 220. He soon plunged happily into the rarefied world of the school's computing center, getting a job as a computer operator the next summer at Stanford and quickly advancing to become a programmer.

The next year, he got a job programming for Joshua Lederberg, a researcher at the university who had won the 1958 Nobel Prize in medicine for exploring the organization of genetic material in bacteria. Working for Lederberg gave him early access to the machine that in some ways could qualify as a truly "personal" computer, the LINC.

Created by MIT physicist Wesley A. Clark, the design of the LINC (the term first referred to Lincoln Laboratory, an early MIT electronics and computing research center, and eventually became an acronym for "Laboratory Instrument Computer") was begun in May 1961, and the following year the machine was used for the first time to analyze neural responses from a cat at the National Institute of Mental Health in Bethesda, Maryland. Each LINC consisted of four metal modules, which together were about the size of two televisions set side by side and tilted back slightly. The machine was a twelve-bit computer and included a half-megahertz processor (in contrast to today's three-gigahertz Intel Pentium chips, which are more than six thousand times faster), a tiny screen, and a keyboard. LINCs sold for about $43,000—a bargain for the era—and ultimately were manufactured commercially by Digital Equipment Corporation, the first minicomputer company. Fifty of the original LINCs were built, and one showed up in Lederberg's laboratory at Stanford.

The machine, which was based on discrete transistors and which stored data on magnetic tape, had several features that would be considered quirky by modern-day computing standards. For example, the LINC had a knob on its front panel that could slow down or speed up its processor, as well as an audio speaker intended to give the user feedback on the internal operation of the system.

Historically, the LINC was an important inspiration for much of what was to come later in personal-computer technology, and it had that impact on Tesler. It combined the research in interactive computing that had begun at MIT in the 1950s with the idea that the entire resources of a computer would be at the disposal of a single user. Although it was an unheard-of possibility at the time, Tesler had the new machine to himself.

He took McCarthy's programming class on LISP, and the following year, while he was still a student, decided to start his own programming company. There were by now a growing number of users who needed computer programs, but very few people who knew how to write them. When Tesler called the phone company to get a listing for his new business, he found that there was no category for programmers, and the phone company was unwilling to create one. He opted instead to list himself under data processing—a category in which there were only five other businesses in the Palo Alto phone book. He took an office in Town and Country Village, a shopping center across the street from Stanford University, and his first clients were graduate students and professors who needed programming assistance.

There was no shortage of interesting projects. He collaborated on a statistical study of a controversial new anesthetic with Lincoln Moses, who was the head of the Stanford statistics department. There had been fears that it was unsafe, but the study proved otherwise, and Tesler's name appeared on the research paper.

Tesler also turned his programming skills toward more traditional collegiate pursuits, helping perfect what was most likely the very first raster-graphics computer program. The earliest computer-graphics displays in the 1960s generally used a monitor and associated hardware that permitted display of geometrically drawn images known as vector graphics. Modern displays, in contrast, use raster or bit-mapped graphics, where information is displayed as rows of pixels that can be switched on and off to create images and text.

But the Stanford students had more ambitious aims. Their display was the student rooting section in Stanford Stadium—seventy-seven rows high by forty-five seats across. Card stunts dated back to the 1920s and had been performed at Stanford since the 1930s. In the early 1960s, both the University of Southern California and Stanford had developed computer programs for arranging card stunts, but only for simple static routines; the computer was used to control printing the individual cards. Two Stanford students developed the new programming system, in which images were first drawn on graph paper, and the Burroughs computer was then used to transform them by stretching them, transforming them, or altering their color. It was a system that was very similar to the Macromedia Flash graphics programming system that is today used extensively to create animations on the World Wide Web. However, it was a tour de force when in the early sixties the students used the computer to generate a series of animations and preview them on a printer. When the correct sequence was arrived at, the computer would do a sort, and then print individual flash cards.

The first version of the language was numeric and was proving difficult for the students to understand. There was a code for move, a code for red, and so on. The original programmer came to Tesler and said, "This is just too hard for them to use, and so I always end up doing all the work myself."

The card project was Tesler's first experience with what would later be called the ease-of-use problem. He found himself working with the student rally commission—a group of people, he realized, who had been chosen for their looks rather than their math skills. He spent the next several years refining the language to the point where student programmers were unneeded. It was excellent training for a path that would ultimately lead Tesler directly to the modern personal computer.

■ ■ ■

Lying west of Stanford are the Santa Cruz Mountains, which are frequently shrouded in fog and covered with a redwood forest that, though spotty, still wanders down to the coast in places. To reach the ocean, it was necessary only to drive past the university out Sand Hill Road to La Honda Road, a winding artery that makes its way from the elite Woodside mansions into a more rustic and rugged world, peopled by a mix of urban refugees thrown together with a rural community of artists, farmers, and bohemians.

Anyone driving to the coast in August 1966 would have been

surprised to see a large banner reading "Welcome Beatles!" while passing through the mountain hamlet of La Honda. The British rock group was in the midst of a triumphant American concert tour and was about to play before thousands of screaming teenagers in San Francisco. The possibility that the Fab Four might make an unlikely detour to this out-of-the-way community created a brief local sensation in the Bay Area. But it turned out to be just a stunt pulled by Ken Kesey's Merry Pranksters, one perfectly suited to the times, which were rapidly beginning to tumble out of control.

Driving down La Honda Road on the way to the coast, at milepost 13.57, just a mile and half from the summit, a visitor would pass a once-nondescript cottage that had been painted with striking psychedelic swirls. Out front, facing La Honda Road, was a huge yin-yang symbol. The cottage was the home of Jim Warren, a chunky math professor at the College of Notre Dame, a small Catholic girls' school located in Belmont.

More than a decade later, Warren emerged as one of the central figures in defining the tone of the personal-computer industry when he created the first West Coast Computer Faire in 1977, a show that became a mecca for computer hobbyists. But long before that, he was emblematic of the cultural, political, and technological forces colliding over the hill from his cottage.

Growing up in San Antonio, Texas, Warren felt like an outsider. His parents had been largely immune to the racism that was endemic in the South in the 1940s and 1950s, and as a young child he had two close friends in his neighborhood who firmly set him apart. One was a black kid who was the son of a woman who worked as a servant, and the other was a Jew. In high school, he spent his time with a dissolute group of blacks who had formed a rhythm-and-blues band and wound up playing rock and roll even before there was such a thing.

In college, he obtained a teaching credential and then took a job teaching math in San Antonio. Several years later, the launch of Sputnik had supercharged the scientific and educational communities in the United States, and Warren was given the opportunity to take a year off from teaching funded by the National Science Foundation, to study for his master's degree in Austin. There he ran into his first computer—like Tesler's, an IBM 650—and threw himself into his studies.

While he was back in school, he traveled with a bohemian crowd on the fringes of the culture that defined the University of Texas campus. His friends included a group of archaeology and anthropology students who were frequently off on field trips to excavate Native American ruins. In the course of their work, they had discovered peyote, which was perfectly legal in some places at the time. Warren was avowedly straight, but he found himself running errands on his trips back to San Antonio. At the time he didn't even drink beer, but he would go to Hogan's Cactus Gardens and pick up three dollars' worth of peyote buds for his friends. One member of the group was a braless and overweight young woman named Janis Joplin, who made no pretense of fitting in and shocked the good students of Texas by smooching with her girlfriend in the cafeteria.

After getting his master's, he went back for what turned out to be his final year as a teacher in San Antonio. He pulled together a class of bright kids and began teaching them what was then being called "modern math": learning underlying principles rather than rote memorization. On the first day, he stood up in front of the class and said, "This is your math book," and then took it, walked to the door, tossed it into the hallway, and came back to the front of the class and said, "Now we're going to learn some REAL math."

He loved teaching, but his sense of alienation from Texas was increasing. In the end there was nothing left about the state he could stand. He knew he had to leave, but for where? The answer came from a friend, who told him quietly, "You might like California."

He decided to buy a truck big enough to haul his belongings and in the summer of 1964 set out for San Jose. Upon arriving, his immediate reaction was "I'm home, I'm finally home."

He couldn't believe his luck. Hedonism and experimentation

were in full swing, and he found himself in a place where the girls actually admitted they liked sex. Warren quickly found a job in Mountain View, which was then a working-class community in the heart of what would become Silicon Valley. It soon became clear, however, that his heart was no longer in teaching junior high school kids, who had all come to seem hormonally unbalanced.

In fact, he was twenty-seven years old, and he was girl crazy. His interests came to encompass other exciting things—in particular, the political crisis that was developing across the bay at the University of California. The Free Speech Movement pitted student activists with a new set of values against an old educational guard. For Warren, the events unfolding were in sync with his own escape from a claustrophobic and reactionary climate in Texas. He quickly began to identify with the student and antiwar groups.

However, the politics of the emerging American left were far from straightforward. Indeed, the various cultural and political factions around the Bay Area and on the Midpeninsula often spent as much time confronting one another as they did society's more conservative institutions. As he complained to his friends, "The problem with the right is they don't have any leaders; the problem with the left is that they have too many leaders."[4]

He began to gravitate toward an increasingly sybaritic lifestyle. His first girlfriend introduced him to nudism, and they were soon regulars at the Lupine Nature Preserve, a nudist colony in the Santa Cruz Mountains. In the mountains he also stumbled across the Merry Pranksters.

Before buying his cottage on La Honda Road, he had rented another place near La Honda. Standing in the new house one morning attempting to deal with the fact that the squatters he found upon moving in were taking their time leaving, he was startled when the door abruptly opened and in walked Neal Cassady, the legendary Beat-era figure who had been the thinly disguised protagonist of Jack Kerouac's novel *On the Road* and who was now driving the Pranksters' bus, trailed by a band of hangers-on.

Without bothering to introduce himself, Cassady and his followers began to search the house while speed-rapping "Got the mash, where's my stash?" which made no sense at all to Warren. The weird scene ended just as abruptly when the entire group headed for the door and piled into a car heading off up La Honda Road, tires screeching.

Warren moved in shortly before Kesey's 1965 drug bust. He knew it was in the offing when his girlfriend stumbled across two gentlemen with coats, ties, and binoculars as she walked along the trail behind Kesey's home.

He found another job and began making the daily commute from the mountains to Belmont, where he was the chairman of the math department at the all-women's college. The sisters of Notre Dame were a relatively liberal Catholic religious order, with a conservative board of trustees. The young women were away from home for the first time, and Warren saw that they had come from repressed families and were enjoying their relative freedom.

With a booming voice and a raconteur's style, Warren was a popular teacher. It was a calling that fit the values his father had instilled in him early: It was important to give something back to society. However, over the next two years he found he was increasingly pulled in three conflicting directions. In addition to his professional role, which was still linked to the National Science Foundation's attempts to increase the quality of math education, there was the self-indulgent, increasingly hippie world of the Santa Cruz Mountains, as well as the growing intensity of the antiwar demonstrations in Berkeley.

All of these forces were converging in 1966. Although he had been a teetotaler, 1966 was also the year that the psychedelic movement swept him up. With his girlfriend, who was part of the Berkeley academic scene, Warren visited an archaeological dig in Sonoma County, where he met a young man who sold him LSD.

He told himself, naïvely as it turned out, "I'll never have a chance to buy this again," and then put the tablets away.

Shortly after that, in his travels in the Berkeley antiwar scene, he met an odd fellow who was a carpenter and a Mensa member. At his house one afternoon, the man offered Warren a joint.

"I've never tried this before," Warren admitted, adding, "I've heard it makes you crazy, and besides, I don't smoke."

His new friend assured him that it wasn't a big deal. In a ritual that was being repeated countless times around the country that year, he put rock music on his stereo and showed Warren how to turn on.

"He was already high, and I kept saying, 'I don't feel anything.'" But then Warren found himself inexplicably pacing back and forth in his new friend's living room. They went to the kitchen, the friend offered Warren a bite of cantaloupe, and all of a sudden Warren felt as if his head were exploding. "I've never heard music like that before," he told the carpenter. The life of the chairman of a college math department was taking a radical turn.

Two of his friends from the Lupine nudist colony told him about a secret beach just down the road from Warren's cabin in a cove north of San Gregorio State Beach. It was clothing-optional, and one hot spring afternoon he decided to drive down and check things out. He had a wonderful afternoon, strolling along the almost two miles of hidden sand, chatting with couples and families, all in various stages of undress. At the end of the day as he sauntered home, he began to invite people to stop in La Honda, pick up food for a barbecue, and come by his cottage on their way home.

When the beachgoers arrived, they ranged from protohippies to IBM engineers, mixed with a smattering of academics. Soon there was a crowd of twenty-five to thirty people making dinner and getting acquainted, and when two of them asked if they could shower to wash off the sand from the beach, Warren thought nothing of it.

Until they returned from the shower without their clothes on.

Warren thought about it for a moment and then, with his characteristic enthusiasm, said, "Wow!"

Nobody else seemed to mind, and pretty soon clothing was coming off everywhere in the house and the garden.

It wasn't a swinging scene or an orgy—that was already happening elsewhere in the Bay Area. And it wasn't the Sexual Freedom League that Warren later dabbled in but found to be oddly repressive in a mirror image to the Texas that he'd left behind: You *had* to be naked and you *had* to have sex. Rather, Warren's home became a center of the emerging California counterculture—he saw it as rejecting the tight-ass mainstream world and a focal point for some kind of vibrant alternative community. A whole range of worlds seemed to intersect in the parties at his mountain cabin: hippies, academics, rock and rollers, and people from the nude beach scene. For Warren it fulfilled a deeply felt need. He was single with no family and divorced parents. He didn't want to get married, but he was looking for something, and this felt like community.

Throughout 1966 and into the next year, the parties continued to grow until several hundred people were attending. They became the stuff of national and even worldwide press coverage. At one point, a BBC crew showed up to film a discreet, backlit scene as part of a documentary on the "Now" generation.

Then the *San Francisco Chronicle* ran a front-page, above-the-fold article that described an unnamed professor who was throwing nude parties in the Santa Cruz Mountains. By then, it was inevitable that the straitlaced religious school would have heard rumors about the activities of its math department chair. He was hardly being secretive about the "really groovy" parties, and word eventually got to the students. With the campus inflamed, the president of the college called him in and said, "Well, is this true?" He responded, "Uh, yes."

And she said, "Well, Professor Warren, you're an excellent professor, we're delighted to have you chair the math department, but I think you'll have to agree that having nude parties is rather incompatible with the philosophy of a Catholic girls' school." Warren allowed that that was almost certainly true, and he asked the president if she would like him to resign. Without pausing, she said, "We would appreciate it very much."

Losing his job left Warren in a quandary, but not for long. All around Stanford University a cauldron of political activism, alternative community, and radical education experiments was boiling. Off campus, the Free University was attempting to encompass every diverse tendency from candle making to Maoism. On campus, student activists had created new organizations in an effort to force the university to loosen up and permit interdepartmental education. There was the Stanford Workshop on Political and Social Issues (SWOPSI) and the Stanford Center for Innovation and Research in Education (SCIRE).

Warren's interest in Utopian communities drew him into the Free University, where amid the chaos of political radicals and hippies he proved to be a natural moderate. He was older than many of the participants and he had already demonstrated that he was a good administrator. He became chair of the group, but since it was a militant volunteer organization in which salaries weren't paid, he was forced to seek some means of support.

He set out to look for a job that wouldn't interfere with his real calling, which was to do the "shit work" to keep the Free U running. One of the alternative school's veterans was a researcher at the Stanford Medical Center, and he suggested that Warren come over and take a job as a computer programmer. Computers were increasingly being used in data collection and analysis in the medical school's research projects.

It was perfect: Programmers were paid relatively well, and the hours were notoriously flexible. There was just one small problem. His experience writing software was limited to a prehistoric IBM computer he had programmed in assembly language.

"No problem," the researcher assured him. "You'll pick it up."

And Warren did. He was handed the manuals for a Digital PDP-8, a minicomputer that had eight kilobytes of memory and a magnetic-tape storage system. At the time, PDP-8s were flooding into the Bay Area, where they were being used for industrial process control.

One of the first Free U regulars Warren met was Larry Tesler, who had closed down his independent programming business and taken a job at SAIL. By now, the Free University was speaking to a growing movement of people who were frustrated with the mainstream university system, which seemed to be increasingly in the thrall of the military-industrial complex. Thousands were attracted to the idea of education beyond the walls of the traditional classroom, and both Tesler and Warren became committed participants, with Warren serving at one point as chairman and Tesler as treasurer.

In the evenings, the two frequently worked at the Free University store on El Camino Real, producing the Free University newspaper in the back room with one of the ubiquitous IBM Selectric typewriters. The machines, with their distinctive bouncing ball, were not just the gold standard for the corporate office world. Used Selectrics were highly prized by community and political groups because they made it possible to inexpensively produce reasonably acceptable-appearing pamphlets, newspapers, and propaganda. With scissors, X-Acto knives, and pots of glue, the two men painstakingly produced the Free U literature.

One evening, Tesler grew frustrated with the slow pace of the work, turned to Warren, and said, "You know, Jim, this is really ridiculous. We have these big computer monitors at the AI lab, and we could really just display these pages up on the screen, and you could just cut and paste right in the screen, and we wouldn't have to do this stuff anymore."

Warren thought that this was a great idea and, after pondering the suggestion for a moment, asked, "Well, how would you get it onto paper after that?"

That stopped Tesler's reverie. "I haven't figured that out yet," he replied.

It didn't immediately matter, and though it would take several years to bear fruit, the idea for interactive page layout was now firmly etched in Tesler's mind.

■ ■ ■

In 1961, Larry Tesler had come to Stanford as a fairly apolitical freshman. During Tesler's first year on campus, Ira Sandperl, the local pacifist and former Stanford student who worked at Kepler's bookstore, came to campus to speak, accompanied by folksinger Joan Baez. Of course everyone wanted to see and hear Baez, a phenomenon at the time. Sandperl discussed at length the philosophy of Mahatma Gandhi, especially nonviolent resistance. The ideas resonated with Tesler but had little direct impact immediately.

After he graduated, Vietnam and the Free University began to have an effect on his thinking. He had married after leaving Stanford and initially focused on his career and family. One of his partners in his small programming consulting business was a former Stanford student who was far more radical than Tesler and who urged him to get more involved in protesting the war. Tesler hadn't thought much about it, but gradually he became politicized, particularly after he began spending time around the Free University.

Because Tesler was married and had a young daughter, he received a draft deferment. Before that, however, he had burned his draft card at a stop-the-draft rally and sent his draft board a letter informing them that he decided he would refuse to fight in Vietnam. His draft board responded by immediately reclassifying him 1A, eligible for military service.

An alarmed Tesler took the letter to a local attorney who was an expert in Selective Service cases. "If you were David Harris or Mario Savio or someone like that, I would take this case and we would fight it all the way to the Supreme Court," the lawyer told him. "But you're nobody, and you don't really want to go to prison, and I urge you very strongly to apologize. Otherwise instead of being in Vietnam away from your child, you're going to be in jail away from your child and accomplish nothing."

Tesler considered his options briefly and then promptly wrote a letter of apology.

Tesler's business initially thrived. He got jobs working for Stanford professors and graduate students, and then as he became better known he found work at SRI, first as a computer operator, where he ran programs for battlefield simulations and even nuclear-fallout simulations, and then later as a programmer. As his business took off, he began getting other jobs from the Valley's start-up companies.

Then, in late 1967 there was a recession, and his business collapsed as people stopped using consultants. He decided to take a job at one of his clients, SAIL. So in early 1968, he began making the trek out to the D. C. Power building to work as a research programmer.

At first, he was enthralled with the esoteric world of machines that one day might think. He was programming in the area of natural-language understanding—a basic technology that would be required for voice recognition and other AI applications, as well as for cognitive modeling, which was supposed to help the AI researchers move toward a better understanding of how the human mind worked. During the next two years, however, he became increasingly disillusioned with the disappointing pace of the field. All around him he could see that the computer industry was exploding, but little progress was being made toward reaching even the primitive goals that the community had hoped would be achievable in the early sixties.

For a while, he tried to convince the Stanford computer-science department to create a computer-graphics program, but he ran into resistance; the professors didn't think there were any significant applications for graphics.

Moreover, while John McCarthy, Les Earnest, and many of the other researchers at SAIL remained deep believers in the idea of time-shared computing, Tesler soon grew skeptical. It seems there is an unwritten law of the computing universe that no matter how powerful a computer is, software will soon be developed that will bring the machine to its knees. At SAIL, where the situation was compounded by the elegant system that farmed the central computer out to as many as sixty-four simultaneous users, performance was a constant issue.

As a result, Tesler and other researchers were forced to sit around for hours waiting for their jobs to run. He began to complain that life had been better in the era of batch computing when researchers had submitted decks of cards to be run one at a time on a mainframe computer. Perhaps because of his early experience with the LINC in Lederberg's office, being forced to share the system rankled Tesler, and he began to think about the possibility of a personal computer, although not by that name.

Finally, in 1969, he decided to do something about it. With Horace Enea, a graduate student at SAIL who was also working for Ken Colby, the psychiatrist, Tesler set out to design a small computer. They took their design to Frieden, the calculator company that had been bought by Singer, the aerospace company. Frieden had released its own minicomputer, but it was doing poorly, and someone had suggested to the two young digital entrepreneurs that the company might be interested in a product that would differentiate it in the new digital world.

Tesler and Enea proposed a tiny computer intended for the office market. Its memory would be optical, using an inexpensive carousel projector and slides to store data in a write-once read-only format, where data files would be stored using a film recorder. The company thought the idea was intriguing, but it had no interest in getting more deeply embroiled in computing markets, and so it offered the two young men programming jobs, which they declined.

Increasingly frustrated, Tesler turned to Les Earnest and told him that he didn't want to work in AI any longer.

"Well, you're a good programmer, and I have several other projects that need doing," Earnest replied. He reeled off a series of programming tasks needed to make the SAIL computer system more useful.

Tesler seized on the idea of creating a new language to make it possible to print high-quality documents. He remembered his late-night conversation with Jim Warren, and it seemed like a perfect task to help bring an end to the era of glue pots and scissors.

Earnest showed him a program that already existed called Runoff, a primitive piece of software that supported basic commands such as ".indent" and ".nextpage" and ".center," but Earnest envisioned something far more powerful. He had been thinking about Chinese character sets, variable fonts, and computer-driven typesetting. That kind of software didn't exist, so Tesler set out to do a better version of Runoff, creating a programming language for printing that would allow the creation of documents with footnotes, tables of contents, underlining, page numbering, and all the controls necessary to publish the highest-quality documents.

He wrote a language called PUB—the cover of the manual for the program was embellished with an engraving of an old British pub—that was a great success. In many respects, it foreshadowed HTML—the markup language that would come to define the World Wide Web and make Internet publishing possible—in that it was the first language to use a feature known as "embedded tags." At the time, the typesetting industry was independently developing similar languages, but they were all specific to a particular machine. Tesler's was the first general-purpose programming language that would do typesetting for any type of device.

While PUB was finding a devoted band of users, Tesler decided he had had enough of AI research. The *Whole Earth Catalog* was having a growing influence on the nascent counterculture, and thousands of people in their twenties were leaving the cities and striking out to create a back-to-the-land communal existence. Tesler found a small group of like-minded friends, one of whom, Francine Slate, had been an employee of the *Whole Earth Catalog,* and together they decided to buy farmland. Slate and several other members of the group had been in a rather unusual upscale commune in Atherton, a town just north of Stanford that was generally known as an elite bedroom community. They all had jobs and had rented an elegant sixteen-bedroom mansion in which they were happily living until the owner decided to move some of his family members back in, and they were evicted. The group eventually bought land in Takilma, a tiny town in southern Oregon near Cave Junction and a perfect place for a rural commune, for $175 per acre.

Just before he was to have left, however, Tesler was contacted by an organizer of an antiwar group that was attempting to mobilize employees of the high-technology and aerospace companies in the Valley. The group was holding a panel to discuss what engineers were doing personally to end the war.

Tesler, with his bushy red beard and rimless anarchist's glasses, showed up to find a room full of white-shirted, gold watch–wearing, married engineers. Many of them were working for Lockheed, and they felt deeply concerned about the war. They weren't radicals, or in most cases even liberals, but were simply troubled by their country's involvement in a war in Southeast Asia. It was an odd scene, and Tesler stood out from the other members of the panel, who were intent on talking about converting defense companies.

"I'm dropping out of my job," he finally said. "I'm going to move to the land with my daughter, and we're going to grow vegetables."

At the end of the evening he left feeling as if he had been the token weirdo on the panel. Tesler finally took off in June 1970 to help build the Oregon commune. It was a month later that a young computer scientist and SAIL researcher named Alan Kay came by for a visit to Tesler's old office.

■ ■ ■

Alan Kay was a passionate believer in the idea of personal computing and had spent almost two years at Stanford and SAIL before leaving to help found a new computing laboratory for Xerox about two miles away from the D. C. Power building, in the Stanford Industrial Park. During 1970, Kay had begun helping with the process of talent spotting, and he thought Tesler would be a good match for the new laboratory, which was supposed to develop the digital office of the future. Tesler's friend Horace Enea told Kay that Tesler had just left to go live on a commune. It was almost three years before Tesler and Kay were to rendezvous at PARC, where the personal computer would flower during the early 1970s.

However, well before PARC, the idea of personal computing was already beginning to have an impact on SAIL. It became a hotly debated subject in the late 1960s, as some of the SAIL hackers began to absorb the consequences of Moore's Law. Early on, one faction at the lab had decided the computer of the future would be like an automobile—something that would be used as needed, and then would sit idle. The idea made no sense to SAIL's founders, McCarthy and Earnest. Why would you want to give up all of the power that was embedded in their shared community resource? Why would you want to go off and attempt to reinvent what already worked so well? Several years later, a testy John McCarthy would use the phrase "Xerox Heresies" to describe the one worker–one computer ideology that was being promulgated just over the hill at the PARC laboratory.

It is hardly surprising that the man who was the father of modern computer time-sharing—an idea that made virtual "personal computing" a reality—would find the idea of breaking up the computer into thousands of less powerful machines to be folly. Indeed, the hallmark of each generation of computing has been that its practitioners have resisted each subsequent shift in technology. Mainframes, minicomputers, PCs, PDAs—at the outset of each innovation, the old guard has fought a pitched battle against the upstarts, only to give in to the brutal realities of cost and performance.

Although McCarthy vigorously resisted the idea of the personal computer, he remained passionately engaged in the wide-ranging discussion at SAIL about the future of computing. There was no shortage of controversy. Perhaps it is because the technological change brought about by the scaling effect in the microelectronics industry is so abrupt that it is quite impossible to predict its future with any degree of accuracy. It is because progress is not incremental but instead happens in discontinuous leaps that Silicon Valley's legions of entrepreneurial "visionaries" are so often wrong. At SAIL, the debate over the future of computing was to have a serendipitous consequence that had a far more wide-ranging impact on the political and economic world than McCarthy or anyone else could have realized at the time.

McCarthy's belief, which was presented in the form of an academic paper prepared for an international conference in Bordeaux, France, in 1970, was that within a half a decade homes would be equipped with information terminals "each consisting of a typewriter keyboard and a screen capable of displaying one or more pages of print and pictures."[5] He foresaw that the terminal would be connected via the telephone network to a time-shared computer, which in turn would store files that would contain all books, magazines, newspapers, catalogs, airline schedules, public information, and personal files.

McCarthy had in effect sketched the outlines of the World Wide Web, which did not become a reality until 1995. At the time, he saw two main advantages and two disadvantages to his notion of home computing: First, it would be possible for anyone to get any document imaginable instantly; and, second, homes would no longer fill up with paper, which meant that trees would be saved and air pollution would be minimized. He also speculated that such a new electronic information system might make it possible to circumvent the homogeneous propaganda that was a consequence of the centralized mass media of the television era. The public might in the end be able to avail itself of a more diverse set of ideas.

Measured against these positives was the expense of the terminal and the fact that, at least initially, it would no longer be possible to read in bed. Moreover, McCarthy worried that the average Joe was actually a TV fan who didn't read anyway, and so a terminal for lovers of text might soon be an anachronism.

Despite efforts by electronic publishers to create videotext terminals, the home information terminal idea was stillborn. The discussion did, however, have consequences. One day while he was
thinking about the challenges of such a system, McCarthy had a
chance conversation with one of the SAIL researchers, a young computer hacker named Whitfield Diffie.

Diffie had read McCarthy's Bordeaux paper and asked an obvious
question about the paperless world that McCarthy envisioned: What
would take the place of a signature in an all-electronic world? It was
a question that was to consume Diffie during the next five years and
ultimately lead to his pioneering work on digital signatures and
public-key cryptography. His research, with Stanford professor Martin Hellman and Ralph Merkle, a Stanford graduate student, ultimately paved the way to both privacy in the electronic world and the
security needed for the commercial services made available by the
World Wide Web. Public-key cryptography not only allowed the secure transmission of digital information between parties who would
never meet face-to-face, it also answered Diffie's original question
by making possible digital signatures. It laid the basis for trust and
authentication in cyberspace.

A native New Yorker and a math prodigy, Diffie had had Mc-
Carthy as a professor in 1962 while he was an undergraduate at MIT
and then came to work for him at SAIL in 1969 to help tackle a challenging software and math problem known as "proof of correct-
ness." Mathematicians believed that it was theoretically possible to
prove formally that a software program had no bugs—or was correct—and McCarthy had Pentagon funding to do research in the
field.

Diffie was one of a legion of bright young men who, were it not
for the Vietnam War, would probably not have considered the idea of
military-funded basic research. But it seemed like a reasonable com-
promise when facing the equally dismal alternatives of being
shipped to Indochina, fleeing to Canada, or going to jail.

As a child, Diffie had come early to a bohemian sensibility. His parents had been in the Foreign Service and had married in Paris in 1928. After returning to America, his father taught history at City College of New York, specializing in Iberia and its colonies, and Diffie had grown up immersed in the academic, left-wing politics of New York City in the fifties and early sixties. In high school, he plunged into the world of mathematics, which led him to MIT, where he took the mathematician's view of that era: Computers were an impure application of a higher art form.

Despite the fact that he was attending an engineering school that was deeply enmeshed in designing technologies for the Pentagon, Diffie became an antiwar activist. He was thus especially averse to being drafted when he graduated in 1965. Finding discretion to be the better part of valor, Diffie applied for work at the MITRE Corporation, a Boston-area military contractor, a move that would exempt him from enlisted service.

His job interview there was with a distinguished mathematician and software designer named Roland Silver, who became his mentor during the next four years. It was an unusual interview by military-contractor standards. It took place at Silver's home in Cambridge, and almost the entire conversation concerned psychedelic drugs: how to prepare them, where to acquire them, what was entertaining, et cetera. Diffie passed with flying colors.

The job was great, and he didn't even have to leave MIT. Diffie worked at the AI lab, writing programs in McCarthy's LISP programming language. It was an insular world that was both technically and socially connected to the West Coast AI lab. When McCarthy's first wife left him in 1968, she moved east and lived with Silver for a year.

In 1969, Diffie came west to work for McCarthy and SAIL, a situation that suited him quite well both politically and culturally. He shared an office with Larry Tesler, who as a single parent was one of the few people at the laboratory who kept nine-to-five hours. For Tesler, it seemed to Diffie, SAIL was only a job. For Diffie it was just the opposite. He had long since gotten over his original mathematician's contempt of computers, and on many days was at SAIL around the clock. He often ended up crashing on a foam mattress he had brought to the office for his programming marathons.

His intellectual partnership with McCarthy, however, never blossomed. They had different views on the proof-of-correctness problem—McCarthy thought it was simply a matter of automating the theories they had applied to very small programs, while Diffie believed the problem was probably so profound that it would likely never be solved. They didn't really argue about it or debate—that wasn't McCarthy's style. Eventually, he just threw up his hands because Diffie was spending all of his time pursuing the problem of digital signatures and cryptography, rather than his Pentagon-funded proof-of-correctness work. Diffie took an indefinite leave from SAIL, although the two men remained friends.

While Diffie was passing through SAIL, another software designer passed through the laboratory nurturing the idea of the personal computer. Alan Kay spent two miserable academic years at Stanford and SAIL and later claimed it was one of the two least productive periods of his life. However, it wasn't a complete waste of time. He acknowledged that he had come to see how beautiful John McCarthy's LISP programming language was.[6] And he was briefly immersed in the world of artificial intelligence, which was then pushing at the edges of computer science. He submerged himself in several of the deductive-logic systems that were being developed by research scientists who were attempting to build abstract planning and reasoning systems, and he dabbled with the idea of developing languages that could be extrapolated from them. But his heart was elsewhere. Deep in the bowels of the time-sharing world, Alan Kay was spending his time obsessing about the impractical idea of notebook "Kiddy Comps," far removed from the concerns of the group of scientists who saw no need for personal toy computers.

Kay had been a star graduate student at the University of Utah, studying under computer scientist David Evans, before coming to Stanford as a junior faculty member. A temperamental child prodigy, he was the son of a university professor and researcher who specialized in prosthetics and worked at a research center funded by the Veterans Administration. Kay's family had moved from Massachusetts to Australia shortly after he was born in 1940, and he had learned to read at the age of three. Fearing a Japanese invasion, the family returned to the United States, where they lived for several years in his grandparents' farmhouse in western Massachusetts. His grandmother was a schoolteacher, suffragette, lecturer, and one of the founders of the present-day University of Massachusetts, Amherst. His grandfather was Clifton Johnson, a well-known illustrator, photographer, musician, and writer. Surrounded by books, even as a child he read widely. His mother had introduced him to music, and it had developed into a passion after he was sent to music camp when he was fifteen. He was not, however, a star student. Intrigued by the idea of studying biology, Kay entered Bethany College in West Virginia, but left the school in 1961 in a dispute with a dean over a Jewish quota system.[7]

That left him vulnerable to the draft, and so in order to avoid the army, he joined the air force, where a mandatory aptitude test led to his becoming a programmer working with an early IBM computer. After the air force, he returned to school at the University of Colorado, where he received a degree in molecular biology and mathematics. While there, he studied music and theater and supported himself by working as a programmer at the National Center for Atmospheric Research, where he was introduced to the earliest supercomputers designed by a Control Data Corporation computer designer named Seymour Cray. As part of his work at NCAR, he was able to spend half a year working in Cray's lab in Chippewa Falls, Wisconsin.

That experience put him in proximity to one of the world's greatest computer architects, but it didn't have much of an effect on Kay, as he had not yet developed a true passion for computing. However, he remained a voracious reader, and he came across the article by Intel cofounder Gordon Moore predicting silicon chips would improve exponentially in performance and cost over many years. As he was then sitting in a room next to a Freon-cooled supercomputer that processed data at ten million instructions per second, the article didn't strike home initially.[8] Indeed, he thought computer design was fun, but he was leaning toward a career in medicine or possibly even graduate studies in philosophy.

Ultimately he did decide to pursue computing, but it was a more or less happenstance event. Enjoying the mountain climate in Boulder, he concluded that wherever he went to school should be above four thousand feet. Boulder didn't have a Ph.D. computer-science program, and his fantasy of going to Wisconsin to study philosophy didn't pan out, so he ended up at the University of Utah, with literally only a dime in his pocket. Kay arrived on campus a little before the beginning of the winter quarter, and he had the good fortune of finding computer scientist David Evans as a mentor.

Evans was then in his mid-forties, although he looked as if he was about twenty-five. At the time, Kay, like almost everyone else he knew, dressed in the obligatory engineer's uniform of white dress shirt and slacks. When he met Evans, the professor was wearing an informal polo shirt.

It was a month before classes were scheduled to start, and Evans asked Kay, If he could do anything he wanted, what he would like to do?

"Well, I've never read the literature," Kay replied. "So if I had my druthers I would just go to the library and read everything that's been written since the mid-fifties, and I'd Xerox all the interesting things."[9]

Evans said that would be fine, gave Kay a photocopying budget, and turned him loose. The new graduate student spent his days in the library reading every technical article he could find in the Association for Computing Machinery journals and all the articles that were published in the fall and spring issues of *Joint Technical Meetings*. And every time he found an interesting one, he copied it for his files.

In addition to Evans, Kay also came into contact with the work of
Ivan Sutherland. The University of Utah was then the nation's leading center of computer-graphics research. (Evans and Sutherland
would found a pioneering computer graphics company nearby in
1968.) Among Kay's readings was Sutherland's doctoral dissertation: "Sketchpad: A Man-Machine Graphical Communication System." Sketchpad had been a striking advance at the time that
computers were still thought of as ponderous calculators. It was a
drawing program in which the user controlled a light pen to create
pictures, blueprints, or architectural drawings. The program made it
possible to edit, copy, or transform a line image in many ways that
were impossible with pencil, paper, and eraser. Evans was handing
out the thesis to all comers and told Kay, "Take this and read it."[10]

The Utah scientists also had a new tradition—Kay was the department's seventh student—that the most recently arrived graduate
student had to take on the project that nobody else wanted to do. It
fell to Kay to get a version of the Algol programming language running on a Univac mainframe computer. He arrived at his desk to
find that someone had placed a magnetic computer tape on it with a
note that said, "This is Algol for the 1108. It doesn't work. Make it
work."

When Kay began to explore the problem, he found that the tape
actually contained a Norwegian programming language called Simula. To make matters worse, all of its documentation had been written in Norwegian and then translated one word at a time into
English. Frequently, he found the terms that were being used to describe things had actually been made up. It also turned out that
some of the terms had different meanings than their English computing counterparts.

Painstakingly, with several other graduate students, Kay engaged
in the Talmudic exercise of deconstructing the machine code found
on the tape. The engineering building at the University of Utah had
extremely long corridors, and the students laid the listing of the pro-

gram out on the floor over more than eighty feet, mulling over it to attempt to understand what the language was doing.

Kay was struggling with a portion of the programming language known as the "storage allocator," and as he probed the arcane rows of numbers he could see that it pointed to other sections of code, forcing him to jump back and forth along the corridor in an almost physical demonstration of hypertext.

Previously, Kay had not fully understood what Sutherland had been doing inside his Sketchpad program to make it a powerful drawing tool, but as he looked at the Simula listing lying on the floor he realized that the two programs shared a basic approach. The insight came to him on November 11, 1966, when he saw that both programs were attempting to create something that was akin to a biological cell mechanism in which simple building blocks are used to create complex systems. As the comprehension dawned on him, he became more and more excited. Traditionally, computer programs have been divided into data structures and procedures. This was an inherently weaker approach to the design of a computation system, he decided. Now he had stumbled across an entirely new way of looking at computation in which all the components are modular, mimicking the cellular structure of living systems. Moreover, it was an idea that was intrinsically parallel—each module could be a complete independent computer. That realization led to another crucial insight. What both Simula and Sketchpad were missing, Kay realized, was another fundamental component of basic cellular mechanisms: the ability to communicate using messages.

In January, Evans arranged a consulting job for Kay working with a brilliant computer hardware designer named Ed Cheadle. Cheadle was developing a small desktop computer that was intended to help with his engineering calculations. The computer was called Flex, and it gave Kay the opportunity to start playing with some of his ideas about programming languages. He received his master's degree in May 1968 for the design of the Flex programming language.

It was while Alan Kay was thinking about the software design of the Flex machine that Doug Engelbart came calling at the University of Utah. Engelbart had filmed a demonstration of his early Augment NLS system, and he was traveling the country showing his work to other ARPA contractors. The Stanford Research Institute scientist lugged with him a sixteen-millimeter Bell and Howell projector that had been customized so that it could freeze frames and even run backward. Few were familiar yet with the idea of a cursor on the screen to use for pointing and selecting, and so it was important to be able to indicate exactly what was happening on the screen at any given moment.

Kay had already begun to think of what he was doing on the Flex machine as "personal computing," and he was absolutely enthralled by the Engelbart video. In Engelbart's system, Kay saw the Promised Land. Indeed, at a time when computing was still largely about data processing, Engelbart had put together almost all of the critical components of modern personal computing: hypertext, graphics, multiple windows, efficient navigation and command input, collaborative work, and a mouse pointing device. The list was a remarkable visit to the future.

The two men shared something else, for Engelbart's demonstration recalled for Kay Gordon Moore's paper on the evolution of computing power. He thought about the tiny computer he was working on, and he was once again struck by the obvious implications of Moore's contention. The thought almost frightened him, for he realized instantly that computing as it was known in the 1960s would never survive. Suddenly, he was certain there would soon be not thousands but millions of computer users. He likened the feeling to the kind of queasiness that those who read Copernicus must have felt when he looked up at the sky after he realized that the sun did not circle around the earth.[11]

It was not a coincidence that the two men who had the greatest impact on the shape of today's personal computer were among the earliest to fully comprehend the impact of the exponential scaling of microelectronic circuits. That knowledge became a powerful weapon that separately allowed them to dramatically change the computing landscape.

One of the most remarkable aspects of David Evans's graduate program was that while students were required to pay their dues in the form of grunt work, they were also treated as full-fledged members of the community. Although their wages were low, they were given a substantial travel budget—Kay wound up logging 140,000 miles. Not only could they get firsthand contact with other researchers all over the world, but graduate students could also accompany Evans to meetings, where they could watch the nation's best technical researchers.

While stumbling upon Simula gave Kay his modular software insight, in February 1967 he attended an educational conference at Park City, Utah, where MIT artificial-intelligence researcher Marvin Minsky spoke. Minsky launched into a diatribe against traditional educational methods and extolled at length the ideas of another MIT researcher, Seymour Papert, who was developing a new programming language called Logo, which he believed could fundamentally change the way children were taught. The concept intrigued Kay, and he made a mental note that he should visit Papert himself.

Evans also took his graduate students to ARPA contractor meetings, where some of the nation's best computer scientists and electrical engineers explored cutting-edge issues. One of the gatherings was held that year at a ski lodge in Alta, Utah. The researchers sat in a circle, while the graduate students sat surrounding them in their own ring, listening. Bob Taylor, the psychologist who had funded Doug Engelbart, was running the session and toward the end asked the graduate students if they had any suggestions on how the meetings should proceed.

John Warnock, who years later was to found Adobe Systems, the company that developed Postscript, Photoshop, and Illustrator, was, along with Kay, one of the early Utah graduate students. He suggested that since the students would soon be colleagues, they should have their own annual meeting. Taylor and his assistant Larry Roberts loved the idea and immediately funded it for the following summer. The plan was that one or two of the best graduate students on each ARPA-funded project would attend.

In the summer of 1968, the ARPA graduate students gathered at Allerton House in Monticello, Illinois. Kay had come prepared with a complex schematic of his Flex computer on a two-by-three-foot chart as a prop for his lecture on the design of the machine. The talk was well received, but the striking moment for Kay came during a campus tour of the nearby University of Illinois. There on a laboratory bench, he discovered a one-inch lump of glass and neon gas that was capable of lighting up different tiny spots on command. It was a flat-panel display, and it left Kay absolutely dumbfounded. It was instantly obvious that not only would it be possible to make a computer personal, but that that computer could be portable as well. Kay spent the next several hours with the other graduate students calculating whether or not it would be possible to place a 512-by-512-pixel flat-panel display directly on the Flex computer. They decided that, according to Moore's Law, it wouldn't be possible until the late seventies or early eighties—an impossibly long time into the future.

During his travels, Kay also visited the nation's best computer-science research centers. He spent time in Menlo Park with the Augment Group, where Bill English took him under his wing and introduced him to many of Engelbart's best young researchers. He traveled to MIT, where he visited with Papert. He traveled to the RAND Corporation and learned about a system called GRAIL that made it possible for a computer to respond directly to human gestures. He was already familiar with the ARPAnet ideas that would ultimately lead to today's Internet. Moreover, in Hawaii, ARPA-funded experimenters were playing with the idea of creating wireless networks, and so it made sense that his notebook-sized Flex machine would have a wireless connection to the outside world as well.

All of these systems and ideas began to bubble together in a hazy synthesis. Early on, however, Kay realized that he had a different worldview than Engelbart's. He thought that Engelbart's concept was more like a "personal dynamic vehicle," which in Kay's mind was still too similar to IBM's bureaucratic and impersonal mainframe railroads. Moreover, the real breakthrough, he decided, would be to create a personal dynamic *medium*. Influenced by Papert, he realized there was no sense in waiting until high school to begin studying computers, using a drivers' education analogy for personal computing. When computing became an ubiquitous medium, it could be extended all the way into childhood.

By December 1968, Kay's time in graduate school was drawing to an end. His girlfriend, who was later to become his first wife, was desperate to leave the confining world of the Mormon-dominated state of Utah. Ultimately, he took a postdoctoral fellowship at SAIL. However, as he finished his work at Utah, Kay heard about the presentation that Doug Engelbart was planning to make at an annual computer-science meeting in San Francisco.

On his earlier visit to the Augment lab, he had seen Engelbart at work at one of the first NLS systems, the Control Data machine with the large display and Bill English's customized mouse and chord-key set. In the months before the demonstration, there was already a buzz that something special was going to transpire. The computing world was about to have its Woodstock.

To his dismay, however, the week before the conference he came down with strep throat, which left him in bed with a raging fever of 103°. From his sickbed, however, he decided there was no way he would miss the planned demonstration. He gathered up some extra blankets to keep warm on the plane and with a group of other graduate students flew to San Francisco a few days before the event.

5 | DEALING LIGHTNING

Doug Engelbart sat under a twenty-two-foot-high video screen, "dealing lightning with both hands." At least that's the way it seemed to Chuck Thacker, a young Xerox PARC computer designer who was later shown a video of the demonstration that changed the course of the computer world.[1]

On December 9, 1968, the oNLine System was shown publicly to the world for the first time. Encouraged by Taylor, Engelbart had chosen the annual Fall Joint Computer Conference, the computer industry's premier gathering, for Augment's debut. In the darkened Brooks Hall Auditorium in San Francisco, all the seats were filled, and people lined the walls. On the giant screen at his back, Engelbart demonstrated a system that seemed like science fiction to a data-processing world reared on punched cards and typewriter terminals. In one stunning ninety-minute session, he showed how it was possible to edit text on a display screen, to make hypertext links from one electronic document to another, and to mix text and graphics, and even video and graphics. He also sketched out a vision of an experimental computer network to be called ARPAnet and suggested that within a year he would be able to give the same demonstration remotely to locations across the country. In short, every significant aspect of today's computing world was revealed in a magnificent hour and a half.

There were two things that particularly dazzled the audience on that rainy Monday morning in December 1968: First, computing had made the leap from number crunching to become a communications and information-retrieval tool. Second, the machine was being used interactively with all its resources appearing to be devoted to a single individual! It was the first time that truly personal computing had been seen.

Engelbart spoke softly in a monotone, his voice given a slightly eerie quality by the reverberations of the cavernous hall. Wearing a short-sleeved white shirt and a tie and seated at a desk on a custom-designed Herman Miller chair, he introduced the world to cyberspace. He showed the nation's best computer scientists and hardware engineers how people would in the future work together and share complex digital information instantaneously, even though they might be a world apart.

For many who witnessed it, it was more than a bolt from the blue: It was a religious experience, inspiring the same kinds of passion that Vannevar Bush's Memex article had given rise to for Engelbart twenty-three years earlier. Computing was just beginning to have an impact on society. Local newspaper articles that preceded the conference noted that there would be discussions of the privacy implications of the use of computers, and a public forum, "Information, Computers and the Political Process," would feature broadcaster Edward P. Morgan and Santa Clara County's member of the House of Representatives, Paul McCloskey Jr.

But Engelbart stole the show. In the days afterward, the published accounts of the event described nothing else. Years later, his talk remained "the mother of all demos," in the words of Andries van Dam, a Brown University computer scientist. In many ways, it is still the most remarkable computer-technology demonstration of all time.

"Fantastic World of Tomorrow's Computer" was the headline in the *San Francisco Chronicle,* which noted that Engelbart had said that his group was consciously steering clear of any artificial "brain" or thinking computer. The more subtle distinction between the opposing goals of augmentation and automation was lost on the writer, but it was at the very heart of the demonstration. Engelbart's system kept the "man in the loop," which was antithetical to the goals of many computer scientists of the era. Engelbart was a heretic, and it was from his heresy that personal computing grew.

With a microphone headset strapped on, he had begun by telling his audience, "I hope you'll go along with this rather unusual setting. . . . The research program I'm going to describe to you is quickly characterizable by saying, if in your office you as an intellectual worker were supplied with a computer display backed up by a computer that was alive for you all day and was instantly responsive to every action you have, how much value could you derive from that?" The new technology would make for an interesting demonstration, Engelbart said, and then added under his breath a barely audible, "I hope."

It was as simple as that. The relationship between man and computer had been turned upside down. From a distance of more than three decades, it is hard to appreciate the power of that simple assertion. However, it was the key to the consequences of personal computing: organizations would be democratized, industries transformed, and a new wave of individual creativity would sweep across the world.

The demonstration had a far greater impact than any of the participants could imagine. It was an instant success, but then the legend grew over time as the world came to realize what Engelbart and his research team had wrought.

One reason the presentation worked as well as it did was because at the other end of the hall, standing on a raised platform, was Bill English, Engelbart's lead engineer. It was easy for Engelbart to wave his hands and conceptualize his computing vision, but someone had to build the demonstration from scratch. And that someone was English. An absolute pragmatist, he had an uncanny knack for making things work. English was the one who had tracked down the remarkable Eidaphor video projector for the demonstration. On loan

from NASA, and with the blessing of Bob Taylor at ARPA, the Eidaphor was the only technology that could create the kind of effect
that Engelbart had in mind. It was a six-foot-high cabinet that used a
blindingly intense arc light, bouncing it off a concave mirror to
make a bright, 875-line video projection. The fact that the device
drew each frame by forming an image with an electron beam in a
sheet of oil that was repeatedly wiped away by a windshield wiper
made the feat only more remarkable.

Engelbart had hesitantly gone to Taylor with the idea in the summer, and the ARPA official had given his blessing to the extrava-
ganza. Later, when the researcher told one of SRI's accountants that
he had ARPA's blessing for the huge expense, he had been told that
it was okay to go ahead, but if the venture failed, SRI planned to
deny any knowledge of its approval.

From his platform behind the audience, English served as the
link between Engelbart onstage and the laboratory researchers who
were connected from Menlo Park to the auditorium by two video microwave links and two modem lines. English served as the director,
talking by telephone to Menlo Park and by a communication link to
a speaker in Engelbart's ear, cuing each part of the demonstration
and controlling the camera views. The researchers had placed a
truck at a strategic point on Skyline Boulevard, high above the
Peninsula, to relay the microwave links to the city, and they had built
two homebrew high-speed modems—1200 baud was high speed in
1968, and each modem carried data in only a single direction—to
connect Engelbart's keyboard, mouse, and key set to the SDS-940 in
Menlo Park.

It required a complicated choreography to mix the images from
the display screen, a camera that was pointed at Engelbart's keyboard, and a second camera in Menlo Park to show demonstrations
by members of the laboratory research team. At times it seemed to
the audience that Engelbart wasn't quite there, that he was listening
to some distant voice. And, in fact, he was. He could hear English
talking to all of the participants up and down the Peninsula, which

made for constantly distracting background chatter. Engelbart referred to the on-screen cursor as a "bug" or a "tracking spot," and there were occasionally odd buzzing sounds in the background as he executed commands at the keyboard. The group had been experimenting with using the computer to generate different tones depending upon what was being executed, as a way of creating auditory feedback.

After introducing the project and the system, Engelbart invited Jeff Rulifson on-screen from Menlo Park. Instantly, there he was on the giant display above Engelbart's head, a serious young man with dark hair, a jacket and tie, and horn-rimmed glasses, holding forth on the internal structure of the Augment NLS. Next came Bill Paxton, another young Augment programmer, whose video image was shrunken into a window in the corner of the display while he discussed using the NLS for information retrieval with Engelbart.

On the surface, it was a dry technical description of a computer-engineering feat. But it was also interactive multimedia entertainment on a scale the world hadn't seen. The computing world was beginning to blend with the counterculture.

■ ■ ■

Operating the camera in Menlo Park for Engelbart's landmark presentation was Stewart Brand, who by then was a twenty-nine-year-old multimedia producer and a friend of English. He had been invited in as a consultant at the last minute to help polish the presentation and help make it an "event." The unstated connection, of course, was Brand's background in helping orchestrate Ken Kesey's Acid Tests. English and Brand had met through Dick Raymond, who along with a quirky independent computer educator named Bob Albrecht and several others had founded the Portola Institute, an alternative educational forum that served as the launching pad for the *Whole Earth Catalog,* the People's Computer Company, and a variety of other experiments.

Raymond had been a consultant in the field of recreational economics at SRI, and Brand had been a longtime friend of the Raymond family, dating back to his days as a Stanford student. After Raymond had left SRI, he had set up his own small consulting firm with a contract with the Warm Springs Indian reservation in Oregon. The tribe was reconceiving its relation to tourists. Raymond thought they needed a photographer, and he prevailed on Brand to take pictures. Visiting the reservation had a profound effect on the would-be photojournalist, who stumbled upon a part of America that was remarkably alien to his comfortable middle-class Midwestern roots. That visit had come shortly after his LSD experience at the International Foundation for Advanced Study in 1962, and as a result of his time spent on the reservation Brand had developed a deep interest in Native American cultures. Starting in 1964, he had begun performing his own multimedia presentation called "America Needs Indians."

Brand was also close to Ken Kesey and the Merry Pranksters, and in 1966 he had helped organize the last of the Acid Tests, which served to launch the Grateful Dead. On the Friday evening of that weekend, Brand's Native American multimedia production had opened the Trips Festival.

Combining his Midwestern roots with a Merry Prankster sense of cosmic adventure, Brand would create in 1968 an irresistible format in the first *Whole Earth Catalog*. A compendium of stuff patterned after the Sears and L. L. Bean mail-order catalogs crossed with *Consumer Reports*, the catalog struck a deep nerve that transcended the counterculture. Brand had come upon the idea of a "Whole Earth" two years earlier, after hearing a lecture by Buckminster Fuller. One day in North Beach, he had been sitting huddled in a blanket on the roof of his three-story apartment building looking out over the city. Having taken "a few mikes of LSD,"[2] Brand was suddenly struck by the fact that the city's buildings were not laid out in perfect parallel lines. It seemed to him that, since the surface of the earth was curved, they actually must diverge just slightly. And then it occurred to him that despite the fact that satellites had been circling the earth for almost a decade, he had never seen a photograph showing the entire earth's surface. He realized that an image of the whole earth might inspire others to have a more complete sense of man's place within the planet's ecology and all of the implications that flowed from such a view of the world. That concept ultimately became a touchstone for the environmental movement that was to spring from Earth Day, first held on April 22, 1970.

Brand ultimately began calling upon NASA to deliver a photograph of the entire surface of the planet. He created a button that read "Why Haven't We Seen a Photograph of the Whole Earth Yet?" and immediately hitchhiked to the East Coast selling copies along the way.

In 1966, caught up with Native American cultures, Fuller's ideas, and the beginnings of an American back-to-the-land movement, Brand also came up with the notion of a mobile "truck store," which he drove around northern California with the intent of distributing goods and information to a new wave of urban refugees who were ill equipped for their newly adopted life. The Whole Earth Truck Store came into existence in Menlo Park just a few doors away from Raymond and Albrecht's Portola Institute, where Brand was an informal fellow-in-residence. In July of 1968, the *Whole Earth Catalog* began to take shape, initially as a six-page mimeographed list of books on topics such as tantric art, cybernetics, Indian teepees, and recreational equipment as well as product samples. Brand, who was tall and gangly and who came equipped with an omnipresent and ambitious Swiss Army knife clipped to his belt, drove around the commune circuit, selling goods and accepting orders.[3]

Later that year in Menlo Park, with a small staff and the help of his wife, Lois Jennings, he put together the first expanded version of the *Whole Earth Catalog,* which was published in January 1969. It was a pioneering effort in desktop publishing. An IBM Selectric allowed different fonts with its easily replaceable "golfball" print head, while a Polaroid MP-3 camera made it possible to copy graphics directly from books and created halftones that could be pasted onto layout sheets.[4] The first edition sold one thousand copies, and ultimately more than 1.5 million copies of various editions were sold. In 1972, Brand would win a National Book Award for his efforts.

The catalog, which became a project of the Portola Institute, had originally been intended as a resource for a way of life less dependent on the power and influence of modern industrial society. Although it resembled mainstream catalogs in many respects, it differed in a manner that struck right at a dualism that Brand himself would coin years later: that strange quality about information that was both easy and freely shareable and immensely valuable. "Information wants to be free," he said, and then he added in typical Brandian fashion, "and it wants to be very expensive."

The first *Whole Earth Catalog* was a full-on tour of the counterculture, a hodgepodge of product descriptions, advice, commentary, and quirky features laid out in a seemingly haphazard fashion, beginning with Buckminster Fuller and ending with the *I Ching;* it became an instant bible and a serendipitous tool for finding interesting stuff. In doing so, it also helped a scattered community that was in the process of defining itself find an identity.

"We are as gods and we might as well get used to it." Brand's introduction began with a phrase borrowed from British anthropologist Edmund Leach that is often remembered and quoted. It was certainly striking, a bit for its arrogance and naïveté, but it also perfectly captured the sense of power and innocence of the movement that planned to atone for its parents' sins and remake the world in a new image. It was the second half of the short introduction that neatly captured the various threads that would soon come together to liberate the computer from large, impersonal institutions: "a realm of intimate, personal power is developing—power of the individual to conduct his own education, find his own inspiration, shape his own environment, and share his adventure with whoever is interested. Tools that aid this process are sought and promoted by the WHOLE EARTH CATALOG."

In the first catalog, there wasn't much computing power to tap into. The HP 9100A calculator, referred to as a computer on the title page, was given a glowing review; Norbert Wiener's *Cybernetics* and the September 1966 *Scientific American* issue on information were also reviewed. The scarcity of material in this particular area didn't matter; the principle of valued tools controlled by the individual was established firmly.

On the verge of publishing the first *Catalog* the following month, Brand saw himself not so much as an entrepreneur but as an artist who was exploring new media, and he was immediately struck by the possibilities of computers that were moving beyond being calculators. He traveled easily between the communes in the backwoods and the computer laboratories. On the day he arrived at SRI, he walked into Dave Evans's office, found a large poster of rock singer Janis Joplin on the wall, and knew he was right at home.

Brand also knew that SRI was deeply involved in planning and weapons design for the war in Vietnam, and he was aware of the antiwar demonstrations that were increasingly beginning to focus on the SRI–Stanford University connection. As a former infantryman, however, he found he had little patience for the antiwar activists. In 1965, he joined Ken Kesey and the Merry Pranksters at a Vietnam Day Committee rally in Berkeley where Kesey had been invited to speak. Kesey climbed onstage dressed in a Day-Glo orange wig and played the harmonica—hardly the passionate opposition to the war the event's organizers had expected. That was fine with Brand, who considered himself to be on the "psychedelic side" in the political dispute over Vietnam.

On one level, Brand had a very conservative political attitude that could be traced back at least as far as his time at Stanford and perhaps even further, to his prep school days in the east. When he was a college student in the fifties, he wrote in his journal, "Just what has the United States got against Communism, anyway? It's an important question." He decided that it threatened his way of life—directly, in a military sense—and his freedom, as well, even his capacity to think for himself. For those reasons, he decided, "I will fight communism in every way I can."⁵

But Brand was no ordinary ideologue. He had a Zelig-like penchant for being intimately involved in a series of key social and technological movements beginning in the 1960s. He always seemed to be surfing on the edge of the most up-to-the-moment events that were transforming California's wide-open culture.

Brand had been brought into SRI because the Augment researchers knew that they were embarked on a project that transcended both engineering and science. They understood that Engelbart's demonstration should involve both media and even entertainment. Brand, for his part, was barely able to grasp what he was seeing. The notion that Doug Engelbart was bombing around—piloting with mouse and chord-key set—in this new kind of information space that didn't even have a name yet was a totally disarming concept.

If he didn't get the computing part, he did have some advice to give that was subtle and yet ultimately had an impact on the demonstration. Brand had an odd perspective: You ought to be able to hear a person think, he decided. He pushed the designers to improve the quality of the sound, as he wanted to be able to hear more than low-quality telephone audio. In the final demonstration, the audience heard from both Engelbart's headset and, from Menlo Park, simple noises like keyboards and the responsive sound of a computer, which added to the impact of what was shown that day.

■ ■ ■

Now, stationed back in Menlo Park at SRI, Brand was running the camera to document the birth of a new kind of computing, and Engelbart publicly thanked him from the stage as he concluded his presentation. Next, he turned to his wife, Ballard, who was sitting in the auditorium with their two daughters, and thanked her for the patience she showed "to a husband who is dedicated in a very monomaniacal way to something that is very wild."

Wild indeed. Engelbart had been lost in the lights onstage and had no hint of how his audience was reacting. But when he finished, there was a standing ovation, and for a second he appeared uncertain of how to respond. The applause went on and on. He nodded several times before glancing up at the screen and just briefly breaking into the sad smile that was becoming his trademark.

In Menlo Park, the Augment team had no idea how the demonstration had been received, as the video wasn't two-way. "Did they like it?" someone asked. It seemed like five minutes before the answer came back from San Francisco, "Yes, they liked it."

Afterward, Alan Kay and another graduate student from Utah watched the crowd flow around several NLS terminals that had been set up to demonstrate the system after Engelbart's presentation. He saw Brown University computer scientist Andy van Dam buttonhole Engelbart in a mob of people. At the time, van Dam cut a striking figure—he looked like a wild man, with his globe of Afro-style curly hair and a goatee. The confrontation between the two men was remarkable, because the previous year van Dam had begun developing a similar system at Brown in collaboration with Ted Nelson, the itinerant poet-sociologist who had a vision that in many ways paralleled Engelbart's. Now van Dam was stunned to find that Engelbart's group had completed what he and Nelson and a group of young students were just starting.

Kay watched van Dam drill into Engelbart. Indeed, van Dam was as intense as Engelbart was mild mannered, and it looked to Kay as if van Dam had an almost desperate need to find out everything about the system, as if he didn't believe it was possible, and he was angry to discover that it existed at all. "How much of this was just a demo?" he demanded. "And how much do you actually *use* this system?"

The Utah graduate student could also sense the Brown computer scientist's integrity. At the end of their confrontation, van Dam was still angry, but it was obvious that he had determined that the demonstration was the real thing. He had decided that it was the best thing he had ever seen.

The NLS demo was a watershed in another less dramatic way as well. For all of those who were present that morning, there were several notable absences, among them Raj Reddy, the graduate researcher at SAIL, and Les Earnest, SAIL's executive officer. The two men were down the hall at the same conference, giving a competing demonstration in which Earnest presented a film of a robot that could see and hear, based on a paper that he had written with Reddy and another researcher. Afterward, no one remembered the talk, which was lost in the brilliance of Engelbart's NLS creation. Indeed, it was the moment the tables turned, and computer science, which had until then been primarily concerned with the esoteric problem of automating human intelligence, would never be the same.

Arthur C. Clarke once said, "Any sufficiently advanced technology is indistinguishable from magic." For many people who saw Doug Engelbart bombing through cyberspace and dealing lightning with both hands in December 1968, that was certainly true. But one young programmer who watched from the audience had a stronger reaction.

Charles Irby had been a student at the University of California at Santa Barbara, where he had worked for Glen Culler, a math professor who independently designed interactive computers for mathematical applications before anyone knew what the word "interactive" meant in that context. By the time he came to the Fall Joint Computer Conference in 1968, Irby had finished his work at UCSB and in order to keep his draft deferment had taken a job at Litton Industries, helping to develop the ground control system for a predecessor to the Skylab orbiting research program.

While he was passionately opposed to the war, he didn't consider himself a radical, and working for Litton allowed him to feel that he was serving his country without killing people. But the work was uninspiring, and now, sitting in Engelbart's demonstration, a missing piece of the puzzle about interactive computing that he had been trying to solve had been filled in. He had already built an interactive system in school, without having had a name for it. Now he saw clearly that his work was just one corner of a very big picture—and that Engelbart had the whole picture.

After the presentation, while other people clustered around Engelbart, Irby sought out the person who seemed to be in charge of the technical details. He took Bill English aside and said, "This is really nifty, and I think I can help you."[6]

English, who was unfailingly polite, responded, "We're looking for a few good men. Why don't you come by?"

That invitation was enough for Irby, and the following week he showed up at the SRI employment office in coat and tie, only to be told there were no job openings.

"Wrong," he responded. "I'm going to sit here until Bill English comes and talks to me."

English eventually came down, and the Augment laboratory ended up hiring Irby, first as a junior programmer and eventually as chief software architect. He ultimately stayed at Augment for seven years. Tremendously loyal to Engelbart and his vision, he left only when it became apparent there was no further progress to be made there.

In the Augment lab, Irby grew into the role of translator between Engelbart and the programmers. It was a job that became increasingly difficult as the Augment founder continued to grapple with the challenge of bringing his idea of scaling not just to computing but also to his larger target of human performance, to the real world.

In some ways the December demonstration was the absolute zenith of Engelbart's Augment experiment. In retrospect, the vision would never again be as clearly communicated and never again capture the imagination of so many people quite so dramatically. In the short run, however, the demonstration also sparked rapid growth for Augment. ARPA funding increased, and there were soon real-world customers for the Augment system, both in the military and in corporations. The head count continued to expand from seventeen at the time of the demonstration to a peak of forty-five in 1976, when the laboratory was sold to the Tymshare Corporation.

But apart from the glare of public notoriety, new tensions had begun to beset the Augment lab. The antiwar movement and the counterculture were now dramatic forces in the Bay Area. The outside world intruded both as political and cultural chaos and in the form of a new wave of skilled software and hardware designers who were drawn to Engelbart's ideas.

Bill Duvall had grown up a couple of miles away from Engelbart's laboratory. His father was a physicist who worked at SRI. During junior high school, the younger Duvall studied at the Peninsula School, an alternative school that had been attended by Joan Baez and her sister and which had a rich tradition dating back to the 1920s. He had started in the public school system, but math and science had always come easily, and the public schools at the time had a policy of no accelerated studies. He was bored, and so in the seventh grade he jumped with a friend to the Peninsula School.

It was like being let out of prison. The staff consisted of the type of people he would have never found in the public school system. Ira Sandperl, the pacifist who had been Joan Baez's mentor, was one of his teachers. Learning was something that the students were free to pursue, rather than having it forced upon them. In the eighth grade, Duvall taught himself calculus from a textbook. Learning how to learn on his own proved one of the most important lessons of his life.

Unfortunately, there was no Peninsula high school, and so in the ninth grade Duvall returned to public school and endured what he considered to be the four unhappiest years of his life. At Woodside High School, anyone who had a natural ability for math and science was classified as a nerd and treated as a social outcast. Duvall resisted becoming a pariah and he went out for track and raced bicycles on his own. In the end, because he was nevertheless one of the top two or three students in science and math, he remained an outcast.

In self-defense, he withdrew into music, often practicing brass instruments for the school band six hours per day.

He applied late to college and only to Berkeley and Harvard. The Harvard interview was a complete disaster. He went to the mansion of a preppie, blue-blazer-clad Harvard alum and immediately realized that he was out of place in his old jeans.

He was accepted at Berkeley and arrived as a freshman in the fall of 1963, just in time to take part in the Free Speech Movement. At the university, however, he felt even more lost than in high school. Berkeley was a huge institution, and he received no mentoring. Instead, his orientation came from the chaos of the student movement, from which he learned two things. First, there was a real political establishment. Second, he discovered an *Alice in Wonderland* world in which, although he had been taught since grade school the importance of free speech in America, the establishment was saying, "Well, no, that person can't speak here."

It was a jarring realization. It wasn't so much that the system was evil, but he saw clearly that there was an order that wasn't going to change easily, and the establishment certainly wasn't going to change the world. He decided he could change things by situating himself outside of the established order.

But while he participated in the demonstrations, he never thought of himself as an activist. One of the values that he held deeply was that each person was entitled to his own position, and he felt slightly guilty in attempting to talk anyone out of a position. It wasn't a good quality for someone caught between the ranks of the students and the Berkeley riot police during the sixties.

But Duvall was extremely opposed to the war in Vietnam, which he came to see as a generational aberration. An entire American generation had been shaped by World War II; they got to be heroes, they got to be in command, and they won. It had been the high point of their lives. Vietnam, he thought, was the legacy of a group of Americans that was reaching its midlife crisis, and to grapple with it they were waging another war. There was no other reasonable explanation.

While in high school, Duvall had taken refuge in music; at Berkeley, it was computing. The university had not yet created a computer-science department, and so it wasn't long before he had taken all the computing courses that the school offered. It was a world he found he was entirely passionate about, and his father, who was a physicist at SRI, got him a job working there in the math department in 1965 during the summer after his sophomore year. Once he stepped into the world of computer hacking, there wasn't anything else in his life for a long time.

He went back to Berkeley for a semester but then dropped out and joined SRI full time in 1966. Although leaving school made him eligible for the draft, by working for a defense contractor he was able to maintain his draft deferment.

His first job was to modify the operating system of the SRI Burroughs mainframe to enable it to time-share multiple users. Like many projects, it never went anywhere. That was followed by an abortive stint as an SRI consultant working with Burroughs and the National Provincial Bank in England. When he returned to Menlo Park the following year, he still had a job at SRI, but he needed to find something to do and Shaky the Robot, an early robotics experiment, seemed like a great project. It, too, proved to be a disappointment. Before long, Duvall decided that he had no intention of ever working again as a menial programmer. His curiosity shifted to the quirky group of programmers down the hall from the AI laboratory.

Even after the Brooks Hall demonstration, within SRI, working on the Augment project wasn't seen as a particularly good career move. The counsel Duvall received was, "Hey, you're doing this serious work on the future of robotics, something that's going to make a difference. You don't want to go down the hall and work with those freaks who don't know what they are doing." But to Duvall it felt different. He had already discovered for himself that the most interesting aspects of computing had little to do with crunching numbers. Even before he had gone to England, he had realized that computers were best used for presenting and communicating information.

It was 1969, and Doug Engelbart had been developing his vision for six years. He had built a loyal group of programmers and hardware designers, what Duvall found to be part engineering culture, part counterculture. In some ways, it was a welcoming world, and in others it was a research group that was as full of politics as any other. Sparks quickly flew between Duvall and Jeff Rulifson, who was one of Engelbart's lead software designers. The way Duvall saw it was that people who had their own clear technical point of view threatened Rulifson. The animosity between the two men grew to the point, at least according to Duvall, that Rulifson withheld source code—the basic programming instructions—from Duvall.

But Duvall also found allies and friends in the Augment Group. He was living over the hill in the redwood forests of La Honda, where his neighbor was David Casseres, the young technical writer. Both men were single, and both of them also owned the same kind of car—offbeat three-cylinder Saab 96s. They were unusual vehicles in the United States at the time, and their owners tended to have a cult devotion to the machines, which were known for their handling prowess in European sports-car rallies.

Shortly after Bill Duvall arrived at Engelbart's lab, he was joined by a young Berkeley physics student who was also looking for a way to avoid the draft and at the same time find something interesting to do. Harvey Lehtman had graduated from Berkeley, and like Duvall he was a veteran of the Free Speech Movement, having been arrested at Sproul Hall. After college, he was tugged a bit by feelings of guilt over his privileged status, but he really didn't want to go to Vietnam.

He was able to visit the Menlo Park laboratory and had a good conversation with a number of the members of the Augment team. He liked them, and they liked him. There was just one small problem: Lehtman knew almost nothing about computers. The visit ended inconclusively, but the computing bug had bitten Lehtman. He discovered a new program that was being started at UCSD in physics and information. He entered the graduate school and was given the responsibility for teaching a computer-science course. Since Donald Knuth's first volume of *The Art of Computer Programming* had recently been published, he got a copy and throughout the quarter managed to keep barely ahead of everyone in the class.

During the summer of 1969 he called Bill English and told him, "I know about computers now." He arrived as a summer intern and then came to work full-time the next year.

The doors of Augment were opened not only to a small technical elite of software designers like Duvall and Lehtman. With time, civilians in the outside world began to get hints of the technology and become curious about it.

Dave Evans was one of the Augment team members who had strong ties to the counterculture, and one evening Stewart Brand brought Ken Kesey by for a look at the NLS system. It was several years after the Merry Prankster era and Kesey's legal problems over a marijuana arrest, and he had become a celebrity as a result of the publication of Tom Wolfe's *The Electric Kool-Aid Acid Test*, in which he was the main character. He was quarreling with Hollywood movie studios over the film based on his novel *Sometimes a Great Notion* and was preparing to retreat to a dairy farm in Oregon.

For an hour, Evans took the system through its paces, showing the writer how it was possible to manipulate text, retrieve information, and collaborate with others. At the end of the demonstration Kesey sighed and said, "It's the next thing after acid."

■■■

The personal computer was indeed fated to be the next big thing, but the Augment project itself was reaching its limit. As great an impression as NLS had made at the FJCC meeting, the program failed to become widely popular in the ARPA community of researchers. Engelbart's plan, supported by ARPA administrators, had been that the Augment lab would serve as a resource center for the newly planned ARPAnet. At an ARPA investigators' meeting in the spring of 1967 in Ann Arbor, he had volunteered the Augment computers as a centralized information repository—it would later became the Network Information Center (NIC)—for the new network. While many of the ARPA investigators were still complaining about how the network might steal their scarce computer resources, Engelbart saw it as an opportunity to proselytize his ideas as well as develop a far greater user community for the NLS software.

At that ARPA meeting in Ann Arbor, Engelbart watched while Bob Taylor and Larry Roberts attempted to sell the investigators on the idea of a research network. Nobody was buying it. The general reaction was, "Well, damn, I'm doing this very important research in artificial intelligence or in time-sharing systems or something. I don't want to fool around and waste time getting all involved and getting my people involved with networks."[7]

Taylor had mentioned the networking idea to Engelbart nine months earlier, and Engelbart's initial reaction had been skeptical. Later, however, he saw that it was directly in accord with the idea of community he was trying to realize.

At the Ann Arbor meeting, there was an open quarrel over the notion of sharing resources. This debate led to a demand from the researchers that ARPA set up a digital library. Engelbart saw the opportunity and seized it. Such a digital library would place the Augment project directly at the heart of the emerging network world. It was indeed a wonderful concept, but because of various delays and the reality of the bureaucracy, it took another three years for the network to be established and the Network Information Center to be created in Menlo Park.

In the interim, the Augment Group added an electronic journal and mail to the NLS system. Engelbart gave the task of designing the journal to Evans, and then Duvall programmed the new function. However, the two men failed to communicate well.

Dealing with Evans was a bit like trying to corral a billiard ball. He had boundless enthusiasm and would get excited about one notion, racing after it and then just as quickly racing in another direction. Finally, Engelbart took him aside and said, "If you can, settle down

Physicist John Von Neumann (far right) and a team of his computer designers, including Hewitt Crane (fourth from right), created the Institute for Advanced Study computer, one of the earliest programmable computers, in the
early 1950s. (*Photograph by Alan Richards, courtesy of Bernice Sheasley*)

Doug Engelbart had a singular vision about augmenting the human mind, which led directly to
the invention of personal computing. (*Courtesy of SRI
International*)

Kepler's Books became a center of the counterculture near Stanford during the 1950s. (*Courtesy of Clark Kepler*)

Fred Moore left his family's home in Virginia in 1959, intent on stopping the fighting in Cuba. (*Courtesy of Irene Moore*)

Robert Taylor was one of the first to fund Doug Engelbart's research. Later he would help create the remarkable computer research laboratory at Xerox's Palo Alto Research Center that designed the Alto. (*Courtesy of Palo Alto Research Center*)

The first mouse was a clumsy device with two large wheels and three buttons, which was the maximum number that would fit in its wooden case. (*Courtesy of SRI International*)

The Stanford Artificial Intelligence Laboratory was located in the hills behind Stanford at the D.C. Power building. (*Courtesy of Bruce Baumgart*)

John McCarthy, a computing pioneer, came to Stanford during the 1960s and created a "Socretean abode" for computer hackers at SAIL. (*Courtesy of Bruce Baumgart*)

Bruce Baumgart, one of the young Stanford graduate students who proto-typed and maintained the SAIL cart robot. (*Courtesy of Bruce Baumgart*)

Larry Tesler would take his crusade for simplicity in computer-user interface from SAIL to PARC, where he joined forces with Alan Kay and Dennis Allison (second from right), who designed Tiny BASIC. (*Courtesy of Paul Freiberger*)

Whitfield Diffie came to SAIL as an AI researcher, but made his most profound contribution in public key cryptography, based on a discussion with John McCarthy about home computing. (*Courtesy of Bruce Baumgart*)

Alan Kay was one of the first to understand that computing would become a new medium.
(*Courtesy of Palo Alto Research Center*)

Bill Duvall and Ann Weinberg worked for Doug Engelbart and later were married. Duvall wrote the software used to send the first ARPAnet message. (*Courtesy of Bill and Ann Duvall*)

Bill Duvall at work on one of the Augment Group's yoga workstations. (*Courtesy of Bill and Ann Duvall*)

Stewart Brand in October 1973. The previous year he had written a *Rolling Stone* article that captured the spirit of the coming era of personal computing.
(© *Ted Streshinsky/Corbis*)

WHOLE EARTH CATALOG

access to tools

Fall 1968
$5

Stewart Brand published the first *Whole Earth Catalog* in 1968. Published twice annually until 1972 it would shape the consciousness of a generation on technology and ecology. (*Courtesy of Stewart Brand*)

Kids learning to use computers at the People's Computer
Company offices in Menlo Park. (*Courtesy of Stewart Brand's Cybernetic Futures*)

As a Stanford student, Bill Pitts discovered the Stanford Artificial Intelligence Laboratory when he attempted to sneak into it late one night. (*Courtesy of Bruce Baumgart*)

Pitts went on to design the world's first coin-operated video game and installed it at the Stanford campus coffeehouse in Tresidder Union. (*Courtesy of Gio Wiederhold*)

As a young programmer working for Alan Kay, Dan Ingalls invented a graphics technique, BitBlt, that became the standard for modern graphical user interfaces. (*Courtesy of Ted Kaehler*)

Ted Kaehler demonstrates the Alto for a Xerox senior manager. (*Courtesy of Palo Alto Research Center*)

The Alto personal computer. (*Courtesy of Palo Alto Research Center*)

The display of an Alto featured windows, text, and graphics. (*Courtesy of Palo Alto Research Center*)

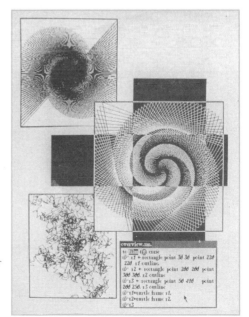

Ted Nelson created the concept of hypertext at roughly the same time that it was pioneered by Douglas Engelbart. He later wrote *Computer Lib*, a manifesto calling for computer power to the users. (*Courtesy of Paul Freiberger*)

(*Covers by Ted Nelson; superstudent by unknown artist commissioned by* Computer Decisions *magazine*)

Lee Felsenstein was a political activist who became the master of ceremonies at the weekly meetings of the Homebrew Computer Club, created by a band of hobbyists in 1975. (*Courtesy of Lee Felsenstein*)

Phone hacker John Draper, another member of the Homebrew Computer Club, was known as "Cap'n Crunch." He was arrested after he was entrapped using a Blue Box to make phone calls from a phone booth in front of the offices of the People's Computer Company. (*Courtesy of Bill Baker*)

Steve Dompier was a computer hobbyist who figured out how to use his Altair computer to generate musical tones. (*Courtesy of Steve Dompier*)

A young Bill Gates makes a presentation at an early computer convention. (© *1976. Photo courtesy of David Ahl, Creative Computing*)

To me, the most critical thing in the hobby market right now is the lack of good software courses, books and software itself. Without good software and an owner who understands programming, a hobby computer is wasted. Will quality software be written for the hobby market?

Almost a year ago, Paul Allen and myself, expecting the hobby market to expand, hired Monte Davidoff and developed Altair BASIC. Though the initial work took only two months, the three of us have spent most of the last year documenting, improving and adding features to BASIC. Now we have 4K, 8K, EXTENDED, ROM and DISK BASIC. The value of the computer time we have used exceeds $40,000.

The feedback we have gotten from the hundreds of people who say they are using BASIC has all been positive. Two surprising things are apparent, however. 1) Most of these "users" never bought BASIC (less than 10% of all Altair owners have bought BASIC), and 2) The amount of royalties we have received from sales to hobbyists makes the time spent of Altair BASIC worth less than $2 an hour.

Why is this? As the majority of hobbyists must be aware, most of you steal your software. Hardware must be paid for, but software is something to share. Who cares if the people who worked on it get paid?

Is this fair? One thing you don't do by stealing software is get back at MITS for some problem you may have had. MITS doesn't make money selling software. The royalty paid to us, the manual, the tape and the overhead make it a break-even operation. One thing you do do is prevent good software from being written. Who can afford to do professional work for nothing? What hobbyist can put 3-man years into programming, finding all bugs, documenting his product and distribute for free? The fact is, no one besides us has invested a lot of money in hobby software. We have written 6800 BASIC, and are writing 8080 APL and 6800 APL, but there is very little incentive to make this software available to hobbyists. Most directly, the thing you do is theft.

What about the guys who re-sell Altair BASIC, aren't they making money on hobby software? Yes, but those who have been reported to us may lose in the end. They are the ones who give hobbyists a bad name, and should be kicked out of any club meeting they show up at.

I would appreciate letters from any one who wants to pay up, or has a suggestion or comment. Just write me at 1180 Alvarado SE, #114, Albuquerque, New Mexico, 87108. Nothing would please me more than being able to hire ten programmers and deluge the hobby market with good software.

Bill Gates

Bill Gates
General Partner, Micro-Soft

Bill Gates became outraged when hobbyists began sharing a version of BASIC he had written with Paul Allen. (*Homebrew Computer Club Newsletter*) and pick just one thing. Let's pick something you can do a thesis on and get that off your back. I want to do this journal, so why don't you do the detailed design for it?"

Unfortunately the idea of a single project didn't really tame Evans, who continued to veer off in multiple directions, albeit this time on one subject. Ultimately, he wrote a five-hundred-page paper describing all kinds of collections of information.

It was left to Bill Duvall to write the code to make the concept a reality. He did it by writing a database that made it possible to create a record of everything that took place on the system. A user could search for documents, group them together, and track changes that were made in each one. Since there was not enough capacity to store the whole journal electronically, it was saved on paper in binders. Today, it can be found at the Stanford University Library in the special collections section, where it stretches for more than four hundred linear feet.

In addition to programming the journal, at the last moment Duvall was given another assignment: to help write the software to connect the Augment NLS system to the ARPAnet. He didn't think much about it at the time, as it seemed to be just one more project in a long list of things that were intended to extend the system and make it more useful, as part of Doug Engelbart's bootstrapping vision. It wasn't supposed to be Duvall's job, but that's the way it ended up.

In March 1969, Duvall traveled to Utah with Jeff Rulifson to represent the Augment Group at a Network Working Group meeting sponsored by ARPA. The first four planned sites of the network were UCLA, SRI, the University of California at Santa Barbara, and the University of Utah. Eventually, it would expand to satisfy Bob Taylor's concept of a single network that would permit information sharing and remote computing among a diverse community of computer users.

Meetings had begun the previous summer between representatives from the four initial sites, and they continued into the fall.

After the March 1969 meeting, Steve Crocker, a member of the UCLA group, had drawn up a preliminary set of notes he referred to as "Request for Comments 1." Such RFCs would become a rich Internet tradition and a simple and efficient way to produce technical standards for the network. The first RFC was based on the group's discussions and outlined a set of understandings about how the host computers at the four sites would communicate through intermediate data processors known as IMPs, which had been developed for the new network at Bolt, Beranek and Newman in Cambridge.

There was something even more revealing about RFC 1, which was essentially the founding document of what was to become the modern Internet. At the end of the paper, Crocker outlined two "experiments." The first called for SRI to modify its NLS software so that it could be operated remotely by teletypes. All of the sites would then use NLS remotely. The second experiment was even more ambitious. SRI was instructed to write a more ambitious "front end" for the complete version of NLS, one that would include graphics. "UCLA and Utah will use NLS with graphics," the report concluded.

There it was, buried in the paper that was to launch a computer network that would stretch around the globe and tie together people in fundamentally new ways. Doug Engelbart's NLS tool was intended to be the first "killer app." The term would become popular a decade later. It referred to a software application that would drive a new wave of growth in the computing industry.

But before that could happen, the low-level task of writing the software to permit remote log-ins and file transfers had to be written. Two days after Crocker's RFC 1, Duvall wrote RFC 2. The document specified an "initial checkout" process to verify that the host computers at UCLA and SRI were actually talking to each other.

At the time, Duvall didn't realize he would also have to actually write the code that he described in the document. SRI had originally contracted the work out to Creative X, a small software-consulting company belonging to Alan Kay and another University of Utah graduate student, Steve Carr. A young woman who had just graduated with a computer-science degree was delegated the actual task of writing the program.

However, as the deadline approached for the first communication, it became clear that the woman was in over her head. Bill English came to Duvall and asked him if he could pitch in and write the routines that would make it possible to permit remote log-ins to the SDS-940 computer.

In RFC 2, Duvall had specified that UCLA and SRI should have a telephone link at the same time they made the first ARPAnet transmission. During the afternoon of October 29, 1969, everything seemed ready, but then the Sigma 7 computer at UCLA crashed, and the two groups waited hours while the southern California computer was restarted. Finally, late in the evening, both computers were running, and the two research labs were ready to repeat the exercise.

As it was recalled by Charley Kline, a UCLA undergraduate who was on the southern California side of the conversation, over a noisy phone line he said, "I'm going to type an L!" Then he keyed it in.[8] (To connect to the remote machine, it was necessary to type "LOGIN.")

From the other end of the phone line, Duvall responded, "I got 114," the base-eight numerical representation of an L.

Everything worked fine until they reached "G," and then the SRI system crashed. Duvall had programmed a feature called "command completion" into the system, and so when the SDS-940 had seen the G it had echoed back "GIN," overwhelming its single-character memory buffer. Duvall debugged the problem, and an hour later they completed the first log-in session over the fledgling network. From his perspective, the event had none of the drama of the first telephone conversation: "Mr. Watson—come here—I want to see you."

Thinking about the power of a network of computers instead of a single machine required a shift in perspective that was slow in coming for many people. Electronic mail did not come to the ARPAnet until almost two years later. But some people got the idea right away, realizing the network gave them new freedom. By the end of 1969, both Bill Duvall and Don Andrews, the young programmer who had

come to Augment from the University of Washington, had independently moved to rural Sonoma County. Neither of them was caught
up in the spirit of the commune of the late sixties, but they both
shared the back-to-the-land ethos that resonated with Brand's *Whole
Earth Catalog* worldview. While Andrews built his own house with
trees that he had cut down on his property, Duvall purchased a small
plane and commuted to work on a weekly basis from his roost in the
country.

Separately, the two men became the world's first telecommuters.
Engelbart was interested in having a remote version of NLS built to
make it possible to use the system widely and spread its utility beyond Menlo Park. Duvall agreed as a condition of his relocation to
program a simple version of the software that would enable him to
work remotely via a telephone line.

From his cabin in the rolling California hills, Andrews became
one of the first people to exploit the power of the ARPAnet. The Augment project was in the process of moving from its SDS-940 computer to a more modern Digital PDP-10, and Andrews needed some
way to test the programs he was writing on the newer computer before it arrived at SRI. It proved to be an ideal opportunity to test the
fledgling network. There was a PDP-10 at the University of Utah,
and so Andrews transferred his program file from Menlo Park to
Utah and then ran it remotely, all from a log cabin in the backwoods
of northern California.

He found the whole concept to be humorous. In the middle of the
night when something went wrong, he would call the computer operator of the PDP-10 in Utah and ask him to do something like
mount a file or reset a piece of equipment. Often, the operator
wouldn't even know that the Utah computer was networked, and Andrews would have to tell him: "Go over to the far corner of the room
where that box is sitting and flip switches three and five and press
the button."9

Now that the network finally existed, it should have been the crowning glory of Engelbart's system for augmenting the human intellect. NLS should have become the original killer app.

It wasn't. The limited bandwidth of the new network, coupled with the intricacies of using NLS, conspired against Engelbart's vision of spreading his system to knowledge workers around the world. For all its power, the NLS system's lack of a welcoming audience beyond SRI was ultimately Engelbart's greatest failure. For those who mastered its complexities, NLS offered editing, retrieval, and communications capabilities that in many ways have not been matched today. But the system was not easy to learn, it required training and a significant personal commitment, and its availability via the ARPAnet did not draw a flood of users.

Responding to the pressure from ARPA to use some of the resources of their new network, John McCarthy at SAIL attempted to use NLS by entering one of his research papers into the system. The experience was a disappointing one. McCarthy recoiled at the hierarchical structure that NLS impressed upon its users. The system, he discovered, forced each document to be broken into chunks of no greater size than one thousand characters and to be in an outline structure. The process was so laborious that when he finished he decided that he had no interest in going through the process again, whatever the benefits. McCarthy came to view both Engelbart's and Ted Nelson's ideas on text editing and hypertext as too dictatorial. He decided structure was imposing an unnecessary restriction on his thought process.

The structure imposed by NLS, which researchers like McCarthy detested, coupled with the training required to become an expert user and the limited network bandwidth that forced network users to use the more awkward remote version of NLS, ultimately became the system's downfall. Moreover, not long after the 1968 demonstration, even while the project continued to grow in numbers, a steady brain drain began taking place from the Augment lab.

Opposition to the Vietnam War was mounting, and the student

movement was increasingly discovering links between the Pentagon and the universities. At Stanford, teach-ins had begun in the spring of 1965. Activists were not yet dominant, however, for that year students from ROTC classes had, at a White Plaza rally against the war, pelted speakers with garbage. By 1968, however, the mood on campus had changed dramatically. In the fall, the Stanford SDS had issued a demand that the university and its subsidiary Stanford Research Institute end all military and Southeast Asia research being done on campus. In March of the following year, the issue sharpened as student activists put increasing pressure on the board of trustees, which included executives from Lockheed, Hewlett-Packard, and other major corporations.[10]

That April, a range of student antiwar groups demanded, in addition to the end of this research, closer control of the laboratory by the university. After the trustees refused to act, more than nine hundred students met on campus, and the majority voted to seize the Applied Electronics Laboratory in protest. One of those who joined the occupation was a young faculty member at SAIL, Jerry Feldman.

Feldman was in an odd position. He was one of the most militant New Left faculty on campus, but at the same time he was in an administrative position at SAIL. He frequently attended ARPA contractor meetings with Les Earnest, where progress reports on projects were presented. There, he and Bob Taylor would have odd conversations.

"You're building robots," Taylor would say. "If we asked you to build a robot that would go down in the tunnels to shoot and kill Vietnamese, would you do it?"

"Absolutely not," Feldman replied.

"That doesn't matter," Taylor said. "The question is if someone from Congress or the press asked you if you would do it, what would you tell them?"

"I'd say I wouldn't be able to do it," Feldman responded.

"Then we won't be able to fund you," Taylor said.

It was just weeks after an LSD arrest, and Feldman was taking a

great personal risk by joining the students in occupying the building. But then something happened that made the whole situation
surreal.

As the students were settling in for a long stay, Feldman noticed
that one of the nerdiest of the SAIL hackers, who he knew had absolutely no political views, showed up.

"What are you doing here?" he asked.

"They told me there is a piece of equipment broken, and I have to
fix it," he replied.

Once inside the "liberated" research laboratory, the students began producing a daily paper, leaflets, and pamphlets, using a printing press they had found in the basement of the building. They
discovered incriminating documents, including one professor's
work on "electronic countermeasures" for the U.S. Air Force. Classified military contracts had been altered to make it appear to the public as if they were basic scientific research.

The occupiers voted to leave the AEL building only after Stanford
promised to end classified research on campus. However, the university still had a direct relationship to SRI. The following month, on
May 16, a pitched battle was fought in the streets of the Stanford Industrial Park as more than five hundred students attempted to
blockade SRI's offices there. Tear gas was used, sixteen demonstrators were arrested, and ninety warrants were issued based on photos
taken by right-wing students.

The next day, students marched on SRI's Menlo Park headquarters. Inside Doug Engelbart's group, there was a brief attempt to use
the new NLS as part of a command center in case the demonstrators
tried to storm the buildings. But the protests were peaceful compared to those in the industrial park.

While demonstrators outside the gates of SRI had made an impact on many of the researchers inside, others remained more or
less unmoved. Bill Duvall was so deeply involved in the innards of
NLS that he barely noticed. He was sitting at his terminal programming when someone said, "The demonstrators are outside." He

briefly got up and went to the window and looked out and then returned to his work. But for others, the presence of the demonstrators created an agonizing time of reassessment. When Hew Crane, Engelbart's coworker from the 1950s, learned of an SRI management plan to ring the perimeter of the labs with a barbed-wire fence, he wrote a letter to the director of security, warning him about what kind of a message that would send.

For David Casseres, the demonstrators' appearance carried with it a stronger message. He realized that he was on the wrong side of the picket line. He had previously gone to the several antiwar marches in Berkeley. Now feelings that had been swirling inside him for a long time were brought to a sharp focus, and not long afterward he decided it was time to leave. He quit and joined a Gandhian commune in Oregon that called its farm Ithilien, a name taken from the *Lord of the Rings* trilogy.

■■■

The Vietnam war, drugs, sexual liberation, women's liberation, the Black Panthers, the human-potential movement, the back-to-the-land movement—at the end of the 1960s, all of these were concentrating with wicked force on the San Francisco Peninsula. And in the midst of the chaos, Doug Engelbart felt that he was beginning to lose control of his vision, the Augmentation Framework.

Everything seemed to be in dispute, even the name of the laboratory, which had for several years been the Augmented Human Intellect Research Center (AHIRC). Although it expressed Englebart's vision precisely, it seemed top-heavy to many of his young researchers. At his low "yoga" workstation, Bill Duvall began flying what amounted to a pirate flag by displaying an abbreviated ARC, for Augmentation Research Center. Finally, after much debate Engelbart agreed to the name change. Thereafter, he was occasionally referred to affectionately as Noah.

Nonetheless, it was an increasingly painful time for Engelbart, who felt isolated as he was pushed and pulled about by his team. He felt that everyone wanted to go in different directions, and nobody was willing to talk to him in terms of his beloved framework. The programmers met separately, the women met separately, and things increasingly seemed to be beyond his control. Years later, he referred to the period as the "beginning of the end" and recalled the pain it gave rise to. He began to feel increasingly lonely and isolated.

In trying to build the organization, Engelbart had found that he didn't understand how to make it scale up while remaining focused on his mission. It was a little bit like giving your teenager the keys to the car for the first time and finding that she has immediately taken it to the beach. He felt a growing sense of frustration as his carefully nurtured group struggled to seize control of his system.

Things began unraveling just as the Augment lab was going through its period of fastest growth. ARC went from being a band of gypsies to a real organization with an actual organizational structure. Engelbart was looking for help in containing his obstreperous work group and felt hammered by people who thought that ARC should be run differently. Frustrated that he could not convey his vision to his researchers, Engelbart sought out Jim Fadiman, the young psychologist who had studied the effects of LSD in graduate school at Stanford and who had worked at Myron Stolaroff's International Foundation for Advanced Study. Engelbart had met him three years earlier when he had experimented with psychedelics, and now he renewed his connection. For more than a year, Fadiman served as a consultant for the researchers, who came to refer to him as the "group shrink." Coming in just one or two days a week, he attempted to sort out the group dynamics with an informal "walk around" approach to observing the workings of the lab. He would stroll into an office and close the door and say, "Tell me how you're feeling."

What Fadiman discovered was an odd mélange of straight engineers and counterculture types. He noted with some bemusement that one of Engelbart's secretaries quietly prepared an astrological chart of each job candidate before he was hired, keeping the results to herself.

Fadiman could see immediately that one major problem of the Augment Group was that it had no management except Engelbart. The psychologist set about creating responsible managers so that every decision in the ARC group didn't need to go through its leader. He could tell that the SRI computer scientist had a vision that he saw quite clearly but was much less obvious to those who worked for him. To many of the young programmers and hardware designers, it seemed as if they had been commanded to follow King Arthur, who was always in the mist. Fadiman could feel their devotion to the cause; the problem was sorting out and actually implementing the vision.

He could also appreciate that Engelbart was unique—his passion was so strong it was almost a psychological state. Fadiman came to Augment meetings and acted as a facilitator, watching the reactions of the team members, gently stopping Engelbart when blank expressions began to form on the faces of his researchers. He would then say, "I don't think so-and-so understood that." He never touched the computers; he simply sat in and listened and attempted to get the group back on track when it threatened to descend into confusion.

The event that best symbolized the disconnect between Engelbart's original vision and the new atmosphere of exploration and dissent that was sweeping through his laboratory was an attempt by Dave Evans to create a meeting of the minds between the Augment researchers and the counterculture community animated by the *Whole Earth Catalog*. Although Evans was close to Engelbart, he was also one of the members of the lab who was connected to Stewart Brand as well as to Jim Fadiman and the human-potential ideas he was exploring.

Evans decided that he would become the interface between the super-straight world of information technology, SRI, and the wild and free world of the embryonic alternative society that was blossoming on the Peninsula.[11] He felt that a lot of the ideas about community that Brand was exploring and the ideas that Engelbart had about a "bootstrapped community" were on the same continuum, and so he started to actively encourage a dialogue between the two worlds. Engelbart, he believed, had a receptive mind.

In 1969, at Evans's urging, Engelbart took a small group of Augment researchers to visit a commune known as Lama that had been started by Steve Durkee and Steve Baer in the mountains north of Taos, New Mexico. Baer was a disciple of Buckminster Fuller and the creator of a novel type of domelike building called a "zome." Durkee was an artist who was Brand's former roommate and mentor/guru.

As hard as Evans tried to bridge the gap, he ended up increasing the stress on Engelbart, who in principle was open to new ideas but who was increasingly obsessing over losing control of his group. Evans continued in his quest and in doing so became one of the main players in organizing the Paradam Conference, an event held on a farm near Santa Barbara the weekend after the Woodstock music festival.

The conference was based on ideas put forward in 1928 by René Daumal, the French alpinist, poet, surrealist, and pupil of George Ivanovich Gurdjieff. The philosophy was based on the idea of the existence of a sacred mountain for the modern world—a peak that is, by definition, impossible to climb. In his novel *Mount Analogue*, Daumal wrote: "For a mountain to play the role of Mount Analogue, its summit must be inaccessible, but its base accessible to human beings as nature has made them. It must be unique, and it must exist geographically. The door to the invisible must be visible." Evans believed this was a perfect philosophical representation for the challenge that Engelbart had set before him in attempting to scale the power of the human intellect.

The event brought together a group of half a dozen of the Augment researchers, including Evans, English, Duvall, Irby, and several others, with Stewart Brand, Steve Baer, and Steve Durkee. Paradam—the term meant "a view through a small lens"—was an effort to tie the two kinds of communities together. Evans believed Engelbart's bootstrapping vision depended on getting a whole host of people on board if he was ever to reach beyond the computer-science types at SRI.

The event itself was a success. Also in attendance were people from Pacific High School, an alternative school located in the mountains behind Stanford, and the Hog Farm, a commune that was then based on a mountaintop near Los Angeles, did the cooking. The Texas Inflatables, a group of New Age architects, created a futuristic plastic environment to walk through.

It was a watershed in many ways. Up until the time of Paradam, the focus of the Augment Group had been on the hardware and software tools; now it was shifting toward a mix of technology and human tools and systems. It was one thing to invent the mouse and prove it was ergonomically superior. It was something else entirely to try to persuade people to work in teams and follow procedures that went against deeply ingrained behaviors in an effort to find ways to increase productivity. It was even harder to attempt to do this in the midst of the growing chaos of the counterculture and the antiwar protests. The Augment lab was developing a real energy of its own, but Engelbart couldn't cope with an eclectic vision that wasn't his. Although he was invited, Engelbart didn't attend the weekend retreat. He didn't like the idea. It was just another symptom of his loss of control of his vision.

6 | SCHOLARS AND BARBARIANS

Years later, Alan Kay observed that you could divide the pioneers of personal computing into two camps: those who read and those who didn't.

When personal computing finally blossomed in Silicon Valley in the mid-seventies, it did so largely without the benefit of any of the history and the research that had gone before it. As a consequence, the personal-computer industry would be deformed for years, creating a world of isolated desktop boxes, in contrast to the communities of shared information that had been pioneered in the sixties and early seventies.

Interactive computing in the sixties had largely been the province of a few scattered laboratories: SAIL, SRI, MIT, and Bolt, Beranek & Newman. Mainstream computing was an exercise in remoteness: You took your problem, captured it in a stack of cards, surrendered it to the priesthood guarding the glass-encased computing machine, and then came back the next day to get the answer on reams of computer-printout paper.

But the potential of computing power had gradually begun leaking out to a widening audience. Seduced by a vision of computing as an interactive medium, as embodied by Steve Russell's Spacewar game, or computing as a tool for augmenting the human intellect, as dramatized by Doug Engelbart's FJCC demonstration, more and more outsiders wanted in. They were mostly young men who had

had enough contact to lust after their own machines, and frequently they weren't even sure what they would do with one once they got it. They were simply captivated by the allure of complex, controllable technology with which they could explore their fantasies.

One of the first people to sense this hunger for computing power was an itinerant former aerospace engineer named Bob Albrecht. Albrecht had first come into contact with computers at the Aeronautical Division of the Honeywell Corporation in Minneapolis during the 1950s. He was intrigued from the beginning, but the computer that he was working with at the time was an IBM 650. Though it didn't inspire a personal bond, it did whet his appetite for more.

He was a skier at the time, and so when he learned that the Burroughs Corporation was entering the computer market, he took a job that allowed him to move to Colorado, where he taught people how to program the Burroughs 205. Albrecht had a math background and was interested in science applications for computing, not the business applications he was teaching. He stayed for a while, but then left for a job he thought would be more interesting, as a research mathematician at the Martin aerospace company in Denver.[1]

That, however, turned out to be a grim experience, as most of his work involved simulating nuclear war. His computers were still using punched cards, but they were transistor-based machines, and somewhat less expensive than the tube-based mainframes that preceded them. He was struck by the fact that his coworkers had no moral qualms about what they were doing. He would run simulations of a war in which forty million people might die in the United States, and his coworkers would be enthusiastic because 120 million would be killed off in the Soviet Union.

The idea of calculating megadeaths finally unnerved him, and so after a year and a half he left Martin to take a job with another computer maker, Control Data Corporation. CDC had just opened a new office in Denver, and his job title was senior applications analyst. It meant teaching programming, and he even found himself teaching a course in remedial Fortran for people who had gone to IBM programming school for a week but hadn't learned anything.[2] Along with his other chores, he began to teach a small group of high school students how to program. He had always taken a get-in-the-water-and-get-wet approach to programming, but in an upper-middle-class Denver high school he had one of those lightbulb-goes-off, changes-your-life experiences. While the adults he had been teaching had all kinds of hang-ups about working with computers, the kids had no such fears. They took to computers enthusiastically. He was teaching with a CDC 160 minicomputer, the same machine on which Doug Engelbart had begun his augmentation research.

The class became extremely popular, and soon the University of Colorado was offering an extension program that involved more than one hundred high school kids. Albrecht took his class on tour, at one point accompanying some of the students from the original Denver school to a National Computer Conference meeting. There they demonstrated their programming skills on the CDC 160 machine, shocking the high priests of computing. At the general conference meeting, there were subsequent complaints that someone had even considered turning children loose on computers! Albrecht, who was already pretty irreverent, simply informed his critics that he had even had success teaching fourth graders to program using Fortran. Later, when he discovered BASIC, he immediately dropped Fortran and began teaching the simpler programming language, which was much more accessible to ordinary people. He even had cards and buttons made up that read "SHAFT—Society to Help Abolish Fortran Teaching."

Like Doug Engelbart and Alan Kay, Albrecht had been introduced early on to the concept of microelectronic scaling. In 1963, Control Data had sent him on a mission to California to discuss educational issues. The company had recently acquired the Bendix Corporation and was hoping to sell Bendix G15 systems to schools. While he was in California, he paid a visit to Sid Fernbach, a pioneering physicist at Lawrence Livermore Laboratory, one of the nation's weapons-design centers. Fernbach had long been intensely interested in education for children. The physicist was a pioneer of scientific computing and several years later was one of the people who coined the term "supercomputer." The two men went on several long walks, chatting about the future of computing. The conversation kept returning to Fernbach's vision of a five-hundred-dollar hand-held machine, a vision that stuck with Albrecht.

Ultimately, he moved back to Minneapolis and created his own job at CDC, which involved producing what he called a traveling medicine show. He would tour the country with a computer and recruit a group from the local high school as volunteers to demonstrate the ease of the process. He would have the kids run their first program within an hour and then write another, and then another, and soon they would be paired off to work on a project as part of a competition for a national convention. He logged over one hundred thousand miles per year, and with his engaging style would frequently set off a frenzy of enthusiasm. It was great fun, but he could keep up the travel schedule for only so long.

In fact, Bob Albrecht was not long for the corporate world. He had never felt completely comfortable in buttoned-down corporate America, and when he left Control Data in 1964 he instantly gave away all of his business suits. He began freelancing, and one day while at work on his first book for Addison-Wesley, *Computer Methods and Mathematics,* he realized there had been twenty-three consecutive days of below-zero weather. "Why am I writing this book here when I could be writing in San Francisco?"[3] he asked himself. He was divorced from his first wife, and California was calling.

He showed up in San Francisco in early 1966 and eventually took an apartment at the top of Lombard, near North Beach. At the time he was still pretty traditional, and his plan was to continue to work as a freelance writer. He had already received a second contract—to write a book for computer math education. But during his first week in town he wandered into Minerva, a Greek restaurant on Eddy Street. He had never been a dancer, but there was something about the Greek music he heard that night that captured his spirit. He plunged into the world of Greek folk dancing. Soon, he was hosting his own Tuesday-evening events combining Greek dancing, computer programming, and wine tasting.

At about this time, he met Dick Raymond, the former SRI consultant. When Albrecht described his social evenings, Raymond responded that he had a nonprofit foundation and that he was looking for a way to explore new educational ideas. It all sounded like great fun, and so Albrecht, who had just remarried, moved to Menlo Park. He hadn't lost any of his passion for Greek dancing, and he decided to offer a class at the Free University. The events were soon thriving, and as luck would have it, a number of them were held in the Atherton backyard of Doug Engelbart, another folk-dancing devotee.

Raymond and Albrecht soon transformed Raymond's nonprofit into the Portola Institute, housed in downtown Menlo Park just off El Camino Real. There wasn't a lot of money involved. Initially, Raymond put in some, as did Hewlett-Packard. It wasn't much for an eclectic handful of staff, which included Stewart Brand and eventually Fred Moore, and essentially just helped cover a desk and a base of operations.

The board of directors was as eclectic as the institute's projects. There was Richard Baker Roshi, the head of the San Francisco Zen Center; Huey Johnson, of the Trust for Public Land; Michael Phillips, the San Francisco banker who would author *The Seven Laws of Money;* and Fanny Schaftel, the head of the education department at Stanford University, among others. The idea was to be radical and exploratory, and the motto of the group was "Fail young." People would literally walk in off the streets with ideas, and the only control mechanism was that the foundation kept careful books and knew exactly what it was funding.

The Portola Institute also served as the umbrella for Dymax, a for-profit publishing spin-off that took its name from Buckminster Fuller's term "Dymaxion"—the conglomeration of "dynamic" and "maximize." Young Marc LeBrun, the SAIL urchin, came up with the idea of using the term. The venture started in a warehouse in Redwood City and soon thereafter spawned a newsletter called the *People's Computer Company*. (The name was derived from Janis Joplin's San Francisco–based rock band, Big Brother and the Holding Company.) The cover of the first issue featured a hand-drawn sketch done by LeBrun, who would become one of the young people who helped make up Albrecht's rank-and-file computer hobbyists. Across the top was written: "Until now computers have been used against people, now it's time for a People's Computer Company."

The secret was out. It was no longer obvious only to engineers and programmers who had access to corporate computers, or to scattered visionaries such as Stewart Brand, that computers could be used for more than just crunching numbers. They were captivating even in their most primitive state—machines that had to be laboriously programmed by toggling switches to enter individual instructions. There was a hidden universe inside the computer, and Albrecht held one key to it.

He created a technology center with his personal imprimatur—as you walked through the doorway, you were confronted by a simulated Greek taverna with tables, a dance floor, blinking Christmas-tree lights, and a slide projector that every fifteen seconds projected another scene from Greece on a large wall.

When Dymax moved to a tiny shopping center in Menlo Park, a "People's Computer Center" was created in the adjacent office, and it soon offered terminals connecting to a time-sharing computer service. People could walk in and program or play games—not Spacewar, which required an expensive and costly graphics display, but rather interactive text-based simulations. Little more than text printed on paper by teletypewriter terminals, the games were still remarkably compelling. The computers, without even the blocky graphics of the first personal computers, were powerful fantasy machines. They were electronic and interactive, and it was possible to become lost in the midst of worlds they created, which were as completely compelling as those invented by any book.

Not long after the center opened, a PDP-8 minicomputer showed up, which Albrecht had arranged to acquire in trade for his technical-writing work. The machine was delivered to Albrecht's house in Menlo Park, which at the time was empty. (He was living out another dream—residing with his new wife and young son on a boat at the yacht harbor in Redwood City.) On the day the computer arrived, LeBrun said he would look after the machine. He was in heaven. He didn't immediately realize that the computer needed a paper-tape reader to input its programs, and, indeed, no software came with the machine, which included only a terse manual. That night, he figured out how to manually input the software to permit the computer to read commands from its keyboard. He entered a low-level program by laboriously toggling it into the computer's memory using a set of switches on the front panel.

By trial and error he managed to bring the keyboard reader software most of the way to life, but it took him all night. When he finished, dawn was breaking and he was so exhausted that he collapsed on a couch. Later that day he woke up and realized he had been sleeping on his back with his mouth open and his tongue had dried out. It was a weird feeling; for a moment he felt like he had woken up with a lizard in his mouth. It didn't matter. LeBrun was ecstatic. He had gotten closer than ever before to having his own computer!

LeBrun was only one of thousands of kids who Bob Albrecht turned on to the power of computing. Albrecht became the Pied Piper of the PC, intent on bringing the power of computing to the people. At one of his Greek-dancing events, he was chatting with Doug Engelbart about computing and kids, and Engelbart said, "Hey, why don't you bring some of these kids over to our laboratory some evening?" For months afterward, every Wednesday night the Augment laboratory would allow groups of ecstatic teenagers to play with the future of computing.

...

That's the kind of place the PCC was: hands-on, run in part by volunteers, and in tune with the power-to-the-people spirit of the late sixties. It wasn't surprising, then, when a bearded draft resister and peace activist named Fred Moore wandered in and soon made himself at home. Fred Moore had won his war of conscience with the University of California, and in the fall of 1962, after the school had finally made ROTC voluntary, he had reentered as a junior, majoring in mathematics. He didn't last long as a student, however, as university life seemed to be increasingly irrelevant to the things he cared about. In January 1963, he withdrew from school and went to work for the Catholic Worker peace organization at St. Elijah's Hospitality House in Oakland.

A tiny peace movement had recently sprung up on American college campuses, led by groups such as the National Committee for a SANE Nuclear Policy, Peacemakers, Turn Toward Peace, and the Student Peace Union, as well as dozens of small newsletters, magazines, and dissident journals. Moore became active in the Committee for Non-Violent Action, one of the first American peace organizations to focus on civil disobedience. In the aftermath of the Cuban missile crisis, he participated in the racially integrated Quebec-Washington-Guantánamo Walk for Peace. The walk began in 1963 in Quebec with groups from other cities expanding its numbers. In Atlanta, some of the marchers were beaten and jailed, and civil rights became a significant issue. Once again, Moore made it only as far as Florida; because of a U.S. ban on travel to Cuba, the marchers stopped in Miami.

After the march, he moved to a CNVA communal farm on forty wooded acres in Voluntown, Connecticut. Although Vietnam had still not become a major issue for Americans, Moore became more deeply involved in the draft-resistance movement. He returned his draft card, and he toured the country several times, speaking out in favor of noncooperation with the Selective Service system. In 1965, he was indicted, tried, and convicted for refusing the draft and was sentenced to serve two years in Allenwood federal penitentiary in Pennsylvania. He refused parole and ended up spending seventeen months in jail, his release coming in April 1967.

By then, the war in Vietnam had exploded onto the front pages of the nation's papers, and a growing draft-resistance movement was sweeping its campuses. In the spring of 1966, David Harris had been elected as president of the student body at Stanford by calling for student independence, equal treatment for male and female students, legalization of marijuana, the end of the board of trustees, and the end of all university cooperation with the war. Later that year, Harris drew national attention when Stanford fraternity members shaved his head to show their disdain for his political views.

Vietnam was rapidly becoming the defining issue at the nation's universities, and the conflict was particularly intense at schools like Stanford, where professors were doing classified research aiding the war effort. Moreover, Stanford, unlike most universities, had active institutions such as the Stanford Research Institute and the Applied Electronics Laboratory that had significant military-contracting operations.

That relationship, which students began describing as the "military-industrial-academic complex," had been formed by design. Stanford's academic laboratories had been instrumental in creating a fledgling electronics industry on the Peninsula as early as the 1920s, and after the Second World War, Frederick Terman, first as dean of the Engineering School and later as Stanford's provost, set about building "a community of technical scholars," an idea that had first come to him at the university and had been refined during the period he spent as director of the Radio Research Laboratory at Harvard during World War II. The community's vision was taken from Terman's reading of history. He envisioned an enclave much like the medieval centers of learning such as Heidelberg, Paris, and Oxford that would debate both new ideas and challenges.[4] By the mid-sixties, that community, which had originally been rooted in the

Stanford Industrial Park just south of campus, was sprawling rapidly into the Santa Clara Valley fruit orchards. The region had already given rise both to a commercial and a military-based electronics industry, and Stanford was playing a crucial role in both arenas.

For students who had moral qualms about America's war in Asia, the relationship of the university to the war effort became an obvious target. As the antiwar movement grew, on-campus specialized student groups sprang up to engage in "power structure research," following in the steps of sociologist C. Wright Mills. One of the first things the young researchers discovered was that supposedly pure academic work frequently involved Pentagon-funded projects directly tied to the Southeast Asian war.

On the Stanford campus, the antiwar movement coalesced in the mid-sixties around draft resistance. It began with a group of young men led by David Harris. Struck by what they believed was the increasingly immoral nature of America's involvement in Southeast Asia, they created an individualist political movement. Borrowing from the ideas of Albert Camus and Martin Buber, the students began wrestling with the complexities of their own middle-class privilege. Before long, there was even a distinctive resistance dialect, and hundreds of political activists were copying the personal style of the movement's leaders. They would gesture white-rapper style while making seemingly profound statements like, "What's important is the way we learn to live our lives, from day to day to day."[5]

In 1968, Harris married Joan Baez, giving the draft resistance a streak of national media visibility. Shortly thereafter, he began serving a two-year sentence in a federal prison in Texas for resisting the draft, leaving a leadership vacuum in the movement. At the same time, the resistance was giving way to more conventional leftist politics in the form of the Students for a Democratic Society chapter, which became increasingly focused on issues of class, imperialism, and racism.

While antiwar and draft-resistance movements were growing on campus, most students clung to their deferments as the easiest way of avoiding the war. There were also tens of thousands of draft-age young men who figured out increasingly novel ways of avoiding the draft, whether it was a letter from a psychiatrist, an old injury, or the sudden inability to pass a hearing test. Failing that, there was Canada. Thousands of other young men fled there, and tens of thousands more were considering it as an option.

An alternative way to avoid the draft was to obtain a "critical industries deferment." And as luck would have it, in the mid-sixties, working in either Doug Engelbart's Pentagon-funded laboratory at SRI or at John McCarthy's AI laboratory at Stanford University would qualify a bright, technically oriented, draft-age young man for just such a deferment.

It was into this world that Fred Moore stepped when he moved to Palo Alto in December 1968. Committed to organizing against the draft, he decided that by persuading the sons of the well-to-do to resist he would have a greater impact.[6] Palo Alto was a perfect setting: the location of the national resistance headquarters and in close proximity to Stanford University and its elite students.

Moore fell in with the Palo Alto draft resistance, which was focusing much of its efforts in attempting to stop draftees at the army induction center across the bay in Oakland. The center itself was a little gallery of horrors, and anyone who ventured inside in the late sixties confident that he might have thought of a scam or a ruse for avoiding the draft would quickly realize the competition was intense. There were young men hanging onto pillars, there were guys talking to themselves, there were guys crying, and there were even guys playing with themselves. Outside, draft protesters were arrested in waves.

The Palo Alto resistance itself presented a classic example of many of the problems that plagued the New Left in the sixties. Although nominally a democratic organization, it was in fact dominated by a small group of young white men. The women did the support work of cooking, cleaning, and running the mimeograph machines. In this world, Moore found himself an outsider. He began to identify with the younger members of the resistance, largely high school dropouts who were facing the draft immediately, and distinguished himself by being among the most militant of the resisters. The group began to focus its organizing efforts on Los Altos High School, an affluent school in a Silicon Valley suburb near Palo Alto. The project consisted of going to campus and trying to engage the students in discussions about the draft. School officials barred the draft resisters, and Moore was arrested several times. He took his noncooperation seriously. When police came to eject the activists, he would go limp, refusing to make any concession to them. As a result, he was beaten up several times.

To Chris Jones, an eighteen-year-old Los Altos High School dropout and a member of the Palo Alto resistance, it appeared that Moore actually constituted a movement of one person, even in an organization that championed individual conscience.[7] There was something inside Fred Moore that set him apart.

There was something else that set him apart: his three-year-old daughter, Irene.

Fred's first wife was Susie "Xenia" Williams. Actually, the two were never formally married. Xenia had been active in the antidraft movement, and they had met during a peace march in April of 1967. Then, some months later, they both wanted to participate in a Committee for Non-Violent Action project that required couples to have a "permanently responsible relationship." They accordingly had a "permanently responsible relationship" ceremony.

Before long, they discovered they weren't in love and that they didn't even like being around each other very much. Xenia was nineteen, and Fred was twenty-six, and she was two months pregnant. She was also in the midst of deciding that she was gay and that the "whole child thing" was too much for her.

They separated, but Fred's sense of romanticism and responsibility led him to urge Xenia to try to get back together or, failing that, to let him keep the child. So in 1968, when Irene was born in a hospital in Northampton, Massachusetts, Xenia's mother went there to claim the infant and help arrange the papers that gave Fred guardianship.

Fred and Irene quickly made their way to California, where father and daughter became itinerants, living in rooms in communal houses in various towns around the Midpeninsula—Menlo Park, Mountain View, Palo Alto—and over the hills in Santa Cruz, the tiny beach town, which had only recently achieved college-town status.

Although he wore his hair long with a bushy beard and sported a rainbow belt, Fred Moore was not a hippie, either by inclination or work style. His father had fought in World War II in India, Burma, and China, and he had instilled a work ethic that crossed political lines. Life was not easy for a single father and a political activist who insisted on living on poverty wages to support his work as a full-time organizer. It meant that much of the time he was both breadwinner and day-care provider, often simultaneously. He frequently spent time on the Stanford campus, often for political meetings that went on for hours. One Saturday morning, a Stanford police officer was called to the Stanford bookstore after a store manager had watched a young girl wandering among the bookshelves aimlessly for more than half an hour. She was wearing pants and shoes but without a shirt. The officer approached the girl and found that someone had scrawled on her back in black marker:

I am not lost; my name is Chiqui (nickname). I live at 345 Willow Road, Menlo Park 325-5315. My daddy is here; his name is Fred Moore.[8]

Officer Calla recognized the young girl immediately; it was the second time she had been found in the bookstore that week. When her father had been tracked down the first time, he had explained to the officer that he had been attending an activist meeting called "A Conference on Alternatives" on the second floor of the Tresidder student union and had told his daughter to stay in the second-floor lobby. He said he became engrossed and had lost track of time. The People's Computer Company had brought some of their computer terminals to the event, and they were linked to a mainframe computer via phone lines, allowing people to play games and generally explore via the pokey modems of the day, which transmitted data at the snail-like speed of about thirty characters per second.

The event, which had been organized by Alan Strain, the radical educator who had once been head of the Peninsula School, proved a catalyst for Moore, the seed that inspired his yearning for his own computer to use as a political organizing tool. It was a unique moment in Silicon Valley history. Forgotten among the thousands of great fortunes since made from the personal-computing industry is the simple fact that the foundation for the industry was laid not by entrepreneurs but rather by a political activist and a group of hobbyists whose original motivation was sharing information.

It wasn't for lack of love that Moore had trouble keeping track of his daughter; he was just a bit overmatched for the challenges of both fatherhood and political organizing. In fact, had he been born in another era Fred Moore might have lived the ascetic life of a saint. Although he had no interest in organized religion, he struggled throughout much of his life with a quasi-religious commitment to Gandhian nonviolence as it was being practiced in the United States: changing the world by setting a perfect moral example and by putting your body in the way when the world didn't listen.

It was the era of "simple living." The New Left was discovering there was a vast imbalance in wealth and resources between the first and the third worlds, and many American activists decided that the best way to right it was by taking voluntary vows of poverty. It meant rejecting America's consumer society and living without energy-consuming devices like cars and all the other electronic gadgets that were rapidly becoming synonymous with middle-class existence.

The gap between privilege and poverty wracked Moore with guilt. He fretted constantly about all the issues and inequities that seemed to face him as an activist. He worried about the energy balance and how he was part of the problem because of the car he used to get around the Santa Clara Valley. "I wonder," he wrote in his journal, "about taking airplane trips to ecology conferences—we do so many contradictory things."9 He worried about male domination of society, noting in his journal that there were images only of men, and not of women or children, on our currency.

But life wasn't all self-vilification. Living as a marginal activist outside the middle class left lots of free time for adventures. Moore was an inveterate hitchhiker, and he regularly took off on open-ended journeys and backpacking trips, bouncing around the country with no fixed destination or timetable. He went camping in the Sierras and in Big Sur, wandering freely in the California wilderness.

Still, despite his membership in political groups and communal households, Moore frequently felt lonely and without a soul mate. Shortly after returning to the Bay Area, he became interested in the older sister of Chris Jones, the young draft resister. When Moore showed up one day at the Jones household in a coat and tie, Chris realized that Fred was in courting mode. Nothing came of the overture. For several years he lived with a woman who had a daughter who was Irene's age, but the relationship didn't last. Feeling isolated and a little desperate, he tried the personals column. His pitch wasn't quite "walking in the rain and drinking pina coladas," but it was certainly a heartfelt approach, from a radical's point of view:

> Looking for a strong, together feminist woman who is pursuing a career, vision, or meaningful cause and wants children. I am a human being, 34 years old, have been mother and father to my daughter, 7, since her birth, have been a nonviolent action radical in the past who now wants to settle down to be a devoted wife and homemaker. Are you she who knows she does need nurturing and understanding care if she is to accomplish her ambitions? Write Fred.10

Throughout his adventures and travails, one thing held reasonably constant: Moore had come to believe that money was the root of evil. "Due to money, we live by proxy," he wrote. "Our life is abstracted from us by the coin we exchange."

The evils of money might have remained his personal political obsession if Stewart Brand hadn't been suffering through deep bouts of depression and plunging into a nervous breakdown. The *Whole Earth Catalog* was a runaway success by 1971, after two years of increasingly popular publications. But Brand was barely holding it together emotionally. His marriage to Lois Jennings, the Native American woman he had fallen in love with after leaving the army, was beginning to crumble. There was tremendous pressure to make each new *Catalog* bigger and twice as impressive as the last, and the effort was beginning to overwhelm Brand. He had never had a break and found he had no idea how to take a vacation.

It seemed that things were starting to close in, and he began to feel agoraphobic. One evening, he went to see *The Swimmer,* a film based on a John Cheever story in which Burt Lancaster steadily goes mad as his world collapses. The movie shook Brand viscerally. He went back to the trailer where he was living on Alpine Road behind Stanford, thinking, *People can really lose it,* and then it occurred to him that maybe he was losing it, too. He kept up appearances, putting out the last *Catalog,* but began to contemplate suicide. In the end he went to several therapists, who helped him sort things out. He realized he was clinically depressed. He thought about the people around him for whom psychedelics had become an all-purpose cure and determined he wasn't going to use drugs as a crutch. Instead, he decided to get rid of things: first his marriage, and then the *Catalog.* With its staff, he arranged to throw a *Whole Earth Catalog* "Demise Party."

Brand had gotten to know Frank Oppenheimer, the founder of the Exploratorium science museum at the Palace of Fine Arts in the San Francisco Marina district, when he had helped Oppenheimer think through some of the museum's plans as it was being developed. So he decided to throw a party with a special twist. The *Whole Earth Catalog* rented the museum's building for an evening, and as a surprise Brand brought along twenty thousand dollars in cash in an inch-thick stack of hundred-dollar bills with the idea that, because he had started the *Catalog* with that amount, it would be fitting to put the money back out into the world and have other things start that might be equally interesting, in a what-goes-around-comes-around way.

It was an unusual event, even by the standards set several decades later during the height of the Internet boom. In the vernacular of the era, it was an out-of-sight party. The Exploratorium provided optical gadgets and illusions, and there were music, dancing, food, and drink. *Whole Earth Catalog* supporters from all over the country showed up, more than one thousand people in total.

No one told the audience what was afoot until a staffer named Scott Beach took the stage at midnight and said, "Sorry to stop the volleyball and the inhaling of nitrous oxide from balloons, but there is \$20,000 that is about to be handed out to the audience." He paused and added, "Oh, I see we have your attention."

Brand had a hypothesis that, under duress, people would come up with the most amazing ideas. It didn't work out that way. Later, he concluded that, rather, under duress people would come up with remarkably stupid ideas.

Brand himself now climbed onstage and said, "I can tell you from working around foundations for three years that they are absolutely strung out about how to use money. They don't know. If we don't know, we can't really complain about them. So we are into frontier territory here. And like on any other frontier we have got to get together and deal with our problem. It may be a creative problem, and that's our task—to find a creative way out of it."

A microphone was set up in the audience, the one-inch-thick envelope of hundred-dollar bills was handed to the crowd, and people started walking up to the mike, taking the envelope, stating what they thought should be done with the money and then handing it to the next person. Brand was dressed in an odd monk's black robe that had belonged to his father, a gesture that was meant as a gentle homage. He stood at a blackboard and began writing down the proposals as people made them in two- to four-word summaries. The hour kept getting later and people kept getting more and more raucous.

It turned out that the assembly had a lot of what Brand thought of as knee-jerk liberal ideas. One guy stood up and said, "Let's give the money back to the Indians."

That prompted Brand's wife, Lois, to go to the microphone and say, "I'm an Indian and I don't want the money."

At one point someone said, "This shouldn't be decided by one chunk. There are a lot of things that can be done with this money. Let's all decide." And then he grabbed a handful and started handing it out into the crowd.

Brand rushed back to the mike and said: "Hey, I think it is more interesting to talk about what to do with $20,000 than what to do with $100. Maybe the money will flow back to the stage."

And miraculously, the money did come back—at least $15,000 of it. The rest disappeared into the night.

In the end, the evening would be Fred Moore's shining moment. He had just returned from a trip to Mexico, and he was deeply involved in a project he had created called "Skool Resistance," which had grown from his draft resistance organizing in high schools as well as from some of the deschooling ideas of Ivan Illich, the radical Chilean educator. Moore, who was almost totally broke and living in a garage in a house on the Midpeninsula, had gotten a ride to the city and arrived that evening with two dollars in his pocket.

But after midnight, when the dispersal of the money was being debated, Moore got angry. This was just like all the bad things that money did everywhere else in the world, he decided. Early on he had gone up to the microphone, removed one of the dollar bills from his pocket, held it up in the air, and burned it. It was a little bit like the Yippies Jerry Rubin and Abbie Hoffman showering dollars onto the floor of the New York Stock Exchange. The point, he argued, was not about money, it was about people. He could see that the money that he so despised was being greeted as a savior and that people were being bought, which was typical. There were big arguments, and it was just the usual downer.

The argument continued, and the hour grew later and later. People

began leaving, and nobody seemed to have any idea that would fos-
ter anything like a group consensus. Out on the floor, Fred Moore
kept talking to people about his idea of helping people directly by
sharing information.

He went up to the microphone again and tried to make his point:
"Now what almost happened with this young person here, who I
don't know, he started to talk about a project that he wants to do in
which he didn't want money for. He wanted help; he wanted to get
together with others. And people yelled that was out of order. . . . Actually, for a moment there we were almost getting down to it. If we
are going to build a change—in a changing new world, or whatever
we want to call it, 'new age,' then it's going to be because we are going to work together and we are going to help each other."[11]

There it was. Out of Moore's frustration with money he was developing a clear idea of how you might go about building alternative
institutions. Call it Fred Moore's No Money Theory of Economics.
Although no one realized it at the time, several years later it would
become the heart of his initiative to build a computer club to share
resources and information freely. It was to lead to one of Silicon Valley's supreme ironies: That an itinerant activist who rejected material wealth as an end in itself ended up lighting the spark of what
became the "largest legal accumulation of capital in the twentieth
century: the PC industry," as venture capitalist John Doerr labeled it.
Indeed Moore would also become the unrecognized patron saint of
the open-source software movement, which in turn has become a
major force in the computer industry.

That evening, however, it was well past midnight and still no decision was reached. Someone finally stood up at the microphone
and read the *I Ching*, which decreed, "Undertakings bring misfor-
tune." Not a good omen.

Finally, there was a vote, just on the question of saving the money
versus spending it. But it ended up solving nothing. To shrieks and
general pandemonium, the vote ended in a 44–44 tie.

Moore stood up again and to applause said: "And I would like again to make my unpopular point—that why do we have to vote to divide this group? Why do you all believe in voting so much? Voting is not the best way to make decisions."

He kept talking, arguing that the people are more important than the rules and that people shouldn't be the pawns of money, but the other way around.

"I would like to suggest that some of us want to get to know each other and maybe write down our names and stick together and not necessarily think that everything just fragmented," he said, adding that he had begun working on a manifesto that might serve as a framework for an ongoing group that would decide what to do with the money. It began: "We feel that the beginning of a union of people here tonight is more important than letting a sum of money divide us."

And that's the way it would end. It was almost dawn, and the Demise Party had agreed to give the money to Fred Moore, with the idea that he would become the steward of the envelope. Stewart Brand just shook his head. It had been an interesting experiment, but he never really expected to see Moore again. *Maybe he'll send a postcard from Mexico,* Brand thought as he left the Exploratorium.

Brand had found a way to get out from under the *Whole Earth Catalog,* to walk away from it while he still had his sanity. For Fred Moore, however, it was like Frodo and the ring, a chapter right out of Tolkien: the ring brought power, but it was impossible to control it.

In the days that followed, Moore felt trapped by all this newfound power and its potential and just froze up. To him, banks were part of the problem, and so not knowing what else to do with the money, he went home and put it in a tin can and went outside in his backyard and buried it.

Word of the strange conclusion to the Demise Party spread quickly. After several newspaper accounts appeared, Moore was besieged with financial requests both by phone and mail.

And like Frodo's ring, the money wouldn't stay in the ground.

Despite his views on the institutions that controlled money, Moore was soon forcibly turned into a "people's banker" when a small group of San Francisco activists who were engaged in building a collective in a warehouse in a tattered neighborhood south of Market Street heard about the windfall. Project One was a single site that encompassed a diverse set of community political projects, ranging from education to organizing to theater to one of the first community time-sharing computer efforts, which was called Resource One and had become the final resting place for Doug Engelbart's SDS-940. Pam Hart, a charismatic Berkeley computer-science graduate student and activist who had been one of its cofounders, had talked the Transamerica Leasing Corporation into donating the machine. Ultimately, the project gave rise to Community Memory, a Berkeley computerized information network that lasted in several different forms into the 1980s.

A few Project One representatives decided to drive to Moore's home in order to make sure that the right thing was done with the money. They arrived one night and forcibly accompanied him out into the backyard, where he grudgingly dug up his tin can. In the end, Sherry Reson, one of the Project One people, was struck by the agony that was etched into his features over the decision about what to do with the money. She felt Moore was about to break down in tears as he walked out into the backyard to retrieve the can.

As uncomfortable as Moore was with the realities of capitalist economics, the Demise Party had propelled him on a quest for an information network to tie all of the community and political activists together. It proved to be a crucial step toward the world of personal computing. As unlikely as it would seem, outside of the computing mainstream, politics and community were converging with technology to create a computing renaissance in the world that was to become Silicon Valley.

■■■

Inside Stanford Research Institute, just the opposite was taking place. Doug Engelbart was still holding tightly to his Augment vision, but it was proving increasingly to be like herding cats. ARPA funding was flowing to it in ever-growing amounts, but as the ARC group grew, the messiness of dealing with all the realities of the staff and managing them proved to be a far knottier problem than writing software programs and building computer systems.

Not only was Engelbart struggling with his own group of engineers, programmers, hippies, hackers, and radicals, he was also still looking for a way to extend the NLS to a much wider world. Engelbart was an older figure in a group that was populated mostly with young engineers and brand-new computer scientists, most still in their twenties. They were growing up designing his system.

Engelbart had come up with a "concentric circles" strategy for expanding the Augment user base by making NLS available first to individuals, then to small groups, and finally to large organizations and ultimately entire industries. The renamed ARC was now being refashioned to be not just a research and software development organization but a sales and training group as well. Now there were real paying customers, the expanding ARPAnet to make NLS available anywhere in the nation, and a variety of new strategies to manage the organizational change that Engelbart hoped NLS would engender.

NLS, meanwhile, continued to add new features, including hypertext, multimedia, and screen sharing, but at the same time there were costs associated with the increasing power of the information tools. Every new feature meant added complexity and added training. For those who were part of the ARC group or committed to the Augment vision, the training was a minimal price to pay for the power that resulted. But for outsiders it presented an intimidating and bewildering array of commands to learn. NLS contained no "user interface" in the manner of modern computer graphical interfaces that are designed to make it easy for a novice computer user to master a range of commands.

For Engelbart, simple user interfaces were beside the point. At one meeting of the Augment programmers, he posed the question,

"When NLS is complete, how many instructions will it have?" He went around the room and asked everyone to answer. They were, of course, all wrong. The right answer was that NLS would eventually have fifty thousand instructions! That would require learning a language a significant fraction the size of English.

In the early seventies, the ARC group for the first time added a business manager. Jim Norton, an SRI business-development specialist, was hired in an attempt to make it more of a traditional business organization. Norton took over many of the responsibilities Bill English had been carrying in addition to his role as engineering manager.

The shift was a relief for English, who had been shouldering the hardware-engineering burden for all of Augment for more than five years. But the change came too late; he was burned out and decided he had contributed as much as he could to Engelbart's dream. In 1971, he quit. It was a painful separation for English, who had several long talks with Engelbart before leaving. They finally came to mutual agreement on his departure. He briefly took another job working with an SRI project developing computer systems for schools, but it soon became apparent the new project wasn't going anywhere.

Not long afterward, English received a call from Bob Taylor, the psychologist who had been instrumental in funding both Augment and the ARPAnet. After spending a year at the University of Utah, Taylor had been approached by Xerox and was busy recruiting a team to put together a computer-systems laboratory on the other side of the Stanford campus from SRI in the sprawling industrial park that was home to companies like Hewlett-Packard and Varian. With plans to challenge IBM in the office-computing market, Xerox was intent on buying itself into the technology race and was ready to spend freely to assemble a team of the nation's best computer researchers at a laboratory to be named the Xerox Palo Alto Research Center.

English had already been offered another job that would have taken him and his family to Spain to work for UNESCO. The idea of going abroad was intriguing, but English and his second wife, Roberta, both had children from previous marriages, which made leaving the country with their kids difficult.

As Taylor sketched out Xerox's ambitious plans to build an office system of the future, coupled with his own interest in taking Engelbart's NLS work and reengineering it in a more commercial setting, English grew excited and began to feel reenergized. Going to work for PARC was the obvious decision.

English became Augment's first great defection, but there were to be more. Over the next five years, a steady stream of the best talents that Doug Engelbart had assembled made their way to the Xerox lab. The exodus grew to such a degree that after a while the ARC researchers jokingly began referring to themselves as the Xerox Research Training Center. And although outwardly he was philosophical about the departures, Engelbart was left feeling bitter and increasingly vulnerable.

In addition to Engelbart's researchers, Taylor cherry-picked the best young researchers from around the country, as well as a team of hardware and software designers who had come by way of the Project Genie time-sharing project at Berkeley and a failed computer company, the Berkeley Computer Corporation. The group included Butler Lampson and Chuck Thacker, a brilliant software and hardware duo, as well as Peter Deutsch, a software wunderkind who had come to Berkeley by way of MIT and who had helped Engelbart's group develop software-design tools for their SDS-940 several years earlier.

Also recruited was Richard Shoup, a serious young electrical engineer who had graduated from Carnegie Mellon and came to Berkely Computer Corporation only a short time before it imploded. Shoup, who had grown up in Pennsylvania, was no radical, but he did have a clear sense of how information technology might empower people. He was an insider compared to the scruffy crowd that was hanging out on the other side of the Stanford campus at the

People's Computer Company, but his worldview was basically the same.

He understood that computers were coming to the office, and he believed there were only two companies that had the economic muscle to make it happen: IBM and Xerox. IBM, in his mind, was a bunch of blue-suited, song-singing, heartless robots. On the other hand, Xerox, he hoped, might be able to do something really good. It had less of an entrenched culture, and it also had more of a progressive vision. Shoup had been inspired by the 1969 speech given by Xerox CEO C. Peter McColough, in which he said that Xerox was determined to develop an "architecture of information" to solve the problems that had been created by the "knowledge explosion." Legend had it that after delivering the speech, McColough had directed one of his scientists to go and set up a laboratory to figure out what he meant.

That turned out to be a blessing for Shoup and his talented partners. They were all counter–computer establishment in a variety of ways and they were proud of it—in some cases even arrogant. Xerox's decision to enter the office-computing market would ultimately have vast influence on modern computing; moreover, the project consciously began with the example of Engelbart's design work from the previous decade.

It should have been Augment's finest hour. Xerox copiers were already in virtually every large office in the United States, and this was what Engelbart had most fervently been hoping for and working toward for more than a decade—to make the NLS a standard tool for the world's information workers.

But when the reality confronted him in 1970 and 1971—Jim Mitchell, an early PARC researcher, wanted to use NLS as one of the building blocks of a futuristic office-information system—Engelbart froze. He was deeply torn and was unable to completely let go of his creation.

Still, with both SRI and Xerox lawyers involved, the two research groups developed a legal framework for cooperation between the laboratories. On the ARC side, Charles Irby did the negotiating for Engelbart, and Mitchell represented Xerox. A licensing agreement was negotiated that would insure that whatever changes Xerox made in the system were given back to SRI and that the Augment team was able to stay in the loop. Despite the best intentions of both sides, however, the alliance never blossomed.

It seemed to Irby that Engelbart was increasingly incapable of taking the obvious next step—to let go of his creation so the world could use it. The experience left the young software engineer feeling frustrated and dispirited, and although he stayed on for several more years after the stillborn licensing effort, it was more out of loyalty to Engelbart and his own feeling of responsibility for holding the team of researchers together. Eventually, at least fifteen members of the Augment lab, including Irby, left and joined PARC.

Engelbart had run out of gas just as PARC emerged. The licensing deal was both a literal and figurative passing of both the torch and the vision.

Engelbart still retained a knack for hiring iconoclastic engineers. A continuous stream of bright young programmers and hardware designers was showing up, drawn by the growing legend that ARC was where the future was being invented. Within straitlaced SRI, however, the ARC group was increasingly coming to be seen as a collection of stoned goofballs who were chasing after the latest human-potential fad. There were beanbag chairs in the bullpen long before they were ever made iconic at Xerox PARC, and the refrigerator was stocked with beer, wine, and other more questionable substances.

Sandy Miranda, a self-styled "child of the sixties," found her way to the Augment Group when she was simultaneously offered jobs in both the SRI AI lab and in Engelbart's lab. She could feel the vibe in the Augment Group the moment she arrived for her first interview. She had walked down the hallway separating the Augment researchers from their AI colleagues, and it felt like walking from a hospital onto Haight Street. People were barefoot, and she could smell pot. The Augment researchers looked like a bunch of hippies.

Whoa, I could fit in here, she thought to herself. It was a different world. Office parties consisted of grabbing sleeping bags at the end of the day, driving to the beach, dropping acid, and spending the night. People brought their dogs to work, and Miranda, who started work as a secretary and was soon promoted to become the first NLS tech-support person, took to bringing her rather large Persian cat, which established residence on her desk.

Miranda became close friends with one of the other young trainers who had been recruited by ARC to spend time in the field teaching NLS to the first commercial users. Ann Weinberg, who would later marry Bill Duvall, was a Stanford graduate student hired by Engelbart. Not long after Weinberg came to ARC, she was sent to Huntsville, Alabama, to train an air force division that was busy using NLS to revise the operations manuals for ICBMs.

NLS was performing well, cutting the manual revision time from months to days. One day Weinberg was asked to give a demonstration of the system to a group of high-ranking air force officers. She was using the remote version of NLS that was running via a terminal over a modem and phone line. In the midst of the demonstration Weinberg discovered she had run out of disk storage in her account. The problem could be easily remedied by logging in as another user and so she "linked"—the equivalent of modern chat or instant messaging software—to her friend Miranda back in Menlo Park.

"Please send your password so I can use your account for a demonstration," Weinberg typed, while the all-male group of officers clustered around and watched the screen.

"I don't think it's a very good idea to share accounts," Miranda responded.

Weinberg was nonplussed. "Oh, come on, I really need it," she typed back. They went back and forth for several minutes, when suddenly Miranda conceded and her password appeared on Weinberg's screen: "cocksucker."

There was dead silence in the room in Alabama.

Among the other new arrivals was Don "Smokey" Wallace, whom Engelbart recruited to help handle the project's operating system needs after the NLS had been moved to more modern PDP-10 computers. By the early seventies, operating systems had become big and complex, and they required the full-time care of a systems expert, a role into which Wallace slipped naturally.

Although he had begun his computing career in California working for IBM in the early 1960s as a marketer for its 360 machine during a period when the company pioneered mainframe computing, by the late 1960s he was firmly a member of the ARPAnet counterculture and a self-described "freak." He had worked at Bolt, Beranek & Newman on the East Coast designing the first generation of ARPAnet hardware and software and then moved back to California. Along the way, he began wearing bib overalls and bought himself one of those Marine drill instructor "Smokey the Bear" hats.

Wallace arrived at about the time Engelbart began experimenting with a variety of organizational and psychological techniques to hasten his pursuit of a "high-performance" work group. In the early seventies, a wild range of social experimentation was going on inside and outside the laboratory. English had introduced Engelbart to the idea of encounter groups, and they had both also dabbled in the more intense and confrontational psychodrama movement.

Although Engelbart found these events at which people would shout at each other and tear down psychological defenses to be jarring, he decided that wasn't bad. The resulting emotional tension created situations in which he made friends and ended up finding a sense of community. Although Jim Fadiman had come on board to deal with personality issues and also help build a real organizational structure in the ARC, Engelbart was looking for a way to harness all of the chaos and step closer to his dream of true Augmentation.

Although he was not a political radical, Engelbart briefly became infatuated with Mao's little red book of quotations. For Engelbart, Mao's revolution represented a great social experiment. But while the Red Guards were sweeping through the countryside in China, one part of the American left was busy deifying the Maoists while thuggishly attempting to apply the theory and practice of the peasant revolutionaries to their middle-class political groups in the United States. Indeed, ARC in the seventies became a constant seething social experiment, and every time the organization began to stabilize, Engelbart would come in with some new idea to stir things up.

One answer to his frustrations and the chaos and the growing disorganization around him was to turn to the human growth and organizational change fads that were then sweeping the Bay Area. By far the most faddish and hip personal-growth business was est, an odd descendant of the Bay Area Zen movement that captured the upper middle class in the early seventies. The ARC laboratory, with notable holdouts, quickly adopted est.

Don Wallace was older than many of the ARC researchers. A Korean War veteran who was something of a bon vivant, he struggled against all of the New Age mumbo jumbo for a long time before he finally came to terms with what he saw Engelbart was doing. After a while, he came to realize that Augment wasn't a technology experiment at all; even though most of Engelbart's employees thought that it was about technology, it was actually a grand experiment in sociology and organizational change.

He began to believe that he needed a mental model of what the goal of the lab was in order to keep sane. Then he realized that every time he finally arrived at an approximate understanding, Engelbart pulled the rug out from under him. At first, it had caused him an enormous amount of emotional pain. Then he got it: The researchers, he decided, were actually lab rats themselves. He sat down and penned Engelbart a memo titled, appropriately, "Of Mice and Men."

Beginning in early 1972, Engelbart, who had a penchant for awkward acronyms, divided the Augment laboratory into three general categories: LINAC, FRAMAC, and PODAC. LINAC would be the "line activities" or technical-development work of the group. FRA-MAC would organize the goal-setting process needed to direct

LINAC, and PODAC would create small groups to pursue "personal and organization development activity."

PODAC was basically a set of ongoing encounter groups responsible for trying to work out the "issues" that had arisen within ARC. The "PODs" had come directly from Engelbart's reading of Mao's little red book, which had been used to retrain the Chinese to be revolutionaries. He correctly understood that you couldn't just drop new technology on people and expect it to work. Minds and behavior had to change as well. He became intrigued by Mao because he was looking for ways to force change. If Augment was going to accelerate the human intellect, he asked, what were the equivalent social and individual changes that needed to be made within organizations?

The Augment employees were broken into one of four PODAC groups with the task of achieving the following goal, as it was described in a journal memo that Engelbart wrote on January 25, 1972, inviting ARC team members to their first PODAC meeting:

> We who tell the world that we are learning how to show other teams how to achieve greater goal pursuit effectiveness must constantly examine ourselves (the "example" that we are working with), as an organization and as individuals, while making a conscious effort to understand how we are doing, and how we can improve.[12]

The PODs were named Cedar, Fir, Oak, and Redwood. Engelbart made an effort to make each group a mix of programmers, hardware designers, and trainers. As might be expected, the weekly meetings quickly became gripe sessions, channeling the researchers' energy into complaints about management:

- There is an impression that Doug goes off in a corner and hatches ideas. People are uncomfortable with all the surprises.
- Doug does not allow enough control, goal setting, participation for ARC in general.
- Doug doesn't do enough selling of his ideas to ARC people.[13]

The PODs also became a vehicle for expressing the uncertainties that were increasingly beginning to plague the ARC research team as the group struggled to define its identity: "Like just about everyone else at ARC these days I'm trying to get my head straight on what ARC is doing, where it's going etc.," read one journal entry in February 1972. "The point of the above is the question, what's our real contribution, why should the galaxy, as WLB [Walter Bass] likes to say, keep feeding us energy units?" added another.

And someone else asked pointedly: "There are tens of thousands of people building computer and computer-people systems and there are only about 30 of us. If we disappeared would it make any difference?"

If Engelbart was seeking consensus or even clarity in the PODs, he didn't find it and the waters soon became infinitely murkier after Walter Bass, one of his young programmers, discovered est.

Former car salesman Werner Erhard had created the manipulative personal-growth "training" series in October 1971. Est soon built a cult following based on a system that was a mélange largely borrowed from other self-help systems, religions, and philosophies. The "training," as it was referred to, was most closely derived from the version of Zen taught by Alan Watts from a Sausalito houseboat during the 1960s.

During the seventies, est swept viruslike through the Bay Area and struck particularly hard in the high-tech world, where educated and relatively affluent young researchers were seeking meaning and community. Est converts tended to proselytize others, telling them that they would understand the benefits of the seminar once they got "it." What "it" was always remained unclear, but there is no question that the movement had a profound impact on those who went through its training sessions.

Almost everyone had at least one encounter with est. A woman who Bob Albrecht, the People's Computer Company guru, had been involved with went through the training and came back transformed into a very un-Zen-like creature. She no longer believed that everything was interconnected, but rather had decided that she wanted it all for herself and would do anything to get it. Curious about what had transformed her so dramatically, Albrecht attended one of the free est introductory meetings, where he discovered they used what he determined was a standard self-hypnosis technique. Albrecht quickly learned to dislike est intensely, and he decided his relationship with the woman had been doomed from the start.

Est had a different effect on Doug Engelbart. Although he couldn't put his finger on it and he was slightly put off by its glibness, Engelbart became convinced that est training genuinely elevated and changed people. He watched as they got up and confessed things to a large audience and then began to glow from getting it off their chests. He figured that Erhard had some special insight into how to get people motivated.

That was particularly true among the members of the ARC group, where Bass reported that the est process had much in common with the ideas underlying the Augmentation Framework. Heavyset and intense, Bass was confrontational and elicited charged reactions from members of the Augment team, but Engelbart was intrigued with the idea of est training and made ARC lab funds available for any of his researchers who agreed to take the seminars.

Moreover, he decided that if he was funding it, he'd better go through the seminar himself, as well. He came away from the two weekend sessions under Erhard's spell, convinced that est was a potent force. It was a two-way street, as Erhard likewise found something special in Engelbart, a receptive and respected scientist who would provide perfect credibility as a member of the est board of directors, which Engelbart agreed to join. Also on the board was psychologist Mary Allen, wife of Don Allen, the former Ampex engineer who had helped run the International Foundation for Advanced Study, which had offered Engelbart his LSD experience. The board meetings themselves were sometimes spectacular events that took the form of parties with distinguished guests. One time, Buckminster Fuller was invited, and Erhard introduced him to Engelbart, describing in detail what the Augment project was attempting, although he had never been to visit or been given a demonstration. Engelbart was impressed.

Still seeking a way to have a broad impact on the world, Engelbart was particularly vulnerable to Erhard's charisma. He came to believe that the self-styled guru was a real genius in the way he could project himself and talk people into things. Although Engelbart realized that Erhard was fundamentally ego-driven, it was a number of years before he began to lose respect for him. He became completely disillusioned only when the est board came under pressure after the organization was accused of financial fraud. Still he chose not to leave the board until Erhard finally closed the operation.

The results of the est experiment, however, were predictably disastrous for ARC. The first wave of est graduates returned enraptured with the experience, but their newfound air of honesty and frankness was not always good for either the group or the individuals themselves. The wife of one ARC programmer came home and told him she had been having an affair with his best friend. Another member of the lab changed her name and several got divorces.

The resulting chaos was chronicled a decade later by Jacques Vallee, a French computer scientist who had come to the Augment Group in 1972 to work on the database that would be the foundation for the ARPAnet Network Information Center that Engelbart had promised the Pentagon managers. Vallee kept a journal, which was published as a roman à clef titled *The Network Revolution: Confessions of a Computer Scientist* in 1982. During the year Vallee worked at ARC, he remained something of an outsider and resisted the pressure to take the est training. He also found himself at odds with prevalent anti-military views of the Augment Group. A French citizen, he wasn't so much pro–Vietnam War as that he had a different perspective than many of the young researchers.

On the floor upstairs from the ARC lab was another group of SRI engineers busy designing laser-guided smart bombs, a project that deeply upset the antiwar engineers in Engelbart's lab. Vallee tried to explain that while he shared their political views, he parted with them on the issue of weapons. He had been born in 1939 in Pontoise, a town on the River Oise next to a bridge that since medieval times had controlled access to Normandy. During the war the Germans attacked the bridges, which were later attacked by the Americans. He recalled that two of his family's homes were blown up and his beautiful small town was virtually leveled. Smart bombs, he decided, might be a very good thing.

In *The Network Revolution*, he described an embarrassing moment when the director of SRI (which he cloaked as Pacific Research Laboratories) brought several high-ranking Pentagon officers to the ARC laboratory (which he named Systematic Thought-Enhancing Machine, or STEM):

> The confrontation became obvious one afternoon when the group, riddled by conflict, wheeled all the terminals into the corners and spread a carpet in the middle of the main room. It was time for a real brainstorm. The programmers, in their blue jeans and colored shirts, took off their sandals and sat in a circle. A bottle of wine and a few joints were produced and a serious encounter session began. The stairway door opened without warning, and who should walk in but the Director of PRL himself, in his gray suit and striped tie, followed by several high-ranking officers from the Pentagon. They were on an official site visit, checking the expenditures of public monies under their jurisdiction.
>
> "And here is our STEM project . . ." the director began, without even looking. Then he looked, and saw, and smelled, when he realized what the unmistakable odor was, he made up some sort of excuse and left in a hurry. The STEM project had just acquired one more crisis.[14]

What struck Vallee most about the infatuation with est was that it created a cultlike atmosphere among the researchers. Only the strongest personalities could resist the pressure to take the training. Don Wallace also looked askance as the est experience destroyed a number of people on the ARC research team. Some people's lives took right-angle turns as a result of the training, which placed them under intense psychological pressures, while others just flipped. Worst of all was that Engelbart was rapidly losing the confidence of his most important backers at the Pentagon.

Taylor's successor, Larry Roberts, believed he was funding Augment to produce the Network Information Center. Engelbart had in fact hired an operating-systems specialist to help manage the NIC effort, but not long after he arrived, Dick Watson discovered that the entire Augment program was at great risk financially. Watson had been a professor at Stanford for several years, and before that had worked with Ed Feigenbaum, then a young computer scientist at Berkeley who would later become a leading AI researcher. He also had industry computer experience working for Shell Oil and, like Wallace, had little tolerance for the est pressure. Moreover, he had studied as a Sufi for several years and had come to the laboratory without any of the emotional insecurity that had led others to turn to est.

His training, however, did not completely prepare him for ARC. Shortly before he started his new job, he had been invited by Engelbart to attend a meeting with visiting ARPA officials, which left him shocked. On January 24, 1972, the day before the invitation to the first PODAC meetings went out, Watson entered his assessment of ARC's relations with its largest backers into the Augment journal:

> On Jan 6 72 I had my first chance to check out my hypothesis about relations with ARPA when Doug invited me down to be around when Larry Roberts visited ARC with Steve Crocker. The visit frankly stunned me. The communication between ARC and ARPA about goals was nonexistent. Larry communicated clearly his displeasure with where he thought ARC was at. . . . In all my five years of selling research and development and interfacing with buyers of various kinds, I had never been in such a tense session; further my experience indicated that unless such a relationship could be reversed it was just a matter of time until funding was cut.[15]

It was clear to Watson that Engelbart simply viewed ARPA as a source of financing for his larger Augmentation scheme, while Roberts wanted a functioning service organization for his new network.

The situation remained tense in May when Watson attended his first ARPA Network Working Group meeting. Roberts now stated clearly that he was supporting ARC only because of the NIC, and he demanded that Engelbart commit the necessary funding to make the NIC functional quickly. During the ensuing months, Watson and Engelbart clashed frequently over resources and NIC's priority. The arguments were often bitter, and yet during the next four and a half years Watson grew to have a genuine respect for Engelbart and his passion. He came to know the laboratory director as a person who could think at a blue-sky level that was wonderful, and in incredible detail as well.

But Engelbart couldn't connect the two realms. For a while he had been fortunate to have people like Irby and English, who could make the connections for him. Watson also realized that Engelbart deeply believed he was a misunderstood outsider. He faced a tremendous barrier in trying to communicate his vision in language that ordinary mortals could understand. A firm skeptic, Watson dismissed the grander vision that more powerful, augmented minds would solve all the world's problems, but at the same time he decided the technology, methods, procedures, and human organization that had emerged might be truly useful.

As the SRI representative to the Network Working Group, Watson got involved in the early "protocol wars" in the ARPAnet community as researchers on both coasts struggled to build the network and make it useful. What could be done to make NLS available to the outside world? he wondered. That goal led Watson, along with ARC programmer John Melvyn, to conceive of the Telnet protocol, which enabled remote users to log in to distant computers via the network. Ultimately, it was Telnet, electronic mail, and ftp, and not NLS, that would generate the demand that led to the dramatic expansion of the computer network.

During 1972, Watson also led the charge at ARC to make NLS more useful to the ARPAnet community. ARPA was under some pressure to show that its new network was actually viable, and articles had already appeared in the computer trade press questioning the entire notion of the packet switching that was at its heart. This was a technique for breaking up digital data into small "packets" so that each packet could be routed separately through a computer network and then resent if necessary. It made it possible to route around network nodes that had stopped functioning, making the network more reliable. Roberts had decreed that in October 1972 there would be an event in Washington, D.C., that would show off the network, in much the same fashion that Engelbart had shown off NLS in 1968 in San Francisco. And so, during the year NWG worked hard to build new software protocols that would make possible new features. When the demonstration happened that fall in the ballroom of the Sheraton hotel in Washington, it was another turning point. People could sit and use the new network. They could see the interactivity; they could see that networking was real.

For the next year, Roberts remained ARC's protector, but in the middle of 1973 he decided that he wanted to leave the Pentagon for a job working for Bolt, Beranek & Newman commercializing the ARPAnet technology. He searched for a replacement, and J. C. R. Licklider agreed to come back in 1974 to take over as the head of ARPA's Information Processing Technology Office again.[16]

Ironically, his return proved to be the death knell for ARC and Engelbart's vision. Licklider had been Engelbart's "big brother" in the 1960s when ARPA funding first launched the project.[17] A decade later, the camaraderie was gone. Within three months of Roberts's departure, Engelbart got a message telling him that ARPA was planning to terminate ARC's funding. At the last minute, there was a reprieve, and there was another year or so of project assignments, but clearly the urge to support anything in the original spirit of Augmentation had ended.

Engelbart concluded he was being accused of not transferring his technology quickly enough to the outside world. He also believed that Licklider felt the project was ferociously overcharging for its services and it had too many people working on support and training. In Licklider's mind, Engelbart believed, this was an admission of the failure of NLS. It simply wasn't possible to teach people how to use it.

In 1974, funding for ARC was finally cut off. Desperate to keep his project alive, Engelbart made a pilgrimage to his first backer, Bob Taylor, at Xerox PARC.

"We have all of this technology, couldn't it prove useful to you?" Engelbart pleaded. But Taylor had no interest; he only wanted to show off PARC's recently acquired electronic-mail capability. It was a sad moment for Engelbart, for his group had been using electronic mail for the past seven years. He had lost his funding, and his people needed a home.

A couple of years later, SRI sold the Augment technology to the Tymshare Corporation. Engelbart and the group of remaining ARC researchers moved offices from Menlo Park to Cupertino. An era had ended, a new one was about to begin, and Doug Engelbart had been tossed out into the wilderness.

7 | MOMENTUM

While the Augment lab was having trouble licensing its technology, on the other side of the Stanford campus SAIL's technology was literally leaking into the outside world, and it showed up first in an unexpected place.

In the early seventies, computer displays were rarities. And so, in the fall of 1971, when one appeared in the Stanford University Tresidder Union coffeehouse, it caused a sensation. In a dimly lit student hangout there was suddenly a luminous computer video screen that showed a white star field on a black background. It was seductive, at least for a group of mostly college-age young men suddenly confronted by an interactive fantasy machine radically different from television. The appearance of the world's first coin-operated video game was even more striking because it was so incongruous. Although the Stanford campus was anything but bohemian, the Tresidder Union coffeehouse in the late sixties felt like a close cousin of Harvard Square or Bleecker Street. A dark room with coffee tables and a counter for food and drinks, it was routinely inhabited by the shaggy shock troops of the counterculture and the antiwar movement, and on weekends it was possible to find high school students looking for something beyond suburban Palo Alto.

Now into their midst came this strange box with two joysticks and a phosphorescent screen on which a pair of two-dimensional outlines of tiny spaceships could duel for the price of a dime.

The coin-operated video game was the brainchild of a Cal Poly student named Hugh Tuck, who had been a high school friend of Bill Pitts, the Stanford computer-science student who had tried to break into SAIL. Pitts had learned about Spacewar as an undergraduate even before he had discovered SAIL in the hills behind campus. He had seen it running at the computer center in Polya Hall, and thought the game was totally magical. Someone told him if he came after midnight he could just load the program and play, so that night he showed up at 1:00 A.M., found the paper tape, and was quickly lost in the imaginary Buck Rogers world Spacewar created. Just as quickly, he was shaken from his reverie by a very angry graduate student who had started a large tape backup shortly before he had begun playing only to discover that Spacewar had killed her program!

Later, while Pitts was still at Stanford, Tuck occasionally came over to SAIL to take part in the late-night Spacewar sessions. While everyone else had been attracted by the compelling fantasy and competition, Tuck had a different reaction. One night in 1969 he said to Pitts, "Boy, if you could make a coin-operated game out of this, you could get rich."

A nice idea, Pitts thought, *but not very practical.* Spacewar required a powerful computer as well as an expensive display system far beyond the reach of any garage shop start-up. The reality was that playing Spacewar was limited to mainframe computers, which were generally billed for several hundred dollars an hour. As a result, the game was usually relegated to periods when the machines were more or less idle.

Two years later, however, Pitts had been hired at Lockheed, the Sunnyvale missile contractor, as a systems programmer. He had been employed to program a PDP-10 computer, the machine that he had mastered at SAIL. The only problem was that Lockheed had never gotten around to actually purchasing the PDP-10, which left him with nothing to do.

While he was waiting for his AWOL computer, he noticed that the year before Digital had introduced the PDP-11, a less expensive minicomputer that was within the budget of a small start-up. It was the height of the minicomputer era, and computing power was beginning to reach a broader circle of people and was about to become a personal and an entertainment medium. Video games would begin as a tiny niche for teenage boys, but with each succeeding generation of computing power they would extend to a broader audience. In a few decades, they would displace movie theaters in revenue.[1]

But none of that was obvious in 1971. After studying the new PDP-11 for a while, Pitts suddenly recalled his friend Tuck's assessment. So he called Tuck, and with funding from Tuck's family, the two young men founded Computer Recreations in June 1971.

The PDP-11 cost about $12,000, and a Hewlett-Packard electrostatic display and related equipment added another $8,000. So for $20,000 the two decided they could pull off building their first prototype. The founders agreed on a fifty-fifty partnership, with Pitts doing the technical work and Tuck providing the money. Fancying themselves to be adept marketers and realizing that at the height of the U.S. involvement in Vietnam, "war" might not be an especially popular term on campus, they renamed the coin-operated version of Spacewar "Galaxy Game" and set to work.

Pitts began programming using the source code that had originally been developed by Slug Russell and his friends at MIT. He wanted to duplicate the initial appearance and feel of Spacewar, but he added some of his own touches as well.

They found a cabinetmaker to build a box for the game, and Tuck, who was trained as a mechanical engineer, did the mechanical design. The game consisted of just the HP display, set on its back and pointing straight up. A mirror was used to project the image on the display; one hundred feet of cabling was used to connect the display and the controls to the PDP-11 computer, which was kept hidden away upstairs in a music room.

When the game was introduced, it was an immediate hit. Crowds of twenty to thirty people would gather around the players, looking over their shoulders. It became a cult scene, and the following year, to increase revenue, Pitts and Tuck introduced a second display so that four contestants could play simultaneously on two screens. Players would put their dimes in a line that sat on top of the case and wait their turns.

While the two young men were working on the prototype, they learned that they had competition. Nolan Bushnell had played Spacewar as an engineering student at the University of Utah. After graduating, he moved to California, first working for Ampex and then eventually bringing his own dream of coin-operated video games to a small arcade company called Nutting and Associates. Bushnell's version of Spacewar was to be called Computer Space.

It was while both small companies were busy designing their games that Bushnell heard about Pitts and Tuck, and so he invited them over for a visit. He told them that he had heard they were spending a lot of money on a PDP-11 to run Spacewar and showed them what he was building. The whole thing, including the case and the electronics, was intended to cost less than one thousand dollars, he said. Pitts was genuinely impressed with Bushnell's prototype, though he decided it was a horrible travesty of the original Spacewar. Bushnell had cut corners to save money and the game wasn't very interesting.

Computer Space was introduced in 1972. It was a commercial failure, but Bushnell went on to found Atari. His next game, Pong, was a huge success, touching off a boom in computer-based arcade and home video gaming. In contrast, Pitts and Tuck struggled for almost eight years before finally giving up on their business. They had originally intended to use their single expensive machine as a means to learn about the market and figure out how cheaply they could build production units. They had priced their games at a dime, or three for a quarter; if you won you could continue to play for free. Their strategy was that, rather than driving people away because it was too expensive to play, they would invite them in and persuade them to sit in front of the machines for hours.

When they saw how much excitement the first machine generated, however, they abandoned their original plan and set out to
build a second one. They moved the new system to the University of
California at Berkeley, where it didn't receive the same favorable reaction as the original Stanford installation, so they installed it instead in a popular bar in Sunnyvale. Unfortunately it still didn't
generate the enthusiasm that greeted the game at Stanford. (One
problem with Galaxy Game was that it required the user to read a set
of instructions that looked like a legal-sized document, which
meant it didn't play well to the masses.) Something about Galaxy
Game had clicked at Stanford. It was a precursor that hinted at the
hunger for computing as a new medium that would lead directly
to the personal computer. In the end, Pitts made it his personal
responsibility to pay off the Tuck family investment of $65,000
and maintained the system at the Tresidder coffeehouse until 1978,
when the debt was settled.

∎∎∎

Galaxy Game was a huge hit even during the chaos of antiwar
protest at Stanford. In 1971, the war in Vietnam was building back
up to a fevered pitch and generating waves of opposition on U.S.
campuses. The Nixon administration was preparing to invade Laos
in an effort to sever the Ho Chi Minh trail, creating growing fears at
home that U.S. military servicemen would soon be fighting in yet
another Asian country.

The previous year, in response to the invasion of Cambodia, the
largest student protest movement in American history had erupted,
leading to strikes that shut down hundreds of campuses and the
killing of students at Kent State University in Ohio and Jackson State
College in Mississippi. Later that year, a bomb planted at the University of Wisconsin's Army Math Research Center killed a researcher.

The violence and the deaths raised the stakes and changed the
tenor of protest and at the same time splintered the antiwar movement. At Stanford in January, Professor H. Bruce Franklin, a

Melville scholar and a Maoist, led a split from the Revolutionary Union, then the reigning Bay Area Marxist-Leninist group, to create a new, even more militant organization called Venceremos ("We will win" in Spanish). Venceremos members were committed to the idea of armed revolution, and their members wore black pins with a red gun. They advocated direct action to stop the war and espoused the idea that prisoners would become the leading force for revolution in the country.

The growing militancy sent Stanford's antiwar movement spinning out of control. On Saturday, February 6, there was an attempted arson at a small wooden building that was the headquarters of the Free Campus Movement, a conservative group whose members frequently took pictures of demonstrations and who were linked by the student antiwar activists to the police. Later that night, Molotov cocktails were thrown into the offices of ROTC, and at the same time false alarms rang out at four different locations on campus.

The next evening, a crowd of six hundred people gathered to watch the San Francisco Mime Troupe in a campus auditorium. Just before the performance began, it was announced that Laos had been invaded. Afterward, leaflets were handed out by an organization calling itself the Inquisition, a student group that was dedicated to ferreting out war research, demanding that the university "release all information on the uses of the Computation Center," where the school housed its mainframe computers. The leaflet alleged that the center was carrying out such work and running a Stanford Research Institute war-planning computer program known as Gamut-H.

Richard Sack, a graduate student who was spending much of his time in the center working on his dissertation, had stumbled upon the program. A close friend who was also a frequent visitor at the center had told him she had seen a program that involved SRI and the Vietnam War and might have something to do with bombing runs. The issue was an especially sensitive one, as students had won a concession from the Stanford administration the previous year forcing classified military research off campus. Several weeks later,

Sack himself found a printout that matched the name of the program his friend had mentioned. Looking around, he warily picked it up and briefly considered taking the computer punch cards that generated the program, as well. He hesitated and then quietly slipped out the door with only the printout in his briefcase.

Sack took the document to the Pacific Studies Center, a radical research group, which operated out of a ramshackle storefront office several miles from campus in a seedy neighborhood called Whiskey Gulch. There, he gave it to Lenny Siegel, a former Stanford student who had been expelled from school two years earlier for his part in the demonstrations against SRI war research and the institute's ties to the university.

Siegel was a heavyset activist who sported Afro-style curly long hair and who was known for wearing an army helmet to many campus demonstrations. He was also a member of the Inquisition. Gamut-H turned out to be a war game, a computerized simulation of a helicopter assault—a modeling exercise for the invasion of Laos, in the students' interpretation. For Siegel and his confederates, it was the perfect smoking gun that could be employed to spark national protests to match the outrage that had greeted the invasion of Cambodia.

On Sunday night after the mime-troupe performance, roaming bands of demonstrators broke more than one hundred windows on campus, police-car windows were smashed, and at 9:30 a bomb threat was phoned to the computer center, which briefly shut down.

The next day, almost one thousand students assembled at the center of campus in White Plaza. At the rally, the Inquisition distributed a leaflet entitled "Do It," which encouraged students "to do whatever actions you feel ready to do." They also circulated an "Open Letter to the Stanford Community," which stated the computation center was being used by the Stanford Research Institute for war research. The letter contained a list of six demands, including making public the identity of all non-Stanford users of Stanford facilities and phasing out all Stanford research funded by the Department of Defense, which of course would have included SAIL, hidden in the hills behind campus.

That afternoon there were various skirmishes and rock-throwing incidents around campus, while at night numerous squads of Santa Clara County and San Jose police patrolled. The stage was set for a confrontation.

The following day, there were calls for a "Cambodia-type strike" protesting the invasion of Laos, and in the evening there was a three-hour meeting at a campus auditorium attended by eight hundred people. A parade of speakers advocated shutting down the computer center, and a rally was called in White Plaza for the next day at noon.

It would turn into the most violent day in Stanford's history. Clashes with the police went on at various places around campus until late into the evening. Three conservative students were beaten while attempting to take pictures of the demonstrators, and an unknown assailant shot two people on campus.

At the rally, Bruce Franklin delivered a speech demanding that the computation center be shut down. In response, a group of about one hundred students walked across White Plaza on their way to occupy the building. Hearing that the building was about to be taken over, the university provost telephoned the center's director and ordered that it be closed. From behind the center *Stanford Daily* editor Felicity Barringer, a twenty-year-old junior, watched a handful of students throwing rocks through the windows. Then the crowd entered the building through a back door. Several minutes later, the mainframe computer itself was shut down after someone pulled a master power switch.

Instead of entering the building with the students, Franklin had gone to a class he was scheduled to teach, but shortly afterward he returned to the crowd that had formed outside of the center. Two hours later, Stanford police used a bullhorn to announce to the students that they were trespassing and were subject to arrest. In response, the students held an impromptu meeting at the front of the building, where it was decided they would voluntarily leave once the police arrived to arrest them. Inside, one of the students saved the computer from destruction, arguing that it was "politically neutral."

An hour later, the police entered the center, and the protesters spilled out the other doorway shouting, "Down with SRI!" and "Get SRI out!"

As a wall of tactical police formed to hold the students away from the building, a Santa Clara sheriff's officer repeatedly ordered the crowd to disperse and was greeted with shouts of "Pigs off campus!" Bruce Franklin, meanwhile, was engaged in a screaming match with one of the deans attending the demonstration as a faculty observer. Whether Franklin was engaged in a debate over whether the faculty observers should remain to watch for police brutality or whether he was egging the students on to resist the order to disperse was bitterly debated after he was accused of inciting a riot on campus and fired by the administration.

Barringer stood with her notebook and watched the scene until with little warning the tactical police charged the crowd. With the other students she turned and ran. What she remembered most clearly was Franklin racing past her in a flash, arms churning while the veins in his neck bulged.

What a coward, she thought.

■ ■ ■

John Shoch, a Stanford senior who was already on academic probation for having been arrested in demonstrations during each of the previous two years, lingered on the edge of the crowd that afternoon. Shoch hadn't joined the students because he wasn't willing to jeopardize his chances for graduating.

He had grown up in a middle-class suburb of Chicago and come to Stanford in the fall of 1967. He began studying physics but over the next two years, after gradually being radicalized by the antiwar protests, took classes in history and political science. In 1969, he was jailed for sitting in at the Applied Electronics Laboratory. The following year, he was jailed again during the Cambodia demonstrations for violating an injunction against political demonstrations from the previous year. He spent a boring week in a Palo Alto jail cell with Lenny Siegel. Back in school, he switched his major from physics to political science, and he started to take computer-science classes because they were more fun than physics and math. Caught up in antiwar politics, he was still not immune from the intellectual challenge of computing. In his senior year, on a lark, he took a course in nonnumerical methods that was cotaught by two young Stanford faculty members, Gio Wiederhold and Alan Kay.

Shoch frequently left a picket line in front of one school building and went to another to take a seat at the back of a classroom behind all of the short-haired, khaki-clad engineering students. He had a different uniform—shoulder-length hair, sandals, torn jeans, and a leather jacket.

Shoch was more familiar with the culture of the political-science department, where if you didn't speak out in class, you didn't get a grade. The computing class was schizophrenic, dealing with an odd assortment of arcane topics ranging from SNOBOL to LISP programming. Wiederhold was European and formal, and Kay was just the opposite, beginning each of his lectures by throwing out an outlandish question for the students. The engineering crowd generally sat there, silent and uncommunicative. Shoch, in contrast, was the smart aleck in the back of the room, frequently engaging Kay in a debate over some esoteric point.

At the end of the semester, Kay handed out a take-home final exam, asking the students to solve one of three programming problems. The first one was completely incomprehensible to Shoch; the second was the obvious one that all of the engineers in the class were going to do; and the third one was an oddball question that he figured no one else would think of attempting. He decided there was no point in competing with the engineers, because they would outdo him, so he undertook the offbeat question, which involved figuring out what a SNOBOL compiler had done at some intermediate state in solving a problem.

He worked on the problem for a long time without progress, until he was finally ready to throw up his hands in frustration. You can't get the system to disgorge this information, he decided. He was worried, for a week had gone by, and he'd waited until the end of the assignment period. So he made an appointment with Kay, gathered all his notes together, and went to the professor's office. "I don't know how you solved this problem, but I don't think it can be done," he told him.

Kay looked up at the frustrated Shoch and said, "Well, I don't know if it can be done or not."

Shoch had prepared a lengthy discussion of what the compiler could and couldn't do. He began painstakingly sketching out what he had figured out about the innards of the compiler, and Kay suddenly cut him off.

"Oh, you're right," Kay said. "You can't get at this information. Don't worry, you've done enough work."

Shoch was stunned. He handed Kay his notes and was preparing to leave when Kay suddenly asked, "So what are you doing this summer?"

"I hadn't really thought about it yet," Shoch replied.

"Well, Xerox is starting this lab in Palo Alto, and I'm going over there to work," Kay said. "Would you like to come and work there for the summer?"

John Shoch went to PARC for the summer, working for Alan Kay. Ultimately, he stayed at Xerox for fourteen years, at one point running the company's personal-computer division.

Alan Kay had always been a bit of an uneasy fit. At Stanford, in John McCarthy's AI world, grappling with dry formal problems in computer science, he hadn't fit the mold. Kay wasn't a political radical or overtly countercultural in his lifestyle, yet his approach to computing and even management was far outside the bounds of normal corporate or academic life.

Now, in a new laboratory funded by a stodgy white-shirt-and-tie, office-of-the-past copier company that was desperate to break IBM's hold on corporate computing, Kay was about to create a small community of researchers that reflected the free-spirited sense of possibility that was synonymous with California in the late sixties and early seventies.

It was to become a legendary experiment, and though it failed in the narrow sense—Xerox never did accomplish its goal of competing with IBM—in a broader perspective PARC served as a funnel for people and ideas from SAIL and Augment, who did change the computing world.

It was, ultimately, the cultural mismatch between the conservative copier company and its California counterculture laboratory that kept Xerox from fully capitalizing on the personal-computing technology that was invented at PARC. Robert Spinrad, the research center's second director, often felt like Clark Kent on his regular weekly flights back from Palo Alto to corporate headquarters in Connecticut. He would step into the plane's lavatory, change into his suit, and emerge looking like a corporate executive.

From today's vantage point, it is hard to recollect how different the computing world was that Kay set out to transform. Virtually all the power and decision making about computing was in the hands of large institutions or a few computer makers, like giant IBM. At the same time, individual computer users were beginning to strain against the limits. "We should be able to do whatever we want with these things" was the mantra.

Indeed, who would think of taking these machines that cost millions of dollars, which were supposed to be kept behind glass walls, and giving them to kids to play with? Kay did things that were just that un-Xerox-like with some regularity. One day early on, he walked into the office of the PARC librarian, set down a copy of the *Whole Earth Catalog*, and told her to order all of the books mentioned in it.

Part of his outrageous behavior was a function of simply not knowing any better. In many ways Kay was completely naïve about corporate culture. He turned to Bill English for support and counsel in figuring out how to build his own research group. One of the first things that English suggested was that Kay come up with a budget for his project.

"What's a budget?" asked Kay.[2]

Although he was a novice at the skills required for corporate in-fighting, for Kay coming to PARC was like opening a dam. Unhappy at SAIL, by 1971 he was preparing to head off to Carnegie Mellon University, where two of the nation's most prominent computer sci-entists, Allen Newell and Gordon Bell, had been actively recruiting him to come build his beloved Dynabook—the portable computing machine that had gradually emerged from his computers-for-kids fantasies. He had met the two researchers when ARPA's technology office director, Larry Roberts, had put him in charge of the idea of a "Super AI" computer for the ARPAnet. It had been one of Roberts's and Bob Taylor's schemes to create "magnets" that would attract peo-ple to use the new network. The idea flourished in 1970 and 1971, and as a result, even while he was a postdoctoral researcher at SAIL, Kay was able to travel widely and meet many of the reigning AI and computer-design gurus.

At the time, however, Kay was deeply into his "interim" Dynabook design project and was mocking up computers to communicate his portable fantasy. Bell and Newell were so taken with the idea that they recruited him. He accepted their offer sometime late in 1970, soon after he had begun consulting for Bob Taylor, who was just be-ginning to build PARC.

When it came time to leave, however, Kay changed his mind. By April and May, PARC was literally throbbing with potential and en-ergy, and it was obvious that the team that Taylor had recruited was going to have an impact on the world. Kay wanted to be part of that adventure. Even better, Taylor, who was familiar with Kay's Flex ma-chine because the two had overlapped at Utah, advised Kay simply to "follow your instincts." He had nothing less than carte blanche to pursue his ideas in concert with the best computer designers in the world.

Kay became a brilliant synthesizer of ideas. Additionally, he was the first person to approach the design of computers from the point of view of an artist rather than that of an engineer. Coupled with an early and profound understanding of the implication of the scaling principle, he also took an important step beyond Engelbart's notion of personal-computer-as-vehicle. He conceived of personal computing as an entirely new medium. In thinking about the computer in this way, he remembered reading about the insight of Aldus Manutius, who some forty years after the invention of the printing press established the dimensions of the modern book by understanding that it must be small enough to fit into a saddlebag. The obvious twentieth-century analogy was that a modern computer should be no larger than a notebook. It was a powerful notion, one that was originally apprehended only by a handful of people, people like Kay and Sid Fernbach, the Livermore labs' supercomputing guru. Once Kay had the concept, though, it was impossible for him to shake it. He would proselytize it widely, and it became one of only two or three true "visionary" ideas that drove Silicon Valley over the next three decades.

Kay's ideas frequently brought him into conflict with Xerox management. He had little patience for the company's top strategic planner, Don Pendery. To Kay, Pendery saw the world in terms of "trends" and thought defensively, asking, "What was the future going to be like and how can Xerox defend against it?"

This drove Kay to distraction, until one day he got so angry he blurted out, "Look, the best way to predict the future is to invent it."[3]

Pendery never bought into either the ideas or the attitudes of the PARC upstarts, according to Kay, and their fundamental disagreement led to a series of papers on the future of technology that became known as the "Pendery Papers." As part of the debate, Kay proposed an ultrathin computer he called a "display transducer," which would include a stylus for writing and drawing, a lenticular lens for displaying a stereo image, a TV camera, and removable memory. It looked striking, like the high-end laptop computers of today.

While he struggled with Xerox management, Kay felt at home in Palo Alto. A cross between an academic town and a middle-class suburb, Palo Alto in the early 1970s was a remarkably comfortable place to live. He never drove a car and became an avid member of the bicycling culture that was being encouraged by a profusion of bike lanes. He grew to love the minimalism that cycling represented and even drew parallels between it and his Dynabook vision. *A bicycle for the mind*—maybe Engelbart's notion about computer-as-vehicle wasn't so wrongheaded. It was an idea that Apple Computer employed in its marketing materials more than a decade later.

With Taylor's blessing, Kay—who was reluctant to become a manager—began to build his own research group, having come to realize that he couldn't do everything by himself. He named his team the Learning Research Group, and it quickly proved to be a reflection of his talent as a synthesizer. He didn't look for scientists so much as fellow travelers and decided that he would recruit only "people who got stars in their eyes when they heard about the notebook-computer idea."[4]

Some, like John Shoch, came right out of school. Others were walk-ons. Diana Merry, who became one of Kay's best programmers, had recently moved from southern California with her husband, who had accepted a job with Lockheed. She had taken several programming classes and, after hearing about what was going on at PARC, figured that it was better to take a secretary's job at Xerox than to start elsewhere in the Valley as a programmer. Merry had come to the lab first as a temporary worker and was then assigned a permanent position as secretary to Jerry Elkind, one of the lab's top managers. Soon, she began following Kay around in the hallways, telling him she wanted to learn to program. Kay took her under his wing, and before long she was writing intricate low-level software for his project.

Others came to Xerox and then were pulled into Kay's orbit, because his group was talking about the most "supercool things" in an already cool place.

Dan Ingalls was working on a separate speech-recognition project across the hallway from Kay's office and soon found he couldn't resist Kay's ideas. Ingalls had come to Stanford in 1966 as a graduate student in electrical engineering. He had grown up in Cambridge, steeped in both old-world wealth and intellectual scholarship. His family had been Virginia landowners for generations, but his father was a Harvard Sanskrit scholar. During the Second World War, Daniel H. H. Ingalls, who could read and write in twenty languages, had joined an elite corps of scholars who had been recruited to the Pentagon, where they applied their language talents to codebreaking. After the war the Ingalls family returned to Cambridge, and ultimately Dan Jr. entered Harvard, where he studied physics. In his senior year, he began experimenting with electronic devices and built several electronic slide rules, assembling them from components that he dredged out of scavenging expeditions to a electronic-surplus shop in Cambridge.

Designing simple electronic circuits grew into a captivating hobby, and upon graduating from Harvard, Ingalls, remembering a childhood visit, decided to head for California's beaches and Stanford University. Once at Stanford, his passion for hardware cooled a bit, and he began spending more and more time trying to pursue the softer side of computing. He took a colloquium taught by Donald Knuth, the Stanford computer scientist who spent his evenings hacking at SAIL.

The Knuth course explored program optimization, the craft of speeding software performance. It opened new vistas for Ingalls, who became deft at designing programs called optimizers—software that would overcome bottlenecks in programs that were inefficient. The Knuth course also led to Ingalls's first entrepreneurial venture and his first business failure when he launched a one-man consulting firm that sought to speed up programs written in Fortran. The venture ran up against an immediate and insurmountable obstacle: The biggest users of Fortran were government laboratories, which had no incentive to speed up their programs because it would undercut their hardware budgets!

At Stanford, Ingalls also plunged into the counterculture. He lived communally and experimented with various psychedelic drugs. Like most college students of his generation, he had been introduced to drugs by a friend who had acquainted him with marijuana, psychedelic mushrooms, and finally LSD. As a hobby, he used his technical skills to design light shows like the ones that had become standard fare at the Fillmore and the Avalon Ballroom in San Francisco. He began playing around with lasers before they became mainstream devices and built his own projecting kaleidoscope. He also altered a television so that it could create modified Lissajous figures, the patterns of crisscrossing lights that gained popularity when they were used in the opening sequence of *The Outer Limits* TV series ("Do not attempt to adjust the picture—we are controlling transmission . . .").

He was open to the entire variety of sixties California experiences, and attended the frequent lectures given by Ram Dass, the former Harvard psychology professor Richard Alpert, who had been involved in the early LSD experiments with Timothy Leary. He stayed on the edge of the student protest, getting involved in just one sit-in on campus. He decided that he differed from a lot of the radical activists, although he was generally sympathetic with the goal of ending the war. He found he was more closely in tune with the looser counterculture philosophy espoused by Stewart Brand's *Whole Earth Catalog*. He began living in a small commune with five other people near the Stanford campus, where they skinny dipped together in the pond behind their house.

He eventually ran another software consulting service. This time, in an effort to find a market for his optimizer, Ingalls rewrote it for the COBOL programming language, and this proved to be more financially rewarding. The problem was that he hated COBOL, a language so inelegant that he couldn't bear the thought of pursuing it as a long-term business. The optimizer did have a silver lining, however, as he was able to use his expertise as a calling card to get a contract with Xerox, working for George White, another alumnus of SAIL, who had been recruited to work on voice recognition at PARC.

It was Ingalls, in turn, who introduced Ted Kaehler, a friend from Stanford, to PARC. The son of a mechanical engineer who tinkered constantly in the garage and flew airplanes in his spare time, Ted Kaehler grew up steeped in science. He went to the newest of Palo Alto's three high schools, Gunn, which was populated to a great extent by the children of Stanford professors, scientists, and engineers. Indeed, Gunn High backed up against the facilities of Fairchild Semiconductor, the company that in 1957 had begun the Valley's grandest start-up tradition when the legendary "traitorous eight" had quit their jobs at Shockley Semiconductor to found the new company.

Ted had decided to build his own computer in the mid-sixties after reading an article about fluidics in *Scientific American*. Using liquid as a computing medium was an odd notion, and luckily he was disabused of it when he obtained a summer job at Fairchild, where he learned to program using Fortran. At Fairchild he met Wendell Saunders, a senior engineer who took him under his wing and convinced the math prodigy that using silicon chips might actually be a more practical idea.

The following year at Gunn, he became a member of the citywide science club, which met every Thursday evening at the neighboring Palo Alto High School. After each general meeting, the bright students from the city's three schools would break into different special-interest groups. Ted chose the programming group, which was led by the father of a fellow student who was a scientist at IBM's science center on the edge of the Stanford campus.

It was not long before Ted had the run of the place and came in every afternoon to use the typewriter terminal that connected to a large IBM mainframe in New York. Not knowing any better, Kaehler used the computers as if they were personal machines. Once, after he was given the password to the maintenance account for a large

Stanford University mainframe, he began submitting a card deck every evening. Several days went by, and he learned that he had used up the entire maintenance-account budget for the month.

It was a mind-set that became a mantra for the PARC researchers. During the 1970s, Kay's team took special pride in the fact that they could bring any piece of hardware, no matter how powerful, to its knees.

■ ■ ■

By the end of 1972, Kay had the beginnings of a remarkable group, but he came close to not having a computer. PARC had been organized into three different laboratories and had initially put its money into the design of time-shared computers. After all, a computer that could do anything at all worthwhile might still cost anywhere from $50,000 to $100,000, and nobody would entertain the idea of committing that kind of expenditure to a single individual, no matter how productive he might be.

To complicate matters, the unconventional computer designers from the Berkeley Computer Corporation had already succeeded in making waves within the Xerox establishment. Instead of using the controversial Sigma 7 computer that was being manufactured by Scientific Data Systems, the southern California computer division that Xerox had recently acquired, the group decided to embark on the design of a prototype computer called MAXC, a clone of a popular Digital Equipment Corporation computer that had become a standard in the fledgling ARPAnet community.

There were good reasons to do so. Many of the researchers felt it was simply a better design than the Sigma machine. Moreover, it had a much broader software library and thus was more useful. The decision, however, created a permanent rift. Because of Xerox's investment in SDS, this brash move sat poorly with both Xerox management in the east and other factions within the company.

In addition to the problem of the Berkeley designers, when Bill English came from SRI, he had started a project called POLOS

(PARC On-Line Office System), which was intended to become an advanced version of Engelbart's NLS. To host POLOS, PARC had invested in a cluster of Data General Nova minicomputers. The idea was to offer distributed computing, so that each user would feel as if he had his own machine. POLOS was in its own way a radical shift in computing design, one that took advantage of the cost efficiencies of minicomputers and created a system of cooperative computers in which software programs slipped between machines in order to balance the computing load. In many ways, it was an idea that was simply too far ahead of its time.[5]

But it was nowhere near the holy grail of personal computing that Kay was pursuing. He had taken to describing his computing ideas in terms of "interim" Dynabooks—prototype machines that would permit researchers to begin exploring the idea of personal computing. One of the ideas he began calling Minicom. Kay made wood-and-cardboard mock-ups of his planned computers to get a better sense of what they would be like. A portable computer after a fashion—it would be a little like a portable sewing machine—Minicom in his sketches looked quite a bit like the Osborne 1, which became the first commercial portable computer in 1981.

To go along with his concept of a portable computer for kids, Kay had also begun to sketch out the first ideas for a new kind of programming language that he called Smalltalk. With a deft marketing touch, he was betting that if he set people's expectations low enough, then anything positive that came out of the language would be warmly received.

PARC continued the grand ARPA tradition of going on retreats to flesh out big-picture ideas. In January 1972, the PARC researchers flew to Alta, the Utah ski resort, to hold a series of meetings to explore the direction of their research. During their days in the mountains, they discussed one another's dreams for future computers. The researchers already knew about Kay's Dynabook, and other ideas were presented as well. Chuck Thacker wanted to build a computer that was ten times faster than a Nova. Butler Lampson wanted a five-hundred-dollar PDP-10 in a suitcase. The visions were starting to overlap.

In May 1972, Kay proposed Minicom at an open meeting of the PARC Computer Science Laboratory (CSL). He wanted PARC to fund the construction of fifteen of the prototypes so that he could put them in a classroom and experiment with their potential. They wouldn't be as powerful as the Novas that English's POLOS group had been buying, but he envisioned something that would basically be configured out of the guts of a Nova. He had already experimented with Sony's new nine-inch black-and-white cathode-ray display tube and discovered that it would make a fine computer screen for displaying both text and graphics and would fit perfectly in his portable machine.

It was an impressive presentation. Kay sketched out all of the obvious uses for a portable personal computer. It was true, he allowed, that PARC would have to spend thousands of dollars to drive the memory for the video display of the computer, but by now it was clear that eventually memory prices would fall dramatically.[6] But his idea was not well received where it mattered most. Jerry Elkind, the manager of CSL, stood up and proceeded to demolish the entire plan. He pointed out that the group's resources had already been spent on MAXC and that the whole notion fell outside of the lab's charter.

Kay was devastated. He had come to the meeting feeling confident that his concepts were the obvious next step, and now, in a few short minutes, the things he believed in most passionately had been thoroughly eviscerated. He slunk out of the room and once back in his office simply broke down and cried for fifteen minutes. The crisis forced Kay to reset his agenda and start over. He turned to Bill English, who had already become something of an older brother and adviser. English sketched out a new approach involving educational research that might make it possible for the young computer scientist's ideas to gain acceptance in the rarefied world of a corporate-research laboratory.

So Kay picked himself up and began scheming how he could go forward, even without a lab full of computers. He had a little bit of money, and so he began thinking about ways in which he could put together an even less costly interim environment for kids. He could still piggyback off the POLOS research, he decided, and so in the summer he began working in earnest using the Nova character generator that veteran NLS hardware designer Roger Bates had come up with. The device basically allowed the display of multiple fonts on a computer screen.

By the end of the summer, Kay's group was able to perfect the first demonstrations of graphical animation and a computer paint system. They also played around with the idea of a musical synthesizer using the Nova and cobbled together a demonstration that offered three separate voices of high-quality digital music—which wasn't quite enough, but it was a start. That summer, Bill Duvall had come to work for English on the POLOS project and had rewritten the NLS text editor. Kay gradually began to tie everything together into what he envisioned might one day be a personal-computing system, and he reached a point where he had a workable demo running on the Nova 800 installed in the room next to his office.

. . .

Then one day in August, Chuck Thacker and Butler Lampson, who were working in one of the other PARC laboratories, showed up at Kay's office door and asked, "Alan, do you have any money in your budget?"

"Yeah," he replied. "I have about $230,000 I'm planning to use for a handful of these terminals to work with the Nova."

"How would you like us to build your little machine?" they said.

On the face of it, it was a surprising offer, because the two designers were far more orthodox than Kay and aspired to a radically different style of computing: Big Fast Iron. At the same time, Kay's was an oddball little project, and they kind of liked the idea. Moreover, Thacker had always had a bit of a soft spot for the idea of helping children with computing and had assisted Kay with his earlier projects.

Behind the scenes, there was another factor at work. Bob Taylor had been nagging his researchers to build what he thought of as a "display-based computer" for several years. The barrier that he faced was that the designers of the era were still deeply immersed in the metaphor for computing that had been pioneered by John McCarthy: Computers were expensive devices that were to be shared. Although Butler and Thacker had ignored him at first, they had finally come around to the idea.

Taylor, whose training was in the new science of human factors in computer design, was obsessed with ideas such as interactivity and high-bandwidth communication between humans and machines. It was obvious, to someone who had spent years working at the slow and clunky terminals attached to early computers, that a large display would change the very nature of computing. This vision of the future had been codified in 1968 when Taylor and Licklider published their essay "The Computer as a Communication Device" in the journal *Science and Technology*. At the front of the publication was a picture of the two men sitting in their Pentagon office, each in front of his own computer screen.[7]

So the plan was hatched to do the machine quickly on the side, while Jerry Elkind had been called away for several months to serve on a corporate task force. Later, the two computer designers admitted to Kay that their motivation was at least in part a bet that Thacker had made with another Xerox engineer that if a computer was simple enough, he could design it in less than three months. Thacker won the bet.[8]

The result was the Alto, a computer that was so striking and so far ahead of its time that a decade later it continued to startle people who came across it. What the Alto represented was a fresh start in computing based on the untried assumption that everything the computer was capable of doing was intended for a single user. It had a black-and-white display with a slight bluish hue, and it was controlled from a keyboard and a mouse. It was as radical inside as outside. For example, two-thirds of the Alto's memory was dedicated to its display rather than its programs, an idea that would have been unthinkable in previous computers. Moreover, almost all of the computer's processing power was dedicated to the display of information on the screen instead of the actual program. The Alto stood the entire history of computing on its head.

For some, it would take a long time to make the adjustment. A number of high-ranking Xerox executives came to observe the Alto, and their reaction was, "Well, this is nice, but can't we have three or four people using it, because it's kind of expensive."

Which, of course, was missing the point. At the end of 1972, Lampson had offered an explanation for the computer in a memorandum entitled "Why Alto." "If our theories about the utility of cheap, powerful personal computers are correct, we should be able to demonstrate them convincingly on Alto," he wrote. "If they are wrong, we can find out why."

When the Alto came to life in April 1973, the first demonstration included a graphic of the *Sesame Street* character Cookie Monster holding a cookie in one hand and the letter "C" in the other.

Even before the Cookie Monster, though, and in true Alan Kay style, the very first graphical display generated on the still-not-completely born machine was the image of the first page of *Winnie-the-Pooh,* looking identical to the real first page of the book, with the embellishment of little graphical Pooh bears blended into the text. The bears were the result of one of Kay's favorite rants, urging his programmers to figure out how to feature variable-width fonts on the display.

For many, seeing the computer was a life-changing experience. Certainly that was the case when Steve Jobs and his Apple engineers were permitted a brief peek at the Alto in December 1979. But Jobs was not alone. Indeed, for anyone who worked with information, the

Alto gave rise to an almost palpable hunger for that kind of computing power.

•••

It was the Alto that finally brought Doug Engelbart's 1968 demonstration to life, making it accessible beyond the boundaries of a computer laboratory. And yet the first true personal computer remained more or less locked away in Xerox's secretive corporate laboratory throughout the 1970s. It had not quite become public when Stewart Brand's seminal *Rolling Stone* article appeared in December 1972.

In an Annie Leibovitz photo that accompanied the piece and captured the long-haired spirit and free-flowing culture of the lab in the Palo Alto foothills, John Shoch's face was hidden, his nose buried in a notebook. Having managed to navigate the antiwar demonstrations at Stanford, Shoch had developed a good instinct for avoiding trouble. Stewart Brand had been hanging around the lab with the photographer, talking to people, and Shoch had a notion that trouble was exactly what his visits might lead to.

This can't be good, he thought, and ducked his head into his notebook just as Leibovitz snapped a shot of a PARC research group relaxing in a corporate office setting that appeared more like a college dorm room.

Shoch's instincts were correct. When the story appeared in the rock-and-roll magazine, it touched off an explosive reaction at Xerox corporate headquarters in Stamford, Connecticut. The copier company's bread and butter was the corporate marketplace, and Brand's comparison of the future of computing to psychedelics was the last thing it wanted to see in print. The initial reaction from Stamford was that anyone who read *Rolling Stone* must be an irresponsible, no-bathing, sandal-wearing hippie—not Xerox's target customer.

The piece ultimately played a positive role in explaining the West Coast computing culture to the Xerox brass, but in the short run the lab managers were called on the carpet, and the lab was tightly locked down to visitors. Brand had exposed the fault line, the division that ran through the expanding high-tech world. In the past was the traditional world, where technology existed to serve the corporate enterprise. Now, something new was emerging: The cultural outlaws in the west were breaking computing from its mold and simultaneously creating a new medium.

The flap blew over fairly quickly, but it did leave the lab publicity shy. When Brand called Taylor later to tell him he was expanding his article into a book, the two men had a testy back-and-forth over whether the company could be named. Finally, Brand agreed to refer to the lab as the "Shy Research Corporation," which satisfied Taylor.

Lampson's "Why Alto" memo had been circulated just two weeks after the *Rolling Stone* piece appeared, outlining a plan to build as many as thirty Alto personal computers to aid Alan Kay in his educational research. The first machines would cost about $10,500 each, he projected. The machine would have four general applications: networked computing to explore whether the files should be kept separately or on a centralized system; the ability to run Engelbart's NLS; personal computing; and computer graphics.

A decade later, Apple Computer made several attempts at commercializing computers inspired by the Xerox Alto prototypes, but it wasn't actually until 1987, with the introduction of the Mac II personal computer, that the technology that Kay and his group assembled in 1973 was finally available to anyone with a few thousand dollars. And it was decades before his original Dynabook concept became a commercial reality.

In 1972, the first microprocessors had just been introduced, and they were far too puny to power anything other than a hand calculator, and so the Alto employed a custom processor assembled from a costly array of chips. The computer itself stood in a floor-mounted housing about the size of a two-drawer file cabinet. The designers had borrowed crucial ideas from work that English's POLOS group had done—in a sense taking Doug Engelbart's original bootstrapping notion to heart. On the whole, the machine was a remarkable tour de force, but there were still some pieces of the puzzle that were missing. They would be filled in by the first person to uncover the gospel of simplicity.

■ ■ ■

It wasn't until February 1973 that Larry Tesler finally came to PARC. He had taken a circuitous route, and the fact that it took so long for him to finally get a job at the lab would always irk him.

The commune idea hadn't worked out. He ran out of money within six months, it being more expensive to live on a commune in southern Oregon than he had thought it would be. Worst of all, it turned out there were no programming jobs anywhere close to his commune.

He did find one computer in Grants Pass, some forty miles away from his farm. The machine was at the local bank, and when Tesler walked in and asked, "Would you like to hire a programmer?" they responded, "We have very few openings for programmers, and when we do we give the job to a bank teller."

"But I have experience," he said.

"Yes, but we have to give preference to our employees," came the reply.

The next nearest computer was in Ashland, which was a two-hour drive and hardly practical. In the end, Tesler went on welfare for two weeks, long enough to hitchhike back to Palo Alto and start looking for a job. On his trip there he stopped by SAIL and learned that Kay had been looking for him because he wanted to recommend him for a job at PARC.

In December 1970, he called PARC and went over for an interview. At that point there were only about twelve people working at the laboratory.

"Do you want a job?" they asked him.

"No," he replied, "I just want to consult because I want to live in Oregon." The PARC researchers said they would consider the idea.

A month later, however, Tesler returned and said, "I've changed my mind, I would like a job." It was becoming clear that his dream of living in Oregon was fading.

"Too late, we've got a hiring freeze," they told him.

So Tesler went back to work at SAIL, on his text-formatting software.

The following year Kay called him again and told them there was a job in Bill English's POLOS group. Tesler was hesitant because it sounded a lot like corporate, not personal, computing. Tesler had been captivated by Kay's Dynabook idea, but there was no budget for more people to work with him. Kay suggested that he might be able to work part-time with his Learning Research Group and part-time with the POLOS group. However, when the job offer finally did come it was barely more than Tesler was making at Stanford.

Tesler was insulted. He had made more money four years earlier when he was working for himself as a programmer, and he believed corporations should pay higher salaries than the academic world. He turned down the job offer. It was the first time anyone had rejected the laboratory.

A year later, however, the job possibility came up again. This time, he was made a slightly better offer and promised that he could work half-time in Kay's group. This time, he accepted.

Once he arrived, however, he immediately clashed with Doug Engelbart's Augment philosophy of complexity, which had arrived with the SRI émigrés. From Tesler's experience at SAIL he had become dead set against the standard structure of programs in that era. In fact, he had been complaining about "modes" since the first time he had used an interactive computer system. Most programs at the time used separate modes to execute different kinds of tasks. In a word processor, for example, you needed to enter a special mode to center a block of text, one that was separate from the mode for entering the text. Tesler believed that modes made learning too difficult for unskilled computer users.

He disputed Engelbart's view that the leverage the computing tools would provide would be so great that the time spent mastering a complex system would be justified. Engelbart's view was that if people were willing to spend three years learning how to speak a language and ten years learning mathematics and years learning how to read, they should be willing to spend six months to learn how to use a computer.

That's ridiculous, Tesler thought. *You should be able to learn how to use a system in a week.*

"Well, I learned in a week," one of the NLS programmers responded.

"Yeah, but I heard about your secretaries and after six months they still barely use the basic features," he responded. "They don't do what you do."

He began conducting user studies—an effort that had rarely been undertaken before. He was aiming to shorten the learning period to a week, but he discovered that if you designed a simple, easy-to-use editor, it would be possible to master it in an hour.

When he first arrived at PARC, he had met with Jeff Rulifson, who had originally helped design the NLS command language for Engelbart. He told Rulifson that he really didn't like all the modes that were present in NLS and explained why he thought they detracted from the usability of the program.

"Where did this come from?" Tesler asked.

"Well, the funny thing is, I designed it," Rulifson replied.

"What was the principle?" Tesler asked.

"None," was the answer. "They had a project to design a user interface, but they hadn't started it yet."

To the Augment programmers the user interface had been an afterthought. In fact, Rulifson had come up with many of the user-interface commands while he was designing a quality-control program for NLS, and they had stuck. In the POLOS group, the programmers continued to believe the NLS user interface was a powerful design, and English had even hired a writer to document the program and explain it.

Both Tesler and Rulifson thought they could do better. They sat down and wrote a paper describing the idea of an iconic filing system. Their idea was a cartoonlike graphical interface, which they called Overly General Display Environment for Nonprogrammers (OGDEN). They made a brief stab at implementing it but didn't get very far.

It didn't matter, for Tesler was convinced the personal-computing approach of Alto was the right idea. But he immediately ran into a brick wall when English told him they needed to finish POLOS before pursuing his simple computing ideas. That seemed like a blind alley to Tesler, who continued to see NLS as needlessly complex and believed that it was recapitulating all of the shortcomings of the SAIL system.

He decided not to give up. During his time working with Kay, he continued to do user studies, playing around with new ideas on user-interface design, continually trying to come up with features that would be more accessible to unskilled nonprogrammers.

He wrote a very simple editor he called Mini-Mouse—it was essentially just an on-screen typewriter—and brought people off the street who had never seen computers to try it. He was able to show that they could almost instantly begin editing text.

He did another user study with a secretary that demonstrated it was possible to create a much more effective way of commanding a computer.

With some trepidation, Tesler wrote up his results in a paper and submitted it to English. He wasn't sure how the POLOS manager would react and worried that he might even be fired.

In fact, the opposite occurred, for English was a pure engineer, and he had never seen real data on user interfaces before. Now he recognized that Tesler had discovered something important. Additionally, one of the Xerox subsidiaries that was helping pay for PARC had recently complained that it wanted something in return. As a result, English took Tesler off the NLS project and gave him the go-ahead to implement his ideas in the form of an editing system.

With Tim Mott, a computer scientist who had been jointly recruited by PARC and Ginn and Company, Xerox's Boston-based textbook-publishing subsidiary, which had demanded support, Tesler developed a more elaborate text editor. The Alto computers were just getting to the point where it was possible to write software for them. There were only five or six of the machines available at the time they started their project. One was being used to develop the operating system, one was being used in the Smalltalk effort, and one was being used for the new office network called Ethernet.

Tesler and Mott commandeered one of the remaining Altos and got to work. They were so afraid that other people would displace them from the computer that they worked overlapping fourteen-hour shifts, writing code day and night for two months. They had set out to modify another word processor written for the Alto called Bravo. Developed by a young Hungarian émigré, Charles Simonyi, who had also worked at the Berkeley Computer Corporation, Bravo was the first what-you-see-is-what-you-get, or WYSIWYG editor. Out of their work came a program called Gypsy, a simple word processor. It was a modeless text editor that worked with a mouse. It included such innovations as cutting and pasting of text, the ability to drag the mouse to select a block of text, double-clicking on a word to select it, and some command menus. (Drag-select had actually been tried first in the Augment Group, but at that time the early wheeled mice were so imprecise it had proved unworkable. But with the aid of a quirky Berkeley engineer, Jack Hawley, Xerox had refined the mouse so that it now rolled smoothly on a single ball, rather than on two wheels set at right angles.)

For years, the significance of Bravo and Gypsy was lost on Xerox's top management. Yet that breakdown lay at the heart of a cultural abyss that the company failed to cross, and it was the core of the reason that Xerox was unable to capitalize on its dramatic information-technology advantage in the 1970s. Shortly before Simonyi left Xerox for Microsoft, where he designed a new version of Bravo, which became Microsoft Word, an episode transpired that made it clear that, despite the remarkable work being done at PARC, Xerox's executives still did not fathom the meaning of personal computing.

In 1977, Xerox chairman Peter McColough and his nine top subordinates visited PARC for a hands-on demonstration of the Alto technology. It was an ambitious two-day effort to bring the corporate executives up to speed on the power of the technology.

The demonstration failed miserably. Not long after McColough returned to Xerox corporate headquarters, he happened across Robert Flegal, a PARC graphics expert.

"I understand you got a demonstration of Bravo," Flegal said. "What did you think?"

The highest-ranking officer of the dominant office-copier company that now had in its grasp a fundamental new technology for creating digital originals with which to make copies responded, "I've never seen a man type so fast."[9]

If the PARC researchers had understood the cultural realities they were facing, they would have had a woman give the demonstration.

Bravo was the first program to take advantage of the Alto's ability to display fonts on the screen and to display documents exactly as they would look when they were printed. However, because Simonyi used modes, Tesler and Mott believed that the program had gone only part way toward the tool they wanted.

To prove their concept, they took the Gypsy system to the Ginn offices, where there was one word-processing specialist who spent days training temporary workers to use the in-house editing system. Gypsy could be learned in an hour, making it worthwhile for the company to bring in temps for as little as a day, whereas in the past they would have to be hired for at least a month to justify the training investment.

There was another dramatic consequence of Tesler's quest to kill software modes. When he had started working on Mini-Mouse, he found he was writing a lot of software routines for scrolling text that involved moving large blocks of the screen. So he went to Chuck Thacker and told him he wanted an additional instruction that he called "rect-op," for rectangle operation. The idea was to take a block of bits on the screen and be able to easily move it, copy it, or invert it.

"No way," Thacker said, totally opposed to the idea. At that point, the Alto ROM—the most basic software operations built directly into the computer's hardware—had a capacity of only five hundred bytes. "We're expanding it to one thousand," Thacker told him, "but the routine you're describing would probably occupy three hundred bytes just by itself. It's not worth spending 30 percent of the ROM on graphics."

Tesler, however, could be persuasive. He mentioned the idea to Kay and Ingalls, who were both supportive. One day, Ingalls informed Tesler that he was pursuing the idea on an even more ambitious level; moreover, he was going to learn how to program in the lowest-level microcode, so that he could do it in a way that extracted all of the power of the hardware.

Ingalls got started on the project after talking to Diana Merry, who had been working on programming the display of text for Kay's group. As he looked at the problem, Ingalls realized it was a general one that showed up not just for text but in many different cases in the display of all information on a computer's screen.

Can't we do all of these individual cases in one way and in one place? he wondered. He worked on the idea for several months and in the end came up with an idea for moving information that was "bit efficient." In other words, he figured out a way that involved picking up a block of information only once and putting it down once inside the computer's memory.

The idea had come to him visually. When you are moving information on the display, whether it is scrolling or copying text or copying a graphical image from one place to another, you have a source and a destination within the computer's memory. In his mind, he envisioned the concept as a wheel that rotated from the starting point to the end point. It was an idea that seemed obvious after Ingalls had conceived of it, and it has been copied widely by all of the graphical computing systems that have followed. Today it remains at the heart of both the Macintosh and Windows computing worlds. In the early 1970s, however, it was a radically new idea. Called BitBlt, it enabled graphical menu systems to "pop-up" instantly on an Alto screen in response to a mouse click. As much as any single software innovation, BitBlt made the modern graphical computer interface possible.

Did the culture or the times have any effect on the discovery? Ingalls had dabbled in psychedelics and smoked pot to put himself in a more creative, introspective mood. There was no dramatic link as in the case of Kerry Mullis's invention of PCR. Years later, however, when people would ask about the inventive ideas in Smalltalk, Ingalls would joke, "Well, where do you *think* these ideas came from?!"

Ingalls demonstrated the new feature to one of the large weekly meetings of the PARC researchers in the fall of 1974. The gatherings were known as "Dealers" and had been instituted by Taylor, who took the name from the book *Beat the Dealer* by Edward O. Thorp, the MIT professor who had developed a system for winning at blackjack. Taylor was taken by the image of a nerdy math professor beating the house. The meetings became forums for both technical presentations and a kind of group interview system for job candidates.

The demonstration of BitBlt had a dramatic impact both inside and outside of Kay's group. One person who watched the demonstration was Don Wallace. (The veteran Engelbart programmer had come over to PARC as part of a technology exchange aimed at bringing NLS to Xerox.) He was involved with a new programming language called Mesa and was still very much in the big-computer-systems mind-set.

But Ingalls's demo was a cathartic event for Wallace. Afterward, he immediately began working on a mock-up of his own idea of a windowing system on a prototype computer known as the Dolphin. It took about a week for Wallace to replicate Ingalls's invention in the Dolphin's software. That machine later led directly to the Xerox Star, the company's tardy, overly expensive entry into the world of office computing.

■■■

Despite the initial resistance, by 1975 the power of the personal-computing paradigm had become overwhelming. Within the research center, the shift in worldview was complete, and PARC was set firmly on a personal-computing path. The POLOS experiment had run its course, and the distributed-computing ideas that English, Duvall, and the others had begun pursuing would not emerge again for more than two decades.

The scientists at Xerox PARC were convinced they were inventing the future, and so in June 1975 when Larry Tesler walked in one day to tell them that there was something important happening outside the walls of the research center, no one really paid any attention.

Possibly, it wasn't simply arrogance, though the PARC researchers did see themselves as the Davids who were busy slaying the Goliath of corporate time-shared computing. It was, rather, something deeper, something that was probably just a function of basic human nature. It was a pattern that had already been repeated a number of times in computing history and would ultimately be repeated many more times. Even with a strong intellectual grasp of the consequences of Moore's Law, it has proved almost impossible for the members of any given generation of computing technology to accept the fact that it will be cannibalized by an upcoming generation.

Many of the PARC researchers were aware of the computer-hobbyist movement, but because the tiny little machines could hardly do anything they were easy to ignore or dismiss as toys. Later, Alan Kay took pleasure in poking fun at the Homebrewers by saying that the hobbyists actually enjoyed their machines more when they were broken, because then they could actually do something with them.

Larry Tesler, however, had seen something that struck his curiosity. He was then living next door to Fred Moore on Homer Lane in Menlo Park. Both men were single fathers, and they shared a radical political perspective. In the *Whole Earth Catalog* spirit, Tesler's activist neighbor argued with him that people were eventually going to build their own computers. Tesler wasn't so sure about that, but when he saw an advertisement in the local paper announcing the visit of a van to Palo Alto to show off the new MITS Altair 8800 computer kit, he thought he would go take a look. It had been only six months since *Popular Electronics* magazine had published a cover story on the Altair, a blue-edged metal box with lights and switches and not much else. Now the Albuquerque, New Mexico, company that manufactured it was sending a bus on tour around the country to demonstrate it.

Tesler went over to Rickey's Hyatt House Hotel on El Camino Real in Palo Alto to attend the presentation, and though he hadn't been very impressed with the machine, he went straight back to Xerox and said, "I just saw something really important."

Perhaps it was Tesler's experience as an activist or his time spent in grassroots organizations like the Free University that enabled him to discern the formation of a social movement and simultaneously the birth of a new industry. PARC researchers had come to believe they had a monopoly on the idea of the personal computer, but Tesler realized there was this other thing happening—another kind of personal computer. He could see that it would be much less powerful, but he believed that it would almost certainly co-opt the name, and that Xerox had better rethink its strategy.

His words fell on deaf ears. He was able to find only a couple of other converts at PARC. Xerox did set up a corporate task force on personal computing, and Tesler and his two allies were able to present their case before the group, but no one else could conceive of how the tiny machines might constitute a threat.

Tesler bought an IMSAI, another early hobbyist PC, with Xerox money, and he set it up in his office to show people. His visitors pooh-poohed the machine, which they thought was ridiculous.

"Once our stuff comes out it will be so much more powerful and easy to use that everyone will drop those things immediately," Taylor told him.

"You don't understand," Tesler protested. "There's a lot of momentum here."[10]

He was right. The walls were coming down around SAIL, PARC, and Augment. Personal computing was coming to the people, and the man who would bring it would be Fred Moore.

8 | BORROWING FIRE FROM THE GODS

The *Whole Earth Catalog* Demise Party had been one of those serendipitous events that had set Fred Moore's life careening along an alternate path. It had done nothing, however, to offer him any clarity in either life or politics. And it had wound his angst over money up to a fever pitch.

He held several meetings in an effort to build a consensus on how to use the $14,905 that he had so grudgingly pulled out of the coffee can in his backyard. He had been working on his Skool Resistance project and to that now he added the Chrysalis Fund, a nonprofit he created to channel the coffee-can funds. He wanted people to think organically, likening the "tool-money" that had come from the three years of the *Whole Earth Catalog*'s existence to the first stage in the life of a caterpillar.

The Demise Party itself, he suggested in a letter that he sent to one hundred people in September 1971, might be thought of as the second stage. Eventually, he wrote, a butterfly might emerge.

However, no beautiful winged creature was immediately forthcoming. The $14,905 was lent out with predictable consequences, forcing Moore into the unenviable position of becoming a loan collector for a group of generally disreputable and unreliable clients. That only added to his stress over money and his general philosophy that it lay close to the root of all evil.

It was all a great hassle, and his internal emotional conflict only deepened when the Point Foundation, a grant-making organization that Stewart Brand had set up to give away more of the Whole Earth project's money, gave him an additional $15,000. "Having it ($15,000), does not seem to bring me closer to any solutions," he wrote in his first progress report to the foundation. "I felt closer when I was broke. Although the daily problems I had when I was broke seemed to prevent much progress toward solutions, because I had to spend time each day providing for survival and doing that within the money economy, part time jobs, expenses for this and that."[1]

Several months later, he penned his continuing frustrations in his journal:

> Can't sleep. Lie Awake. Head full of thoughts—things to do, things that are needing to be done—details, mail, my change of address has been fouled up. But most of what bothers me is that I am full of confusion. My life daily I see is fragmented, at cross-purposes. I'm caught in a multitude of contradictions. . . . I need to be part of a community. I need to move from here. Or radically alter my living pattern here. I would like my life–daily living to be all of a piece/peace. I want to settle down—but where?[2]

His life was an ongoing jigsaw puzzle, and he kept struggling to put the pieces in order. The Alternatives conference, where he had forgotten his daughter, Chiqui, was one of those pieces. One project from the conference had been to create a computer database of all the people who had attended—they came from throughout the country—and output a listing with their addresses and categories representing their interests.

The database was eventually generated at the Stanford Medical Center, where Moore had known several of the computer operators. The center had a surplus of computing power and an eclectic group of people managing the machines. Both Larry Tesler and Jim Warren had worked there, and the center maintained a relatively open-door policy, supported by people such as Walt Reynolds, an electrical engineer who worked for medical researcher Joshua Lederberg. Politically sympathetic and involved in the Free University, Reynolds had become a friend and mentor to Moore when he arrived back on the West Coast in 1968.

Coming in contact with computers proved to be another piece of Moore's puzzle. During the sixties, Moore had largely left behind the science and math he had pursued in high school and college, but he had retained a special aptitude for creating useful tools from simple components.

Now his friendship with Reynolds and other activists who were working at the medical school gave him access to computers, and it set him thinking about using the machines to help his organizing efforts. He would return to the center for hours at a time—occasionally leaving his daughter outside in his Volkswagen bus—teaching himself basic programming skills.

At the same time, although the machines were compelling, he remained ambivalent about computing. From the point of view of the counterculture, mainframe computers were synonymous with Big Brother and bureaucracy. Yet it was increasingly obvious to Moore that if the power of computing could be liberated, it would become a useful organizing tool.

He began to think about the idea of an information network that would connect the people on the Alternatives conference list. What if there was a way to enable communication between people who were involved in all kinds of organizing efforts all around the world? Moore, in fact, was an organizer's organizer. He was an inveterate list maker and note taker, and he always carried with him a small spiral-bound notebook to jot down addresses of the people whom he met in his draft-resistance travels.

In June 1972, he wrote a series of funding proposals for an information-access network to be based at the Whole Earth Truck Store on Santa Cruz Avenue in Menlo Park. Initial reactions were lukewarm, and no funding was forthcoming, but he kept playing with the idea, and in October he established a nonprofit information network aimed at tying together all the disparate odds and ends of the counterculture.

As he envisioned it initially, the information network would be a nationwide project that would be run through the mail to draw together all the people who were interested in building the alternative institutions and technologies that were featured in the *Whole Earth Catalog*. Using the catalog as a classification system, a person would join for a nominal fee and in return he or she would be sent a list of all the people who shared similar interests. At this juncture, the system wasn't computerized but was only Fred Moore, opening the mail, keeping records on three-by-five file cards, and preparing the lists.

That there was a better way to carry on the basics of political and community organizing was staring Moore in the face. Just across town was the People's Computer Company, holding out the promise of smaller computers that could not only free workers from manual drudgery but shift the balance of power away from giant corporations.

■ ■ ■

It was an idea that was attractive not just to activists like Moore but to some of the insiders as well, engineers who loved the machines as ends unto themselves.

The same long-ago fall that Fred Moore had made his stand on the steps of Sproul Plaza at the University of California, another young man had arrived in Berkeley. Dennis Allison was a tall, dark-bearded, and somewhat detached physics undergraduate who had transferred from UCLA in part because Berkeley was where the physics action was and in part because he was—unsuccessfully, as it turned out—chasing a young woman. After graduating, Allison spent another year and a half hanging out on the fringes of the Berkeley student scene until economic necessity forced him to look for work.

The job he took, it turned out, was an interesting but lonely one. Allison's physics degree was a commodity that was in demand at Stanford Research Institute. He was hired there and soon found himself in an isolated part of Florida, downrange from a missile test site that was tracking the flight of various military rockets. He was responsible for the esoteric radio equipment that was used to plot the trajectories of missiles in the atmosphere. Because Allison's expertise was in radio physics, he wound up with a night job, since most of the missiles were fired at 3:00 A.M., when they were least likely to disturb civilians. For the most part, the work was highly technical and uneventful. There was, however, the evening of the third day of the Cuban missile crisis, when other military radars tracked one of the experimental launches, and planes were scrambled from a nearby air force base. The launches were temporarily put on hold.

When Allison came back to the West Coast, he initially spent time working for the classified side of SRI, but soon, like many others, he became more intrigued with computing. The classified division had a growing need for computing power, and it had a second SDS-940 machine, similar to the one used by Engelbart's group, to which Allison had ready access. Because of the security rules, the classified computer was not a time-sharing system, and Allison was able to use it as his own personal device much of the time. He built software compilers for projects at SRI as well as other programming-development tools, both for his own use and other groups at the institute. He became friends with some of the people in Engelbart's group, and for a while he was chairman of the local chapter of the Association for Computing Machinery. Ultimately, he was seduced by the open computing world, and when Engelbart gave his demonstration in San Francisco in December 1968, Allison was able to watch the remote half of the presentation from a corner of the Menlo Park laboratory.

An incurable software hacker, he helped out another group of programmers at SRI who were creating a version of BASIC for a mainframe computer. Several years later, his experience with the language, which had been designed as an educational tool, proved fortuitous.

Swept up by the Midpeninsula counterculture, Allison became an active member of the Free University, helping to create an informal alternative salon called the Woods Seminar, after its birthplace in Los Trancos Woods, in the hills behind Stanford. At the Free U, he met Jim Warren and then briefly became Warren's professor at San Francisco State University, where he was teaching in the medical informatics program.

One day at an ACM conference in San Francisco, Allison stopped by an interesting booth where Bob Albrecht, computing enthusiast, was pitching the idea of computers for kids. Albrecht had already created Dymax, as well as the People's Computer Company newsletter. Albrecht had decided that a nonprofit home for the newsletter would be useful, which Allison thought was a great idea. They exchanged phone numbers and before long had incorporated the People's Computer Company.

Allison was still working at SRI at the time, plus he had a family and two small kids, so Albrecht did most of the work, with Allison and Stewart Brand's wife, Lois, as the other two founding board members. Albrecht lived the PCC day and night, swapping computers for technical writing, hustling donations, and attracting an unruly crowd, mesmerized by the computing world. Although the PCC was only a storefront, early on it attracted a much wider following than its tiny physical size would suggest.

The PDP-8 computer that Albrecht had acquired wasn't a personal computer, but it was, after a fashion, certainly a desktop computer, albeit a bulky one. It had a front panel complete with plastic toggle switches and blinking lights, and it served an array of four terminals that could print out a line at a time on a roll of computer paper. It was possible for anyone to come in off the street and rent computer time on the system to play games or do word processing or program for a nominal twenty-five cents per hour.

Every year the Japanese Ministry of International Trade and Industry (MITI) sent a delegation to the large industrial computer meetings, and the delegation of a dozen or so Japanese businessmen and technocrats would invariably be taken on a tour of Silicon Valley companies. More than once, the delegation stopped by to visit PCC's minuscule operation.

It was definitely a collision of cultures. In their carefully pressed suits, the Japanese seemed truly mystified by the ragtag, long-haired corps of volunteers and hangers-on. On one occasion, however, the visitors included a young Japanese engineering student named Kazuhiko Nishi. The jowly and bright-eyed Nishi understood English, had a flair for business, and was remarkably enthusiastic, as he immediately saw gold in the fledgling operation. He returned to Japan and became the Japanese distributor for PCC publications while he was still a college student. Soon after that, he started a computer-publishing firm called ASCII. In 1978, Nishi tracked down a young Bill Gates and played a crucial role in the events that led to the IBM PC and Microsoft's MS-DOS operating system.

Among other visitors to PCC, perhaps no other was as influential as Theodor Holm Nelson, a college friend of Andy van Dam, the Brown University computer scientist. Nelson had coined the term "hypertext" as part of his vision of a worldwide electronic publishing system he dubbed Xanadu, and the two men had collaborated in developing the editing system van Dam was pursuing when he saw Engelbart's 1968 demonstration.

The son of actress Celeste Holm and film director Ralph Nelson, he had read a history of American bohemianism in fifth grade and decided that he had found his milieu. Later, he would assert that while he was a student at Swarthmore he had coauthored the first rock musical, in 1957. Ted Nelson had also studied with the conservative Harvard sociologist Talcott Parsons. At that time, he discovered computers and independently hit upon some of the same ideas that were beginning to float openly in the computer labs surrounding Stanford in the 1960s and early 1970s.

In 1974, Nelson lashed all of his ideas together in a self-published computing manifesto that openly imitated Brand's *Whole Earth Catalog*. Organized as a mélange of useful information about computers as tools, it actually consisted of two books, *Computer Lib* and *Dream Machines*, published as one: a reader could begin either by simply turning the book over and reading from the opposite direction. Printed in the same oversize format as the *Whole Earth Catalog*, the cover of *Computer Lib* was emblazoned with a stark white power-to-the-people clenched fist on a black background beneath the imperative: "You can and must understand computers NOW."

A potpourri of useful and useless information, Nelson's book attempted to establish clearly that the computer was a universal medium: "Forget what you've ever heard or imagined about computers," he instructed his readers. "Just consider this: The computer is the most general machine man has ever developed."

"I have an axe to grind," Nelson wrote in the introduction. "I want to see computers useful to individuals, and the sooner the better, without necessary complication or human servility being required."

In his quest Nelson found common ground with the radicals: "A chant you can take to the streets," he thundered, "COMPUTER POWER TO THE PEOPLE! DOWN WITH CYBERCRUD!" To Nelson's thinking and to the minds of the People's Computer Company hobbyists, cybercrud was the embodiment of the dull, gray, IBM-dominated world of the computing professionals. His book, he explained, was his break with the world of computer professionals, who had once been genuine computer fans but who had unfortunately grown older and become reactionary.

It was another mark of the digital divide between the class of experts who controlled the machines from within the glass rooms and the unruly outsiders who had begun to glimpse the idea of computing as a medium, one they could control for their own means.

By the early 1970s, Menlo Park had become ground zero for the new search for community that had evolved from the antiwar politics and the drug culture of the previous decade. Just blocks from where

Jim Fadiman and Myron Stolaroff had introduced hundreds to the spectral intoxication of LSD, there was now a thriving community network ranging from the Whole Earth Truck Store, Bob Albrecht and Dick Raymond's Portola Institute, the People's Computer Company, and the Midpeninsula Free University store and print shop. In 1975, the Briarpatch food co-op was added to the community.

Because all these organizations shared the common values of making access to tools and information freely available, it was not surprising that that view would be likewise applied to the software that was necessary to animate the machines that were beginning to become accessible to organizations like the PCC.

The PCC model was a simple one—part hobbyist, part political counterculture. You made the software available for free, and anyone could do anything they wanted with it. If they wanted to make money on it, that was just great.

As part of his work at SRI, Allison had helped develop a mainframe BASIC programming language called Interaccess BASIC. Interaccess was a time-sharing firm that had been started by a small group of SRI alumni, who had contracted with the think tank for the software as part of their plan to compete with the dominant time-sharing company Tymshare. The group had bought a handful of CDC 3800 computers that had been sold as surplus by the nearby Air Force Satellite Control Facility in Sunnyvale. At the time, the machines were the cheapest computing system you could possibly purchase. Their business plan positioned them to be a Tymshare competitor for one-third the price.

When in early 1975 an Altair 8800 computer showed up at the PCC office, Allison carefully looked at its specifications, and what he discovered horrified him.

"Two hundred fifty-six bytes of memory! You can't do anything with this machine," he said. He had been a consultant at Intel on the first microprocessor, the 4004, and so he had a clear sense of how much code was necessary to make the newer 8080 microprocessor do anything useful.

"How much do you have to have?" Albrecht asked. "This memory costs an awful lot of money."

Allison thought about it for a moment and replied, "I don't know, maybe two thousand bytes."

At the time, makers of add-in memory cards were just starting to introduce their products, and so it was possible to buy the computer starter kit and then expand it by adding peripherals. But the severe constraints of the hobbyist machine served as a challenge to Allison, and as a result Tiny BASIC was born. While it couldn't do the more ambitious things his mainframe BASIC made possible, his notion was to make the programming language absolutely as small as possible in part by insuring that it reused its different internal functions as frequently as possible. Soon it would lead to the first open clash between the world of shared software and the industry created by Bill Gates, the young software hacker who was destined to become the world's richest man.

After a fair amount of friendly coercion, Albrecht had persuaded Allison to draw up his outline for this simpler BASIC, which he sketched as a "participatory project" in the PCC newsletter. The idea was to create a framework for the language in a three-article series, and Allison, who was a bit of a procrastinator, would generally write each of them in an afternoon the day before the publication was supposed to go to press.

The first issue went out, and Allison and Albrecht were immediately overwhelmed with an unexpectedly enthusiastic response. Hobbyists deluged the magazine with different versions based on Allison's rough sketch. It was a foreshadowing of what was to come, for even at the onset of the personal-computing revolution, the forces that two decades later would drive the free-software movement were already very much alive.

The first working version of Tiny BASIC was created by a couple of guys in Texas. It showed up written in machine language, ready to be printed and distributed by the PCC within three weeks after Allison's original proposal had been mailed out. Other hobbyists who tested the program immediately began mailing in bug reports and suggesting improvements. The reaction was so strong that Albrecht suggested that PCC begin publishing a Tiny BASIC newsletter to be cranked out on a Xerox machine in an office across the street. From a list they had created from the replies to the Tiny BASIC article, they sent out an announcement of the newsletter to four hundred or five hundred names. Almost 100 percent of them asked to subscribe, and it was not long before the Tiny BASIC newsletter morphed into a full-blown magazine for hobbyists and programmers.

The magazine took its name in the typically informal PCC manner. The typesetter at the PCC was a mysterious young man named Eric Bakalinsky, who was also editing a black community newspaper, although he himself was not black, rather Jewish, with a large Afro. He was then working at the PCC doing typesetting in exchange for personal access to the typesetting equipment. Bakalinsky was a rather unusual guy whose father was an anesthesiologist in San Francisco. Everyone agreed he had a way with words, including the ability to formulate a succession of puns one after another, often leaving the PCC volunteers on the floor in laughter.

One afternoon, Albrecht and Allison gathered all of the articles for the first expanded issue, tossed them on Bakalinsky's light table, and said, "Why don't you put this together?" The two men were heading out the door to what they liked to call PCC's "executive conference room," which in fact was around the corner at the Village Host pizza and beer joint.

Bakalinsky called out, "What should I call it?"

"You're bright, you'll figure it out," Allison replied.

Bakalinsky went around the office asking, "What's this about?"

"Oh, it's about Tiny BASIC," came the reply.

"What's Tiny BASIC?" he asked.

"BASIC is an exercise in computer programming," was the answer.

"Well, what's tiny about it?" he wanted to know

"Oh, it doesn't use very many bytes of memory," they told him.

"Who created it?" he queried.

"Oh, Dennis and Bob put it together," they responded.

That was enough for Bakalinsky. Dennis and Bob became Dobb. An exercise in computer programming was calisthenics, and not many bytes of memory was avoiding overbite.

There it was: *Dr. Dobb's Journal of Tiny BASIC Calisthenics and Orthodontia.*

Allison soon realized that he would never have the time to edit a magazine. While he was grappling with that reality, he received a call from Jim Warren. Warren had just lost his research assistantship and been bounced out of the Stanford computer-science program, where he had been studying for several years. He hadn't really fit into the school, which had been demanding he write a theoretical dissertation. When the faculty member to whom he was closest lost his tenure bid, it was time to start looking for something else to do.

So Warren began contacting his friends, seeing if they had any odd jobs, and when he reached Allison his reaction was, "I have the perfect job for you. Let's get together and talk about it over dinner."[3]

For $350 a month, Warren took over as editor of the new magazine and quickly revised the name slightly to read: *Dr. Dobb's Journal of Computer Calisthenics and Orthodontia: Running Light Without Overbyte.*

In his first issue, Warren spelled out the goal for *Dr. Dobb's:* "The Journal is explicitly available to serve as a communication medium concerning the design, development, and distribution of free and low-cost software for the home computer." Since at the time there was neither a real personal-computer industry nor a mature software industry, today's sharp debate between proprietary and shared software was not broached. However, the roots of the bitter conflicts surrounding digital information ranging from free software to file sharing were being laid.

As it grew more and more popular, the PCC became perhaps the oddest of cultural and technical intersections. Long hair was the rule, along with torn jeans and sandals, but it was also host to a sprinkling of serious engineering types and no shortage of kids. In

1975, the People's Computer Company was pulsing with energy. Reflecting Albrecht's frantic style, it had become a community center housing all kinds of interests, ranging from an artist's studio, to a place to bring kids for birthday parties. There were bookshelves that contained an eclectic range of materials including a shelf devoted to science fiction. The community spirit spilled over into regular Wednesday-night potluck dinners, which attracted an eclectic crowd. The idea had been pure Albrecht, who would confide in an unguarded moment that his real agenda in hosting the potlucks was to teach Greek folk dancing, which he would do at the least provocation. For the assembled crowd, the evenings fueled the deeper desire for obtaining their own computers, machines they could control on their own.

On Fridays, the PCC would host "game nights," when the building filled up with testosterone-charged teenage boys all bent on playing at the Teletypes. The PCC organizers would look the other way and pray that not too much damage was done. There were lots of games, some of which had names like Hurkle, Snark, and Mugwump. A version of *Star Trek* that was written in BASIC and designed for the Teletype terminals allowed imaginary space battles to be played out in a galaxy consisting of sixty-four squares laid out in an eight-by-eight array. The field of play was repeatedly typed by the printer after each move, leaving almost everything that happened to the computer user's imagination.

In contrast with today's hyperrealistic PC video-game graphics such effects might seem pedestrian. However, as the early computer-game company Infocom said in its 1980s ads for text-adventure games, "The best graphics are in your head."

Indeed, one of the most popular versions of these games was Wumpus, which was written in 1973 by Gregory Yob. Wumpus was a maze game that was a precursor of the more ambitious text-adventure games.

Yob had visited the PCC and seen early maze efforts. He later wrote that when he looked at the games, his reaction was "ECCH!!"

He decided that there had to be a hide-and-seek adventure that wasn't dependent on grids and dots.[4]

He began meditating on the phrase "Hunt the Wumpus" and went home and wrote his own maze game, in which the computer responded interactively to a user by presenting him with a text scene that could be navigated through. He dropped the program off at PCC, where it soon became hugely popular and was later published in the PCC newsletter.

Yob realized that he had created a hit about a month later when he attended the same Alternatives conference where Fred Moore had lost track of his daughter, Chiqui. "Many far-out folk were gathered to share their visions of improving the world," he wrote.[5] He also discovered that PCC had brought over a few terminals, which were left running in the conference room. To his shock, all of them were running Wumpus, and scraps of paper littered the floor, with scrawled numbers on them indicating that "much dedicated Wumpus-hunting was in progress."

Another person who was attracted to PCC early on was Howie Franklin, who had studied applied mathematics at Brown University under Andy van Dam and come to Stanford for graduate school in 1969. He didn't last long, having been radicalized in 1970 by the National Guard shootings at Kent State. All of a sudden, studying numerical methods didn't make sense. At a campus teach-in, he listened to Ira Sandperl talk about pacifism and Gandhi. Franklin hadn't connected at all with the SDS types on campus, but Sandperl's words rang true.

He dropped out of school and joined a War Resisters League bus that was traveling through the South organizing against the war. When he came back to Menlo Park in 1973, he ended up living down the street from the PCC. He walked in one day and immediately hit it off with Albrecht. He loved the center and soon became one of its driving forces. Where previously his computing skills had seemed without purpose, he now connected computing to his politics within a hippie culture. Franklin eventually coauthored *What to Do After*

You Hit Return with Albrecht, an introduction to programming games in BASIC that soon became a hot seller.

Another of the potluck regulars was Lee Felsenstein, who would arrive each Wednesday evening by train from San Francisco, where he was tending an SRI mainframe computer that had been donated by the Transamerica Leasing Corporation to Project One community activists who had taken over a warehouse in the city's South-of-Market district. For Felsenstein, the PCC was a glimpse of the future, as forecast by Nelson and Albrecht.

A veteran of the Berkeley Free Speech Movement whose career had already run the gamut from being a junior engineer at Ampex to working on the editorial collective of the *Berkeley Barb,* Felsenstein, like Lenny Siegel at Stanford, was an antiwar activist who was not anti-technology. Instead, he was committed to using his technical skills to help the cause. During the Free Speech Movement, Felsenstein had performed pedestrian tasks such as running the mimeograph machine, which was routinely delegated to the nerds. One night, he was hanging around the student-group headquarters when somebody came running in and—erroneously—reported that police had surrounded the campus. It seemed to Felsenstein that everybody went into a frenzy and turned to him in unison, yelling, "Quick, make us a police radio!"

Flustered, he responded, "You don't understand—you can't do something like that that quickly."[6]

The incident led him to realize that he would never be able to come up with technical solutions on demand, and so he decided to take the responsibility for working on useful technologies ahead of time. Several years later, he was using his ability as an engineer to do things like build bullhorns and maintain radios for the antiwar movement. He had decided that he would actively shy away from the intensely political leadership meetings, instead styling himself as a movement technician.

"You decide, I'll just implement," he had concluded.

Felsenstein's people's technology—bullhorns, radios, and shields—played a significant role in the Oakland Stop the Draft Week protests in 1967, but afterward he was not one of the seven leaders who were indicted. He came to realize that technology by itself had the power to invisibly transform political events. He had had an impact, but he hadn't showed up on police radar screens. It was a powerful lesson.

As the antiwar movement wound down, Felsenstein returned to school at Berkeley and rekindled an early love affair with computing. The seed had been planted, and now it led to a new kind of politics. Perhaps, he thought, power no longer grew from the barrel of a gun, perhaps it would in the future accrue to anyone who owned a computer. Felsenstein came to embody a populist computing spirit, ultimately designing several early personal computers including the hobbyist Sol and the first portable, the Osborne 1.

It was also inevitable that Bob Albrecht and Fred Moore would meet. Moore had been playing with computers at the Stanford Medical School computing center and was running his information network out of the Whole Earth Truck Store while scheming to find his own computer to move the project into a real database. Moore began making an effort to find out more about the computing resources around the Midpeninsula. He called Alan Kay at Xerox and had lunch with him at Rossotti's, the beer garden on Alpine Road west of Stanford University. He made a number of visits to the Stanford Artificial Intelligence Laboratory, although he came away skeptical about the possibility of machines mimicking humans. He also found his way to Doug Engelbart's Augmentation Research Center and talked briefly with one of Engelbart's business managers.

Despite his wariness about technology, Moore found himself increasingly drawn to computers. He was not really a programmer, but he had begun to teach himself the fundamentals. He spent hours at the medical center, and afterward, walking outside, he would feel as if he were returning from another world. He would feel as if his head were spinning and that he had been spending his time in a narrow tunnel, almost as if he had been inside the machine itself.[7]

Albrecht had a room full of small computers and terminals, and when the two men did meet, in his typical open style Albrecht invited Moore to relocate his information network to the PCC. It was a great move for Moore, who got relatively steady work teaching classes on how to write computer games. At one point he was teaching as many as thirteen classes each week and was making more money than he had ever made before. Albrecht and Moore also teamed up to teach a course they called Electronic Magic Boxes at the Peninsula School, the Menlo Park alternative school. It was a simple course in the fundamentals of electronic design, using digital components to make things like coin tossers, electronic dice, metronomes, and burglar alarms. Teaching was a perfect position for Moore in another sense, as it fit with his notion that people shouldn't go to school to get educated but rather should teach themselves and one another.

Moore's antiestablishment, alternative community outlook was a perfect match for the world of hobbyist computing. He took a political view of his time spent teaching at the People's Computer Company, figuring that it would help demystify computers, putting them directly in the hands of the people.

Perennially searching for community, Moore became a regular at the PCC potlucks. Even though he wasn't on the technical level of many of the other participants, he loved the idea of a shared passion, and it fed his growing dreams of having his own computer. It would be great, he decided, to have a machine that could justify columns of text and give him some control over the fonts for the flyers he wanted to print.

The do-it-yourself spirit of the crowd that showed up for Howie Franklin's weekly pot of spaghetti was also a perfect realization of Fred Moore's grassroots economic ideas. Larry Tesler had been skeptical about the notion of people building their own computers in the Heathkit style of the electronic experimenters, but here was a group that badly wanted to do just that.

Joan Koltnow, a teacher whom Franklin and Albrecht had met at a math conference and recruited to work at PCC, was one attendee who was a little put off by the Wednesday-evening scene. Computing and folk dancing was an odd enough combination, but to make matters worse it was a remarkably scruffy crowd, which in general took the notion of potluck to mean contributing a family-size bag of potato chips.

One of those who set Koltnow most on edge was an unusual character who referred to himself as Cap'n Crunch and who brought with him an obsession for using technology illicitly. Crunch was John Draper, a former air force technician who had worked with radar and secure communications equipment while in the military. After leaving the service, he had bounced around the Bay Area working as an engineering technician at National Semiconductor, as a radio engineer for a local FM station, and at Hugle International, a small electronics company, where he had begun to design a cordless phone before the effort had collapsed and he left to study at De Anza Community College.

Draper's life had taken a strange turn in the late 1960s when he met a young blind man named Denny who had demonstrated how the whistle that came in the Cap'n Crunch cereal box was tuned to the precise frequency that enabled it to control the long-distance calling switches of the AT&T telephone network.[8] Draper subsequently found his way into a subterranean cult of young "phone phreaks," who explored the innards of the vast global telephone network with the passion of a Bilbo Baggins setting out from Hobbiton. Draper became notorious under the name Cap'n Crunch after his antics with the telephone system were described in an article in *Esquire* magazine by Ron Rosenbaum, titled "Secrets of the Little Blue Box," which appeared in the October 1971 issue.

Margaret Wozniak, whose son Steve was then studying at the University of California at Berkeley, saw the article and mailed a copy of it to him at his campus dormitory. Wozniak was entranced. He had never been so excited, and he started sharing the story with anyone who would listen to him. Several days later, a friend from high school came by to visit, and as he listened to Wozniak expound on the character known as Cap'n Crunch, interrupted him and said, "I know who Cap'n Crunch is."

"What do you mean? Nobody knows who he is! The FBI doesn't even know who he is!" Wozniak shot back.

"I worked at KKUP in Cupertino," his friend answered. "He worked there. A guy by the name of John Draper said he was Cap'n Crunch."

Wozniak was determined to find Crunch and enlisted another high school friend, Steven Jobs, in the hunt. Jobs was back in the Bay Area after having dropped out of Reed College and traveling in India for several months. When Draper heard they were searching for him, he drove to Berkeley.

Mustached and wearing horn-rimmed glasses, Draper strolled into Wozniak's dorm room and with a flourish announced, "It is I!"[9] Draper tutored Wozniak and Jobs in the art of building their own blue boxes, devices that were capable of gaining free—and illegal— access to the phone network. The two novice entrepreneurs sold the blue boxes door to door on the Berkeley campus, several years before they founded Apple Computer.

After the *Esquire* article came out, Draper became a target for the FBI and local telephone-security agents. He was arrested, convicted, and sent to jail for phone fraud several times during the 1970s. During his first stay in prison, he was beaten up badly enough to scar him both physically and psychologically for years afterward.

Draper would eventually become one of the most tragic figures of the personal-computing era. Several years later, he wrote the first word processor to come bundled with the IBM PC, which would make him quite wealthy. Later, having squandered his fortune, he found himself homeless. For a while he worked with Ted Nelson at Autodesk, an early PC software company. Years later, during the dot-com boom, he did pioneering website design while on the Goa coast in India.

...

By 1975, though PCC, the nation's first storefront educational computer center, was booming, tensions that had long simmered below its surface started coming into the open. Bob Albrecht could be a difficult guy to get along with. He could be argumentative and had the ability to bicker seemingly interminably over minor decisions. Koltnow decided that it was easier to simply say, "Yes, Bob," and let the matter slide than to take the time to make a point.

The issues eventually became difficult enough that Dennis Allison was forced to broker a breakup of the center. People's Computer Company would remain dedicated to its original publishing mission, but the activists, including Franklin and Moore, decided to create a new entity to be called the People's Computer Center, the mission of which was to focus on outreach and computer education from the storefront on Menalto Avenue.

Ever the organizer, Moore took notes during the meeting at which the split was formalized:

a Computer Center

Thrust of center on 8080 technology (low cost computer)

That a Corporation be formed known as Peoples Computer Center at this address consisting of personal [sic] working there and that corporation be separate from P.C. Company. . . .

A legal separation so that there is no liabilty of PCCenter to PCCompany or PCCompany to PCCCenter

Newspapers are communication, centers are local and different.[10]

In the end, Albrecht was a gentleman about the divorce, and the People's Computer Company contributed money and equipment to the new venture.

The split didn't solve all the problems, however, or end all of the bad feelings. Some of Albrecht's staff and volunteers felt that he was taking their hard work for granted. That was particularly true of Moore and another regular, Gordon French. A programmer with a military security clearance, French was a bit of an odd duck among the computing hippies at PCC. He was an engineer in the optimistic American tradition of the fifties and sixties. He had already built his own personal computer from the ground up and named it Chicken Hawk. Personal computing was simply one in a series of hobbies that included a remarkably ambitious model train set.

French, in particular, didn't get along well with Albrecht. He had been turned down in his request to become a board member of the People's Computer Company. He believed the PCC founder was jealous of potential competitors and complained that he was going to be taken advantage of and conned into working on a book on assembly-language programming for Dymax. The same was true of Fred Moore, who had also begun to feel that his labor was not being recognized and was doubly irritated that he had been pigeonholed by Albrecht as someone who would do all the grunt work.

The conflict came to a head over the PCC quarterly newsletter that Moore was helping put together. From time to time Albrecht gave Moore encouragement, telling him that he planned on retiring at some point and that Moore could replace him as editor.

One day, a reporter from *Datamation,* a computer-industry magazine, showed up to write a profile about the People's Computer Company.

"What's your role?" the writer asked Moore.

"Basically a lot of shit work," he answered. "I'm also assistant editor."

After the reporter left, Albrecht dressed down Moore, complaining that he had overstated his responsibilities. Moore was stunned. He began to realize that there wasn't a lot of room for others in the limelight at PCC. He decided that Albrecht had a remarkable talent for bringing together smart and creative people but wasn't generous about sharing the credit.[11]

Moore continued to dream of building his own personal computer. He was still keeping his tiny information network going while he was at PCC, but three-by-five cards had real limits. Once his list had grown beyond fifty to sixty names, he came to recognize that the variety of categories and key words he had chosen quickly overwhelmed his hand-sorting abilities.[12] Why not, he thought, give a class where people would build their own systems from scratch? When he approached Albrecht with the idea, however, he ran into a stone wall. Albrecht had no quarrel with the idea of the class, but he didn't feel any obligation to supply Moore with the PCC's money or other resources to sponsor it.

At the same time, the split between the People's Computer Company and the People's Computer Center was leading to the phasing out of the potlucks. After one of the last Wednesday evenings, Moore and French stood outside and talked about how they were going to miss the events and how there was no longer going to be any regular forum for people who were interested in building their own computers to stay in contact.

Wouldn't a computer club be the best way to keep up the spirit of exchange? French offered his garage as a meeting place and loaned Moore five dollars for the cost of producing the flyers to announce the formation of the group.

The next day, Moore scribbled the wording for his flyer in his notebook and then took the final announcement around by bicycle and mailed it out to a small list. It read:

Amateur Computer users Group
Homebrew Computer Club . . . you name it.

Are you building your own computer? Terminal, TV typewriter? I/O
Device? or some other digital black-magic box?

Or are you buying time on a time-sharing service?

**If so you might like to come to a gathering of people with like-
minded interests. Exchange information, swap ideas, talk shop,
help work on a project, whatever . . . [13]**

One person who saw the flyer was Allen Baum, who was working
at Hewlett-Packard at the time with his friend Steve Wozniak. The
two had met in high school when Baum had seen Wozniak sitting in
his homeroom class drawing strange graphics in a notebook.

"What are you doing?" Baum asked.

"I'm designing a computer," was Wozniak's reply.

It turned out that Baum had on his own become intrigued with
computers just months earlier after his father, who had moved the
family from the East Coast, took a job at Stanford Research Institute. Shortly after they arrived, he had brought his son to the laboratory one Saturday morning. As they walked down the darkened
hallways, they passed one office where the lights were on. Baum
ducked his head in and saw a man with prematurely silver hair operating a machine that sat next to what seemed like an immensely
large television screen. He was sitting in front of a keyboard and
controlling a hand-sized device that he was sliding along the surface
of the desk.

It was Doug Engelbart.

Baum and Wozniak had remained close friends through college,
and Baum had helped Wozniak get a job at HP. Now he phoned his
friend to tell him about the flyer, and they both decided to show up
for the meeting.

The event itself was something of a disappointment for Baum,
who had access to much more powerful machines than the anemic
Altair that Bob Albrecht brought to the meeting to demonstrate. For
the rest of the thirty-two people who showed up that evening, how-

ever, the first Homebrew event was a revelation. Computing was still basically locked up inside corporations and research laboratories, but a crack had just opened in the wall.

Albrecht showed up for the first meeting but came only infrequently afterward. The Homebrew hackers were quickly descending into a world that was far too arcane for him, and he recalled later that he understood only about one out of every three words that first night. Dennis Allison also came to the first meeting and stood with other hobbyists out under the streetlights in the mist from the wet night, waiting for Gordon French to arrive and open his garage. He had to leave by the time the meeting actually started, as he had young children and dinner responsibilities to attend to.

People came that evening from as far away as Berkeley and Los Gatos. Three Palo Alto High School students—Bob Lash, Mike Fremont, and Ralph Campbell—showed up after they found a flyer that Moore had posted in the school's computer-terminal room. Because there weren't enough chairs to go around, people sat on the cold concrete floor. The meeting was held in the grassroots political style that Moore favored. Six of those who were present at the first meeting had already built their own computers. People went around the room making their introductions and then immediately got down to the important business of sharing technical information and gossip. The information-sharing sessions became a hallmark of the Homebrew experience over the next decade.

Steve Dompier, a long-haired Berkeley computer hobbyist, told about a visit to MITS, the New Mexico–based maker of the Altair. The company couldn't keep up with demand, he reported, and already had back orders for four thousand machines. Ken McGinnis showed off a Phi-Deck digital tape drive that could store an unheard-of half megabyte of data at reasonable cost. Lee Felsenstein noted that he was at work on what he called a Tom Swift terminal, effectively a people's computer distinguished by an integrated video display, an idea he had come upon after reading Ivan Illich's *Tools for*

Conviviality. Illich was a radical theologian whose ideas helped shape a radical technology movement in the 1970s based on the notion of from-the-bottom-up control of tools. Illich's influence had earlier found expression in Stewart Brand's *Whole Earth Catalog*.

French chaired the first meeting, while Moore took notes for the newsletter that he would send out ten days later. It was a single-page flyer in which he reported that the group contained a good cross section of hardware and software expertise. He also offered an editorial note or two including the observation that "I expect home computers will be used in unconventional ways—most of which no one has thought of yet."[14]

As the meeting ended, Marty Spergel, the owner of a small electronic-parts firm, in the spirit that would come to characterize Homebrew, stood up and gave away an Intel microprocessor chip.

The second meeting took place two weeks later at John Mc-Carthy's SAIL. The number of attendees had already begun to swell, but the father of computer time-sharing still turned a blind eye to the looming reality of personal computing. In the second Homebrew newsletter, he posted a small note suggesting the formation of a Bay Area Home Terminal Club, to provide computer access on a shared Digital Equipment Corporation computer. He thought that seventy-five dollars per month, not including terminal and communications costs, might be a reasonable fee.

For the third meeting, the group moved again, and Steve Dompier stole the show.

Dompier had come to Berkeley after getting out of the navy at the height of the antiwar movement in 1969. On the day he arrived, tactical police squads were posted all over town, and helicopters were spraying tear gas on the students. "This is cool, there's something going on here," he decided.

He supported himself as a carpenter while studying electrical engineering, and though he wasn't an activist, his home became a crash pad for an assortment of sixties political and cultural figures. At different times, Joni Mitchell and Jane Fonda slept over, and once

Abbie Hoffman and John Draper crashed at his house on the same night.

Draper, whom Dompier had met at the Lawrence Hall of Science in the Berkeley Hills, became a regular guest, taking advantage of an upstairs computer terminal in Dompier's house to break in to remote mainframe computers. The house rapidly became a center for phone phreaks and hackers. As many as twenty people would assemble on some days, fiddling with the phone lines, placing illegal prank phone calls to places like Hanoi and the White House. Finally, after a phone-company truck with a suspicious antenna drove by, Dompier became paranoid and threw everyone out.

A devotee of games such as *Star Trek*, Dompier had been badly bitten by the computer bug, and in the weeks before the first Homebrew meeting, he flew on the spur of the moment to Albuquerque to appear in person at the MITS factory in an attempt to hurry the arrival of his four-thousand-dollar Altair kit. He found out that he wasn't the only hobbyist that desperate. A secretary at the firm told him that there was someone else who had parked his motor home in the company lot and refused to leave without a computer kit.

His computer finally showed up piece by piece after the first Homebrew meeting, and he spent the ensuing weeks doing little more than playing with it. At one point, two other hobbyists showed up at his home with a card they were attempting to sell as a peripheral for the computer and managed to turn the machine into a smoking wreck.

Painstakingly, he resuscitated it and brought it with him to the third Homebrew meeting, this time at the Peninsula School, which was housed in a converted mansion in Menlo Park. There was no desk available, so Dompier set up shop on the floor, but when he plugged in his new computer, nothing happened. His heart sank, because Moore's tape recorder was already connected to the same socket and seemed to be working just fine.

With a little bit of experimentation, they determined that the recorder was actually running off batteries, and so after several extension cords were commandeered and run upstairs to a working socket, the computer sprang to life. As it had nothing so luxurious as a keyboard or a monitor, Dompier entered his program by toggling it in via the switches on the control panel at the front of the Altair. Each instruction had to be laboriously input in the computer's native hexadecimal language.

In the weeks he had been playing with the computer, he'd gotten pretty fast, but before he could finish someone tripped over the extension cord, and the computer went dead as the program instantly vanished from the Altair's memory.

Dompier started again, and this time he succeeded. Previously he had discovered that the unshielded computer could be programmed to generate tones by interfering with a transistor radio. He spent hours figuring out how to create a musical scale. Then he used the radio as an output device for the computer. At the Homebrew meeting lightning struck when, unexpectedly, strains from the Beatles' "Fool on the Hill" emerged.

When the song ended, the crowd crammed into the room jumped to their feet offering thunderous applause. After the audience calmed down, the song was repeated and then, foreshadowing a world of vastly more powerful computers, the Altair broke into a rendition of "Daisy," raising the specter of the almost conscious HAL from the movie *2001: A Space Odyssey*.

For the first time there was a computer that you could build yourself that actually did something!

Felsenstein eventually calmed the crowd down and noted, "Okay, there is music, but we're not exactly changing the world." Nobody cared. Everyone wanted to hear it again, and so Dompier hit the button, and the music started all over again. When it ended, he received another round of applause.[15]

Gordon French chaired the first three meetings, but he seemed to be out of sync with the anarchistic style of the hobbyists. He would stand in front and lecture on computer science until his monologues drove people who wanted to gossip out of the room. At the Peninsula School meeting, Felsenstein noticed that half of the audience had left the room while French was speaking. He decided there was what he labeled "lateral communication" going on out in the hallway; a community was forming.

At the next meeting, French was gone. He had gotten a contract to work for the Social Security Administration and had temporarily moved to Baltimore. Marty Spergel proposed that Felsenstein run the meeting officially, and nobody thought it was a bad idea.

And so, taking a long pointer in hand, he took over. He was to run the meetings in a simultaneously autocratic, democratic, and anarchistic style until the Homebrew era came to an end almost a decade later.

Felsenstein was more than a bit of a ham and not averse to using the pointer as a weapon to help subdue the unruly audience. Indeed, his pointer served many purposes, including as a stacking tool for collecting the paper-tape programs that the hobbyists brought to share with one another. From the start, Felsenstein encouraged this gift economy, urging the hackers, "Bring back more than you take." In the hobbyist's culture, software was not business. In fact, the idea that the codes were intellectual property was actually laughable to the experimenters. The instructions were simply necessary to imbue the machines with life.

Eventually, the Homebrew meetings settled at the Stanford Linear Accelerator auditorium, located west of the university along Sand Hill Road, where at roughly the same time Silicon Valley's venture capitalists were beginning to take up residence. The meetings just grew and grew until routinely as many as four hundred people showed up for each one.

For the first six meetings, Fred Moore sat up front, took notes, and afterward sent out the club newsletter. With another member, he drove up to San Francisco in early April to see about starting a spin-off. A group of ten people met, and Moore shared his enthusiasm for the new club.

The striking fact that a new industry was forming was already sinking in. "What if someone comes up with a circuit and gives it away for free?" he asked the people assembled around a table. "A club should have nothing to do with making money, but individual people all have their own desires. . . . It's like a marketplace of ideas."[16]

At every opportunity, he repeated his mantra of sharing. But the entrepreneurial explosion he had touched off was unstoppable. It was the odd consequence of all of the pain and suffering that he had gone through during the previous years while attempting to develop an alternative economics from the money that had fallen into his lap at the Demise Party. He had been deeply frustrated by the corrosive power of money and then overnight had helped create a powerful community in which the free sharing of information was not just an aspect of it but the essential reason for its existence. The deep irony is that Fred Moore lit the spark that burned brightly in two contradictory directions—toward the creation of powerful information tools that made information remarkably easy to share and increasingly valuable at the same time.

The Homebrew Computer Club was fated to change the world, but when the change came, it was not the one Moore had hoped for. The Homebrew Club wound up serving as the catalyst for what venture capitalist John Doerr was to call "the largest legal accumulation of money in history."[17] At least twenty-three companies, including Apple Computer, were to trace their lineage directly to Homebrew, ultimately creating a vibrant industry that, because personal computers became such all-purpose tools for both work and play, transformed the entire American economy. Moore's pursuit of democracy and community proved to be more than a footnote, however. With Ted Nelson's computing-power-to-the-people rallying cry echoing across the landscape, the hobbyists would tear down the glass-house computing world and transform themselves into a movement that emphasized an entirely new set of values from traditional American businesses.

Moore might have stayed longer and been drawn more deeply

into the industry that he had helped create. However, his relationship with a woman he was living with in Menlo Park was ending painfully. It was also clear to him that the Homebrew Club was heading in an entrepreneurial direction, and was not going to be a vehicle for his politics of nonviolence.

So in the summer of 1975, Moore took his daughter to stay with her grandparents and headed east, a vagabond hitchhiking across the country, picking apples for a while and eventually getting arrested and going to jail at a Seabrook nuclear-power plant protest in New Hampshire. His interests turned toward applying technology in the developing world. Years later, after viewing the devastation of the forests in Central America, he invented a simple stove that used wood fuel efficiently for cooking. He remained a restless peace activist until he died in an automobile accident in 1997.

Although he had left at the very moment the personal-computer industry was born, Moore's crusade left its mark. The spirit of sharing with which he founded Homebrew left its mark on the industry that grew up around the club.

That spirit, in turn, foreshadowed the chasm that has come to divide the digital world, underscoring all of the struggles that today are reshaping both the consumer and business computing worlds from Napster to open source.

The chasm first appeared when the MITSmobile arrived in Palo Alto as a result of the efforts of a marketing-savvy sales representative named Paul Terrell. Terrell had approached MITS about the possibility of distributing their new Altair computer. Although the company was planning on selling the machines by mail order, Terrell met with MITS's founder Ed Roberts at the National Computer Conference in Anaheim, California, in 1975 and reached an agreement where he would promote Altairs in northern California and in return receive a commission on the machines sold in the region.

MITS planned a nationwide bus tour for its Altair 8800, giving many people their first hands-on experience with a personal computer. The company had equipped a van as a mobile showcase, and

Terrell reserved a conference room at Rickey's Hyatt House, a Palo Alto hotel. The room held eighty people, but more than two hundred showed up in response to advertisements in local newspapers, including Larry Tesler, who would later unsuccessfully try to convince his colleagues that he had seen the future.

By then, just three months after Homebrew had been founded, many of the hobbyists had already bought Altairs, but there was still little software to be found for the computer. During the chaos of the event, which was run by two MITS employees (one of them an attractive blonde who distracted a number of the hobbyists), someone "borrowed" a copy of Altair BASIC, the first commercial program from a tiny Albuquerque company named Micro-Soft, recently founded by two young Harvard University students, William Gates and Paul Allen.

Thus "liberated," Altair BASIC—stored as a set of punched holes in a long paper tape—was shared among the members of the Homebrew Computer Club. The identity of the thief has remained a mystery for more than a quarter century. Both Steven Levy in *Hackers: Heroes of the Computer Revolution* and Stephen Manes and Paul Andrews in *Gates: How Microsoft's Mogul Reinvented an Industry— and Made Himself the Richest Man in America* hint the culprit was Steve Dompier. Yet Dompier has long denied that he was the guilty party. He points out that he already had his own copy of the program, which he had received directly from Bill Gates in order to beta test it. Nearly three decades later, Dompier still has the original paper tape stored at his home, and he will take it out to show a visitor, complete with a note of thanks for his testing help from Gates. Dompier remembers keeping quiet about his copy of Altair BASIC because it wasn't public at the time and he was already getting calls from all over the world begging him for his music program.

What is not in dispute is that somehow the tape reached Dan Sokol, a thirty-one-year-old semiconductor-engineering manager, who took it back to his company, where he had access to a high-speed paper-tape-copying system. He made more than seventy copies, handing them out at the next meeting of the Homebrew club. Sokol's gift touched off a frenzy. People stampeded to the front of the room for a copy, and he held them back, making the hobbyists who had ordered their Altairs but had not yet received them stand in line behind those who already had a machine.

Sokol, who had attended the first Homebrew meeting but hadn't signed his name to the list that Fred Moore had passed around, had become a good friend of both Wozniak and John Draper. He shared the attitude of many of the hobbyists that they were being ripped off by software developers who were charging five hundred dollars for a programming language that was freely and widely available within the academic world. There were already many versions of BASIC that had been written for larger mainframe and minicomputers, as well as PCC's volunteer-written Tiny BASIC. The hobbyists thought it reasonable to charge perhaps a nominal fee or even bundle the cost of the software as part of the purchase of the hardware, but the idea of paying a huge fee was highly offensive to them.

At the same time, the theft outraged a twenty-year-old Bill Gates, who saw nothing in the stunt but the outright victimization of his tiny company. He wrote an angry letter to the computer hobbyists, which was reprinted in a number of publications, including the People's Computer Company quarterly. "As the majority of hobbyists must be aware, most of you steal your software," Gates complained. "Hardware must be paid for, but software is something to share. Who cares if the people who worked on it get paid?" It was pure Bill Gates—an aggressive and sarcastic attack on the hobbyists. Later, after he was widely criticized, he wrote "A Second and Final Letter," noting that he was not a MITS employee but was not backing down from his original stand.

This initial confrontation between Gates and the anarchic cadre of programmers and hardware tinkerers forged a basic tension that has enveloped not just the computer industry but now the music world, other technology industries, Hollywood, and the entire publishing world as well. A confrontation at the dawn of the personal-computer era exposed a fault line that today has become the bitterest conflict facing the world's economy.

On one hand, Silicon Valley has long been motivated by what author Michael Malone called "The Big Score"—more simply put, greed. In fact, it was not long after the Homebrew Computer Club's first meeting in Menlo Park that the hobbyist conclave began spawning names such as Apple, Osborne Computer, Cromemco, and North Star, owing their roots, directly or indirectly, to the enthusiasm that was captured in the initial club meetings.

At the same time, the Valley has also long been driven by the more idealistic motive expressed by Fred Moore's passion for sharing information freely. The collision of the two motives during the sixties and early seventies around Stanford forged the ethos of the personal-computing industry. Today there remains a direct connection between that past and the modern computer industry. Its idealistic side finds clear expression in Linux—a freely available operating system that has been developed and supported by volunteer programmers.

Stewart Brand expressed the fundamental tension most clearly: "Information wants to be free," he said, "and information also wants to be very expensive."

That is the legacy of the forces that collided three decades ago around Stanford. The collision created a conflict that is still reshaping the landscape in the consumer electronics, digital entertainment, and computer industries. And it will become even more of a factor as digital computers increasingly define every aspect of modern life.

Its origin lies in the separate passions of Doug Engelbart, Fred Moore, and Myron Stolaroff. Engelbart and Moore were two sides of the same coin, both committed to an ideal to the exclusion of almost everything else in their lives. Both felt deeply they were outsiders. Stolaroff's zeal for exploring the potential of the human mind, meanwhile, dovetailed perfectly with a culture intent on seizing and remaking the tools of the establishment in a new image. Certainly Stolaroff's impact on the history of the computer was less direct than those of Engelbart and Moore. But his obsession with creativity and psychedelics unleashed forces the impact of which has never been adequately acknowledged.

In their individual ways, all three men helped lay the groundwork for the personal computer, which in turn during the past three decades has given risen to the information economy. Today, that industry embodies some of what all three men dreamed of.

It has spread the conflict over the dual nature of digital information into every nook and cranny of modern life. In league with Hollywood and publishers, Microsoft and Intel have now embarked on a crusade to build computer software and hardware that wraps information with a protective layer of encryption designed to prevent sharing via computer networks. At the same time, the open-source software community has begun attempting to redefine the idea of copyright, more in keeping with the spirit of the framers of the Constitution. The computer hackers' urge to share and the entrepreneurs desire for wealth—it is a confrontation that will inevitably define new technology revolutions. The stage is set for a clash of values that echo the very forces that created Silicon Valley.

ACKNOWLEDGMENTS

Let me first pay my respects to those who have gone before me. From 1981 to 1984, I worked with both Paul Freiberger and Mike Swaine at a start-up weekly newspaper, *Infoworld,* which had set out to become either the *Rolling Stone* or *Sports Illustrated* (it was never quite sure which) of the personal-computer industry. I watched the two of them struggle through the exercise of writing history while it was still being made as they researched *Fire in the Valley.* At about the same time, a New York–based *Rolling Stone* writer, Steven Levy, showed up at our Palo Alto offices and took me out for pizza at the Roundtable on University Avenue in downtown Palo Alto. Steven had come to Silicon Valley to do research for what would become *Hackers: Heroes of the Computer Revolution,* an account that seventeen years later is still the definitive work on the culture of the modern computing world. More recently, Steven was kind enough to dig through his old boxes to share transcripts from his original interviews.

Also, I have to give special thanks to friends who were willing to listen to me chatter endlessly about what my reporting had dug up. Paul Saffo has been one of the sharpest thinkers in Silicon Valley for more than two decades, with a wonderful critical eye. Michael Schrage was once upon a time a competitor at *The Washington Post* but was one of the first people to give me encouragement. Kevin Kelly helped me explore the idea of what was special about a certain time and place. Gregg Zachary has taught journalism with me at the University of California at Berkeley, and at Stanford, and when he covered Silicon Valley for *The Wall Street Journal* during the 1990s he was the competitor I dreaded most. Steve Lohr preceded me on a *New York Times*–sanctioned book leave and filled me with fear, trepidation, and ultimately hope, as from a safe distance I watched him labor on his own book.

Mark Seiden, a veteran Unix hacker and computer-security expert, read an early draft of the manuscript for technical nonsense and other idiocies. John Kelley took the time to carefully read several chapters and offered solid advice. Tom Buoye read a draft and obsessed over World War II fighter planes. Steve Most also read an early draft and offered extensive and helpful comments.

Michael Keller, Stanford's head librarian, was kind enough to offer me a library fellowship and access to the university's invaluable special-collection materials. Henry Lowood and Alex Pang, Stanford University archivists and historians, took time out of their schedules to answer my questions.

Paula Terzian was a wonderful transcriber on a moment's notice.

Finally, Leslie Terzian Markoff was there for me when I needed her most.

NOTES

Preface

1. Stewart Brand, "We Owe It All to the Hippies," *Time*, special issue, spring 1995.
2. Stewart Brand, "Spacewar: Fanatic Life and Symbolic Death among the Computer Bums," *Rolling Stone*, December 7, 1972.
3. The meaning of the term "hacker" changed beginning in the early 1990s, when it came to refer to teenagers who used modems to break into computers. Originally the term was used to describe a group of almost exclusively young men who were passionate in their obsession with computing and computers. This book uses the term in its original sense.
4. George B. Leonard, "Where the California Game Is Taking Us," *Look*, June 28, 1966.
5. William Gibson, interview with Paul Saffo, Director, Institute for the Future, Cyberthon, San Francisco, 1994.

1 | The Prophet and the True Believers

1. Oral history, interview by Henry Lowood and Judith Adams, Stanford University, December 19, 1986. This interview is the clearest and most comprehensive account of Engelbart's career, and I have relied on it extensively.
2. Ibid.
3. Ibid.
4. There is some confusion on this point. At various times Engelbart has said that he found the original article in the library and at other times he has said he believed he first read the *Life* account of Vannevar Bush's Memex. Whatever the case, it had a defining impact on him.
5. Vannevar Bush, "As We May Think," *Atlantic Monthly*, July 1945.
6. Lowood and Adams, oral history.
7. Ibid. Twenty years later, a young Steve Wozniak, then a brand-new HP engineer, would ask the company if they wanted to sell a personal computer. HP said it wasn't interested, and Wozniak went off to cofound Apple Computer. It was the second time the Silicon Valley pioneer missed an opportunity to define the future of computing.
8. Ibid.

9. Jack Goldberg, Stanford Research Institute, e-mail to author.

10. Author interview, Charles Rosen, Menlo Park, Calif., October 10, 2001.

11. Douglas C. Engelbart Collection, Stanford Special Libraries, Stanford University.

12. Author interview, Don Allen, Menlo Park, Calif., August 31, 2001.

13. Myron Stolaroff, *Thanatos to Eros, 35 Years of Psychedelic Exploration* (Berlin: VWB, 1994), p. 18.

14. Stolaroff, *Thanatos to Eros*, p. 19.

15. Ibid.

16. Ibid, p. 20.

17. Jay Stevens, *Storming Heaven: LSD and the American Dream* (New York: Grove Press, 1987), p. 53.

18. Stolaroff, *Thanatos to Eros*, p. 23.

19. Ibid., p. 25.

20. Kary Mullis, *Dancing Naked in the Mind Field*, New York: Pantheon Books, 1998.

21. Author interview, Don Allen, Menlo Park, Calif., August 22, 2001.

22. Vic Lovell, "The Perry Lane Papers (III): How It Was," in *One Lord, One Faith, One Cornbread*, eds. Fred Nelson and Ed McClanahan (Garden City, N.Y.: Anchor Press, 1973), p. 173.

23. Robert Johnson, Elsa Johnson, Eve Clarke, "The Fight Against Compulsory R.O.T.C.," Free Speech Movement Archives, http://www.fsm-a.org/stacks/AP_files/APCompuls ROTC.html.

24. Ibid.

25. Personal collection, Irene Moore.

26. Ibid.

27. Ibid.

28. "U.C. Student Fasts to Protest ROTC," *Oakland Tribune*, October 19, 1959.

29. "UC Student on Strike Over ROTC," *San Francisco Chronicle*, October 20, 1959.

2 | Augmentation

1. Don Nielsen, SRI vice president, personal communication, November 4, 2001.

2. Draft paper, 1961, Douglas C. Engelbart Collection, Stanford Special Libraries, Stanford University.

3. Memo, March 14, 1961, Douglas C. Engelbart Collection, Stanford Special Library, Stanford University.

4. Doug Engelbart, "The Augmented Knowledge Workshop," in *Proceedings of the ACM Conference on the History of Personal Workstations*, ed. Adele Goldberg (New York: ACM, 1988), p. 190.

5. D. C. Engelbart, "Augmenting Human Intellect: A Conceptual Framework," prepared for Director of Information Sciences, Air Force Office of Scientific Research, October 1962, p. 5.

6. Ibid., p. 6.

7. Douglas Engelbart, oral history, interview by John Eklund, Division of Computers, Information, and Society, National Museum of American History, Smithsonian Institute, May 4, 1994. http://americanhistory.si.edu/csr/comphist/englebar.htm.

8. Oral history, interview by Lowood and Adams.

9. M. Mitchell Waldrop, *The Dream Machine: J. C. R. Licklider and the Revolution That Made Computing Personal* (New York: Viking, 2001), p. 217.

10. Oral history, interview by Eklund.

11. Author interview, William English, Sausalito, Calif., May 11, 2001.

12. Author interview, Don Andrews, Menlo Park, Calif., September 27, 2001.

13. Oral history, interview by Lowood and Adams.

14. Bill English, "Early Computer Mouse Encounters," presentation sponsored by the Computer History Museum, at the Xerox PARC Auditorium, October 17, 2001.

15. Stevens, *Storming Heaven*, p. 177.

16. San Mateo *Call Bulletin*, January 5, 1963.

17. Stewart Brand, personal journal, 1962, Green Library Special Collection, Stanford University, Stanford, Calif.

18. David Evans, e-mail to author, August 30, 2001.

19. Engelbart, "Augmented Knowledge Workshop," p. 194.

20. Oral history, interview by Lowood and Adams.

21. Author interview, Bob Taylor, Woodside, Calif., August 12, 2000.

3 | Red-Diaper Baby

1. Author interview, Les Earnest, Los Altos Hills, Calif., July 12, 2001.

2. Anonymous, "Take Me, I'm Yours, The Autobiography of SAIL," June 7, 1991, http://wwwdb.stanford.edu/pub/voy/museum/pictures/AIlab/SailFarewell.html.

3. Author interview, John McCarthy, Stanford, Calif., July 19, 2001.

4. J. M. Graetz, "The Origin of Spacewar," *Creative Computing*, August 1981.

5. Ibid.

6. John McCarthy and Patrick J. Hayes, "Some Philosophical Problems from the Standpoint of Artificial Intelligence," Stanford University, 1969, http://www-formal.stanford.edu/jmc/mcchay69/mcchay69.html.

7. Author interview, John McCarthy.

8. Author interview, John McCarthy; Lenny Siegel, Mountain View, Calif., July 9, 2001.

9. Author interview, John McCarthy.

10. Steven Levy, *Hackers: Heroes of the Computer Revolution* (Garden City, N.Y.: Doubleday, 1984), pp. 27–33.

11. Brian Harvey, "What Is a Hacker?" http://www.cs.berkeley.edu/~bh/hacker.html.

12. Ibid.

13. Les Earnest, "My Life as a Cog," *Matrix News* 10. 1 (2000): 3.

14. Ibid., p. 7.

15. Ibid., p. 8.

16. Horace Enea, e-mail to author, November 10, 2001.

17. Michael L. Mauldin, "Chatterbots, Tinymuds, and the Turing Test: Entering the Loebner Prize Competition," paper presented at AAAI-94, January 24, 1994.

18. Sean Colbath's e-mail from Les Earnest, posted to alt.foklore.computers, February 20, 1990.

19. Les Earnest, e-mail to author, September 15, 2001.

20. Les Earnest, comments during a seminar at the Hackers Conference, Tenaya Lodge, Caif., November 11, 2001.

4 | **Free U**

1. Larry McMurtry, "On the Road," *The New York Review of Books,* December 5, 2002.
2. Midpeninsula Free University catalog, spring 1969.
3. Ibid., fall 1969.
4. Author interview, Jim Warren, Woodside, Calif., July 16, 2001.
5. John McCarthy, "The Home Information Terminal—a 1970 View," in *Man and Computer,* Proceedings of the First International Conference on Man and Computer, Bordeaux, 1970, ed. M. Marois (Basel: Karger, 1972), pp. 48–57.
6. Alan C. Kay, "The Early History of Smalltalk," *ACM SIGPLAN Notices* 28:3 (March 1993): 11.
7. Dennis Shasha and Cathy Lazere, *Out of Their Minds: The Lives and Discoveries of Fifteen Great Computer Scientists* (New York: Copernicus, 1995), pp. 40–41.
8. Kay, "The Early History of Smalltalk," p. 4.
9. Author interview, Alan Kay, Glendale, Calif., July 31, 2001.
10. Ibid., p. 5.
11. Ibid., p. 7.

5 | **Dealing Lightning**

1. The origin of the phrase "dealing lightning with both hands" is intriguing. It was first reported in Stewart Brand's seminal *Rolling Stone* article about PARC and SAIL in 1972 and attributed to Alan Kay. However, Kay does not remember if he used the phrase first, while Chuck Thacker has a clear recollection of exclaiming, "He sat on stage for an hour and a half dealing lightning with both hands," after watching a video of Engelbart in 1970 or 1971. Robert Taylor, director of the computer-science laboratory at PARC, also remembers Thacker using the phrase first. Thus it is ironic that Michael Hiltzik chose the phrase "Dealers of Lightning" as the title of his thorough history of Xerox PARC, when in fact the term was first used to describe Engelbart's work.
2. "Whole Earth Visionary: Stewart Brand," *The Guardian* (London), August 4, 2001, p. 6.
3. Sam Binkley, "Consuming Aquarius: Markets and the Moral Boundaries of the New Class, 1968–1980," Ph.D. dissertation, New School University, 2002.
4. *Whole Earth Catalog: Access to Tools, Thirtieth Anniversary Celebration* (San Rafael, Calif.: Point Foundation, 1998), p. 2.
5. Stewart Brand, personal journals, Stanford University Special Collections, March 24, 1957.
6. Charles Irby, "The Augmented Knowledge Workshop," in *A History of Personal Workstations,* ed. Adele Goldberg (Reading, Mass.: Addison-Wesley, 1988), p. 185.
7. Oral history, interview by Lowood and Adams.
8. Katie Hafner and Matthew Lyon, *Where Wizards Stay Up Late: The Origins of the Internet* (New York: Simon & Schuster, 1996), p. 153.
9. Author interview, Don Andrews, Los Altos, Calif., September 27, 2001.
10. Dave Pugh, "The Anti-War Movement at Stanford: 1966–1969," September 14, 1999, unpublished draft, available from author.
11. Dave Evans, e-mail message to author, August 30, 2001.

6 | **Scholars and Barbarians**

1. Bob Albrecht, unpublished interview with Steven Levy, August 1982, private collection.
2. Ibid.
3. Ibid., 1982.
4. AnnaLee Saxenian, "Creating a Twentieth Century Technical Community: Frederick Terman's Silicon Valley." Paper prepared for inaugural symposium, "The Inventor and the Innovative Society," The Lemelson Center for the Study of Invention and Innovation, National Museum of American History, Smithsonian Institution, November 10–11, 1995. Available at http://www.sims.berkeley.edu/~anno/papers/terman.html#_ednl.
5. "The Resistance," Palo Alto draft resistance pamphlet, n.d., author's personal collection.
6. Fred Moore, unpublished interview with Steve Levy, n.d.
7. Author interview, Chris Jones, Berkeley, Calif., October 3, 2001.
8. Fred Moore, personal journal, April 7, 1973, courtesy of Irene Moore.
9. Ibid., n.d.
10. Ibid., n.d.
11. Demise Party tape recording, courtesy of Irene Moore.
12. Augment journal, January 15, 1972, Stanford University, Special Collections.
13. Cedar POD notes, Augment journal, January 1972.
14. Jacques Vallee, *The Network Revolution: Confessions of a Computer Scientist* (Berkeley, Calif.: And/Or Press, 1982), p. 103.
15. Augment journal, January 24, 1972.
16. Waldrop, *Dream Machine*, pp. 394–96.
17. Ibid., p. 217.

7 | **Momentum**

1. Ben Fritz, "Vidgame Biz Buoyed," *Daily Variety*, January 26, 2004, p. 8.
2. Alan C. Kay, "The Early History of Smalltalk," *ACM SIGPLAN Notices* 28:3 (March 1993): 13.
3. Ibid.
4. Ibid.
5. Ambitious distributed computing projects like Microsoft's .Net and IBM's Websphere indicate the persistence of this goal.
6. Michael A. Hiltzik, *Dealers of Lightning: Xerox PARC and the Dawn of the Computer Age* (New York: HarperBusiness, 1999), p. 164.
7. Author interview with Robert Taylor, Woodside, Calif., June 17, 2003.
8. Hiltzik, *Dealers of Lightning*, pp. 168–69.
9. Author interview, Adele Goldberg, San Francisco, Calif., July 15, 2001.
10. Author interview, Larry Tesler, Menlo Park, Calif., August 27, 2001.

8 | **Borrowing Fire from the Gods**

1. Fred Moore, letter to Dick Raymond and Point Agents, February 28, 1972, personal papers, courtesy of Irene Moore.

2. Fred Moore, personal journal, March 24, 1972.

3. Author interview, Dennis Allison, Palo Alto, Calif., July 28, 2001.

4. Gregory Yob, "Hunt the Wumpus," in *The Best of Creative Computing*, vol. 1, ed. David H. Ahl, 2d ed. (Morristown, N.J.: Creative Computing Press, 1976), pp. 247–50.

5. Ibid.

6. Author interview, Lee Felsenstein, Palo Alto, Calif., August 9, 2001.

7. Fred Moore, unpublished interview with Steven Levy, n.d.

8. John Draper website http://www.webcrunchers.com/crunch/story.html.

9. Author interview with Steven Jobs, Cupertino, Calif., June 2000.

10. Fred Moore, personal journal, 1975.

11. Fred Moore, unpublished interview with Steven Levy, n.d.

12. Ibid.

13. Homebrew Computer Club newsletter 1, March 15, 1975.

14. Ibid.

15. Author interview, Lee Felsenstein, Palo Alto, Calif., August 9, 2001.

16. Tape of San Francisco computer-club planning meeting, April 1975, courtesy of Irene Moore.

17. Doerr's remark would later be linked to the dot-com era, but he made the claim first with respect to the personal-computer industry.

BIBLIOGRAPHY

Abbate, Janet. *Inventing the Internet.* Cambridge, Mass.: MIT Press, 1999.

Ahl, David H., and Burchenal Green. *The Best of Creative Computing.* Morristown, N.J.: Creative Computing Press, 1976.

Anderson, Terry H. *The Movement and the Sixties.* New York: Oxford University Press, 1996.

Bardini, Thierry. *Bootstrapping: Douglas Engelbart, Coevolution, and the Origins of Personal Computing.* Stanford, Calif.: Stanford University Press, 2000.

Beers, David. *Blue Sky Dream: A Memoir of America's Fall from Grace.* New York: Doubleday, 1996.

Bergin, Thomas J., and Richard G. Gibson. *History of Programming Languages II.* New York and Reading, Mass.: ACM Press, Addison-Wesley Pub. Co., 1996.

Black, David. *Acid: The Secret History of LSD.* Berkeley, Calif.: Frog Ltd, 1998.

Braunstein, Peter, and Michael William Doyle. *Imagine Nation: The American Counterculture of the 1960s and '70s.* New York: Routledge, 2002.

Ceruzzi, Paul E. *A History of Modern Computing.* Cambridge, Mass.: MIT Press, 1998.

Cohen, Robert, and Reginald E. Zelnik. *The Free Speech Movement: Reflections on Berkeley in the 1960s.* Berkeley: University of California Press, 2002.

Cowan, Ruth Schwartz. *A Social History of American Technology.* New York: Oxford University Press, 1997.

Coyote, Peter. *Sleeping Where I Fall: A Chronicle.* Washington, D.C.: Counterpoint, 1998.

Edwards, Paul N. *The Closed World: Computers and the Politics of Discourse in Cold War America.* Cambridge, Mass.: MIT Press, 1996

Engelbart, Douglas C. *Augmenting Human Intellect: A Conceptual Framework.* Director of Information Sciences, Air Force Office of Scientific Research, 1962.

Evans, Christopher Riche. *The Micro Millennium.* New York: Viking Press, 1980

Farber, David R. *The Sixties: From Memory to History.* Chapel Hill: University of North Carolina Press, 1994.

———. *The Age of Great Dreams: America in the 1960s.* New York: Hill and Wang, 1994.

Flamm, Kenneth. *Creating the Computer: Government, Industry, and High Technology.* Washington, D.C: Brookings Institution, 1988.

Frank, Thomas. *The Conquest of Cool: Business Culture, Counterculture, and the Rise of Hip Consumerism.* Chicago: University of Chicago Press, 1997.

Freiberger, Paul, and Michael Swaine. *Fire in the Valley: The Making of the Personal Computer.* Berkeley, Calif.: Osborne/McGraw-Hill, 1984.

Gitlin, Todd. *The Sixties: Years of Hope, Days of Rage.* Toronto and New York: Bantam Books, 1987.

Goldberg, Adele. *A History of Personal Workstations.* New York and Reading, Mass.: ACM Press, Addison-Wesley Pub. Co., 1988.

Gross, Michael. *My Generation: Fifty Years of Sex, Drugs, Rock, Revolution, Glamour, Greed, Valor, Faith, and Silicon Chips.* New York: Cliff Street Books, 2000.

Grossman, Wendy. *From Anarchy to Power: The Net Comes of Age.* New York: New York University Press, 2001.

Hafner, Katie, and Matthew Lyon. *Where Wizards Stay Up Late: The Origins of the Internet.* New York: Simon & Schuster, 1996.

Hajdu, David. *Positively 4th Street: The Lives and Times of Joan Baez, Bob Dylan, Mimi Baez Fariña, and Richard Fariña.* New York: Farrar, Straus and Giroux, 2001.

Himanen, Pekka. *The Hacker Ethic, and the Spirit of the Information Age.* New York: Random House, 2001.

Lee, Martin A., and Bruce Shlain. *Acid Dreams: The Complete Social History of LSD: The CIA, the Sixties, and Beyond.* New York: Grove Weidenfeld, 1992.

Levy, Steven. *Crypto: How the Code Rebels Beat the Government, Saving Privacy in the Digital Age.* New York: Viking, 2001.

———. *Hackers: Heroes of the Computer Revolution.* Garden City, N.Y.: Anchor Press/Doubleday, 1984.

Ludlow, Peter. *Crypto Anarchy, Cyberstates, and Pirate Utopias.* Cambridge, Mass.: MIT Press, 2001.

McNally, Dennis. *A Long Strange Trip: The Inside History of the Grateful Dead.* New York: Broadway Books, 2002.

Margolis, Jon. *The Last Innocent Year: America in 1964—The Beginning of the "Sixties."* New York: William Morrow and Co., 1999.

Metzner, Ralph. *The Ecstatic Adventure.* New York: Macmillan, 1968.

Mullis, Kary B. *Dancing Naked in the Mind Field.* New York: Pantheon Books, 1998.

Mumford, Lewis. *The Pentagon of Power.* New York: Harcourt Brace Jovanovich, 1974.

Nelson, Fred, and Ed McClanahan. *One Lord, One Faith, One Cornbread.* Garden City, N.Y.: Anchor Press, 1973.

Nelson, Theodor H. *Computer Lib; Dream Machines.* Redmond, Wash.: Tempus Books of Microsoft Press, 1987.

Phillips, Michael. *What's Really Happening: Baby Boom II Comes of Age.* Bodega, Calif.: Clear Glass Pub., 1984.

Pinch, T. J., and Frank Trocco. *Analog Days: The Invention and Impact of the Moog Synthesizer.* Cambridge, Mass.: Harvard University Press, 2002.

Raymond, Eric S. *The New Hacker's Dictionary.* Cambridge, Mass.: MIT Press, 1993.

Reynolds, Terry S., and Stephen H. Cutcliffe. *Technology & the West: A Historical Anthology from Technology and Culture.* Chicago: University of Chicago Press, 1997.

Rheingold, Howard. *Tools for Thought: The People and Ideas Behind the Next Computer Revolution.* New York: Computer Book Division/Simon & Schuster, 1985.

Roszak, Theodore. *The Making of a Counter Culture: Reflections on the Technocratic Society and Its Youthful Opposition.* London: Faber, 1970.

———. *From Satori to Silicon Valley: San Francisco and the American Counterculture.* San Francisco: Don't Call It Frisco Press, 1986.

———. *The Cult of Information: A Neo-Luddite Treatise on High Tech, Artificial Intelligence, and the True Art of Thinking.* Berkeley: University of California Press, 1994.

Segaller, Stephen. *Nerds 2.0.1.* New York: TV Books, 1998.

Selvin, Joel. *Summer of Love: The Inside Story of LSD, Rock & Roll, Free Love, and High Times in the Wild West.* New York: Dutton, 1994.

Smith, Douglas K., and Robert C. Alexander. *Fumbling the Future: How Xerox Invented, Then Ignored, the First Personal Computer.* New York: William Morrow, 1988.

Smith, Merritt Roe, and Leo Marx. *Does Technology Drive History?: The Dilemma of Technological Determinism.* Cambridge, Mass.: MIT Press, 1994.

Solnit, Rebecca. *River of Shadows: Eadweard Muybridge and the Technological Wild West.* New York: Viking, 2003.

Stevens, Jay. *Storming Heaven: LSD and the American Dream.* New York: Atlantic Monthly Press, 1987.

Stolaroff, Myron J. *Thanatos to Eros: 35 Years of Psychedelic Exploration Ethnomedicine and the Study of Consciousness (Series Ethnomedicine and the Study of Consciousness = Reihe),* Verlag for Wissenschaft Und Bildung, 1994.

Vallee, Jacques. *The Network Revolution: Confessions of a Computer Scientist.* Berkeley, Calif.: And/Or Press, 1982.

Waldrop, M. Mitchell. *The Dream Machine: J.C.R. Licklider and the Revolution That Made Computing Personal.* New York: Viking, 2001.

Wayner, Peter. *Free for All: How Linux and the Free Software Movement Undercut the High-Tech Titans.* New York: Harper Business, 2000.

Wolfe, Tom. *The Electric Kool-Aid Acid Test.* New York: Farrar, Straus and Giroux, 1968.

Zachary, G. Pascal. *Endless Frontier: Vannevar Bush, Engineer of the American Century.* New York: Free Press, 1997.

INDEX